378.1981 BRE

Learning Resource Centre
Ashford College
Elwick Road
Ashford,
Kent TN23 1NN
Tel: 01233 743027
Email: **ashfordlrc@ashfo**

D1614595

E-Hub
Resource

SOUTH KENT COLLEGE

L12202W0589

A SOCIAL HISTORY OF STUDENT VOLUNTEERING

Georgina [signature]

HISTORICAL STUDIES IN EDUCATION

Edited by William J. Reese and John L. Rury

William J. Reese, Carl F. Kaestle WARF Professor of Educational Policy Studies and History, the University of Wisconsin-Madison

John L. Rury, Professor of Education and (by courtesy) History, the University of Kansas

This series features new scholarship on the historical development of education, defined broadly, in the United States and elsewhere. Interdisciplinary in orientation and comprehensive in scope, it spans methodological boundaries and interpretive traditions. Imaginative and thoughtful history can contribute to the global conversation about educational change. Inspired history lends itself to continued hope for reform, and to realizing the potential for progress in all educational experiences.

Published by Palgrave Macmillan:

Democracy and Schooling in California: The Legacy of Helen Heffernan and Corinne Seeds
   By Kathleen Weiler

The Global University: Past, Present, and Future Perspectives
   Edited by Adam R. Nelson and Ian P. Wei

Catholic Teaching Brothers: Their Life in the English-Speaking World, 1891–1965
   By Tom O'Donoghue

Science Education and Citizenship: Fairs, Clubs, and Talent Searches for American Youth, 1918–1958
   By Sevan G. Terzian

*The Founding Fathers, Education, and "The Great Contest":
The American Philosophical Society Prize of 1797*
   Edited by Benjamin Justice

Education and the State in Modern Peru: Primary Education in Lima, 1821 – c. 1921
   By G. Antonio Espinoza

Desegregating Chicago's Public Schools: Policy Implementation, Politics and Protest, 1965–1985
   By Dionne Danns

A Social History of Student Volunteering: Britain and Beyond, 1880–1980
   By Georgina Brewis

A Social History of Student Volunteering

Britain and Beyond, 1880–1980

Georgina Brewis

A SOCIAL HISTORY OF STUDENT VOLUNTEERING
Copyright © Georgina Brewis, 2014.

All rights reserved.

First published in 2014 by
PALGRAVE MACMILLAN®
in the United States—a division of St. Martin's Press LLC,
175 Fifth Avenue, New York, NY 10010.

Where this book is distributed in the UK, Europe and the rest of the world,
this is by Palgrave Macmillan, a division of Macmillan Publishers Limited,
registered in England, company number 785998, of Houndmills,
Basingstoke, Hampshire RG21 6XS.

Palgrave Macmillan is the global academic imprint of the above companies
and has companies and representatives throughout the world.

Palgrave® and Macmillan® are registered trademarks in the United States,
the United Kingdom, Europe and other countries.

ISBN: 978–1–137–37013–6

Library of Congress Cataloging-in-Publication Data

Brewis, Georgina.
    A social history of student volunteering : Britain and beyond,
    1880–1980 / by Georgina Brewis.
        pages cm
    Includes bibliographical references and index.
    ISBN 978–1–137–37013–6 (hardcover : alk. paper)
        1. Student movements—Great Britain—History—20th century.
    2. College students—Political activity—Great Britain—History—
    20th century. 3. Voluntarism—Great Britain—History—20th century.
    I. Title.

LA637.7.B69 2014
378.1'981—dc23   2014005644

A catalogue record of the book is available from the British Library.

Design by Newgen Knowledge Works (P) Ltd., Chennai, India.

First edition: July 2014

10 9 8 7 6 5 4 3 2 1

For Iain and Toby

CONTENTS

FIGURES

SERIES FOREWORD

Students outnumber professors, administrators and staff at every college and university in every nation. But they are rarely the central figures in most histories of higher education. Like the seasons, students come and go. One cohort of students replaces another, each leaving an imprint on their institutions and the larger society while often remaining elusive as historical subjects. Generalizing about the aims, beliefs, and behavior of students—both in the classroom and on- and off-campus—has always been difficult, especially as enrollments in higher education boomed in many nations during the last century. Scholars thus tend to focus on the history of the curriculum, governance, corporate relations, and other aspects of college and university life.

Georgina Brewis is that rare historian who places students front and center. Drawing upon a treasure trove of primary sources, *A Social History of Student Volunteering: Britain and Beyond, 1880–1980* examines vital aspects of student life since the late Victorian period in England, Scotland, and Wales, as well as in Ireland and Northern Ireland. Long before "service learning" became fashionable on many campuses in the United States and elsewhere, students in Britain frequently engaged in a breadth of voluntary activities. This not only provided opportunities for professional development and civic engagement but also nurtured connections with a wider student movement beyond national boundaries.

Whether they studied at Oxbridge, the new civic universities, or at more modest schools, students often found voluntary work appealing for a variety of reasons. While most students in higher education were often preoccupied with other concerns, many tried to advance a social or political cause, prepare for a career, or do both simultaneously. They sought real-life experiences to learn about the world beyond their homes and classrooms, leading to careers as teachers, social workers, or administrators in an emerging welfare state. Many were animated by concerns about poverty, social injustice, and the horrors of war that would plague millions of people in the twentieth century.

Still others were apolitical and simply sought relief from the boredom of school and yearned for something more vital and exciting.

Students participated in a wide range of activities. They often joined academic or athletic groups and reveled in student rags that raised money for charity. Many joined missionary associations to promote Christian values at home and in Britain's far-flung empire, while others championed pacifism in the 1920s and 1930s and then aided the sick and wounded during wartime. Women in particular played a central role in the history of voluntary action. They volunteered at day care centers, aided the homeless and unemployed, and assisted student refugees escaping war-torn lands. Some students made the headlines when they served as strike-breakers in the 1920s, refused to defend king and country in the 1930s, and campaigned for disarmament after the Second World War and against America's war in Vietnam. More typically, voluntary activities attracted little public notice but were no less vital in the lives of students.

By placing students at the center of the history of voluntarism and higher education, Georgina Brewis has recast our understanding of Britain's educational past in this model, landmark volume.

WILLIAM J. REESE
and
JOHN L. RURY

ACKNOWLEDGMENTS

The idea for this book arose when I was a researcher at the Institute for Volunteering Research (IVR) and this book would not have been written without the initial encouragement of colleagues both at IVR (including Nick Ockenden, Daniel Hill and Angela Ellis Paine) and at student volunteering charity Student Hubs, where I am grateful for the support and practical assistance of Sara Fernandez and Adam O'Boyle. I am most grateful for the input and advice of many others including my PhD supervisors John Marriott, Derek Robbins and Mike Locke, my series editors Bill Reese and John Rury, Nicholas Deakin, Carol Dyhouse and Clare Holdsworth as well as the anonymous reader and my editorial team at Palgrave Macmillan. Thank you also to colleagues from the Voluntary Action History Society, Hisory of Education Society UK, Voluntary Sector Studies Network and the Students in Twentieth Century Europe Research Network with whom I have discussed this research at numerous seminars and conferences over the years. I should like to thank Student Hubs for initial seedcorn funding and the Economic History Society and St John's College Oxford for supporting the 'Students, Volunteering and Social Action: Histories and Policies' project in 2010–2011. The award of my John Adams Fellowship at the Institute of Education, University of London (IOE), enabled me to complete the book. At IOE I would particularly like to thank my mentor Gary McCulloch for his encouragement and help in getting the project to publication stage, as well as colleagues in the Newsam Library and Archives, Sarah Aitchison and Becky Newman.

I should like to thank all those involved in student volunteering and social action in the past who spoke to me over the course of this research or granted access to privately held materials, notably: Steve Butters regarding Returned Volunteer Action; Jamie Clarke for allowing access to the People and Planet papers in Oxford; Mike Day on the National Union of Students; Clare Gilhooly for letting me see the records of Cambridge House; Alan Phillips for material relating to World University Service; and Mike Aiken, Erica Dunmow and

Debbie Ellen for additional papers on the Student Community Action movement. Thank you also to the "witnesses" of student volunteering past: Graham Allcott, Mike Aiken, Alan Barr, Jamie Clarke, Mike Day, Kelly Drake, Erica Dunmow, Debbie Ellen, Rich Lott, Nick Plant and Ray Phillips. The hard work of Anjelica Finnegan means that the papers of the Student Community Action movement from the 1970s can now be consulted by researchers at the London School of Economics. I would also like to thank the archivists and librarians at the British Library, the Cadbury Research Centre at Birmingham University, Cambridge University Library, Hull History Centre, Liverpool University Library, London School of Economics, Modern Records Centre at Warwick University and the National Library of Wales.

The book could not have been written without the ongoing help and support of friends and family, particularly my in laws and my parents in providing childcare over the past year, enabling me to attend conferences and compete the manuscript; so a huge thank you to Shirley and William Smith and Neville and Felicity Brewis. Lastly, my love and thanks to my husband Iain and our son Toby for living with the book over the last few years.

CHAPTER 1

Introduction

University students have been a significant cultural force in modern Britain. Popular culture abounds with student stereotypes, from the gown-wearing nineteenth-century scholar to the undergraduates of the Brideshead era and the bearded radicals of the 1960s and 1970s. Yet our understanding of what it was like to be a student over the period 1880–1980 remains limited. The eminent historian of education Harold Silver recently repeated his call for academic work to pay greater attention to the student experience.[1] Although new studies have begun to address students' lives, interest in the more overtly political activities of universities and colleges has meant other forms of student social action have been neglected. A closer look at extra-curricular activities reveals that participation in voluntary action—ranging from support for university settlements in the 1880s to antifascist relief in the 1930s and Student Community Action (SCA) in the 1970s—was a common experience for successive generations of higher education students. Indeed the very emergence of a distinct student movement in twentieth-century Britain can be ascribed to the unifying force of social service and social action across a higher education system otherwise noted for its heterogeneity.

This book is not a history of any one voluntary or student organization or any one cause or campaign. Rather, it is an attempt to synthesize a wide body of secondary work and published and unpublished primary sources on student voluntary action over a hundred-year period, in the belief that this will make an important contribution to our knowledge and understanding of the histories of both higher education and voluntary action. The focus is largely on activities at universities and university colleges in England, Wales and Scotland (and to a lesser extent in Ireland and Northern Ireland after 1922), but it is by no means only a study of developments in Britain. British students have always looked outward for causes to support and have played a leading role in the creation of international student networks. At different periods of history they have worked closely with American, Commonwealth or European peers in what has been often been called "international student friendship."[2] The book sets developments in international comparative perspective by giving center stage to important though often neglected student networks including the Student Christian Movement (SCM), the World's Student Christian Federation (WSCF), and International Student Service (ISS). While successive generations of students sought to distance their models and methods of voluntary action from those of earlier cohorts, there is value in a long view because it reveals that the outcomes of involvement in voluntary activity have often been remarkably similar across time and place.

The book uses student voluntary action as a lens through which to examine some central themes of modern history in Britain and beyond. First, it takes the rich story of voluntary service, fundraising, campaigning and protest at universities and colleges as a means to explore the changing experience of being a higher education student across the period 1880–1980. Unlike the United States, where there is a longer tradition linking civic engagement and higher education, it was largely in the absence of formal citizenship instruction that students and tutors in Britain developed a wide array of voluntary associations to bring them into contact with communities outside colleges and universities. The book relates developments in student voluntarism to wider changes in access to higher education, student funding and patterns of residence, and considers the gendered nature of voluntary action across a hundred-year period. It situates student voluntary action in the context of the ongoing development of a wider associational culture at universities and colleges. Although undergraduates at the older universities of Oxford and Cambridge did not readily identify themselves as "students" for much of the period under study, those at other universities and colleges in Britain and elsewhere did, and this term is used throughout the book. Uniting student voluntarism at different periods are several strands that will weave across the story. For instance, a strong strain of seriousness and earnestness in student discussion of social and political questions was tempered by the tendency to imbue social action with high-spirited delight in larks and pranks and with carnivalesque features. Student voluntarism also drew strongly on the Platonic notion of "guardianship," of educated talent in the service of society, as students across the generations sought to demonstrate the special contributions they could make to communities and good causes.

Second, the book argues that voluntary social service was core to the emergence of a distinct "student estate" in twentieth-century Britain and central in the development of an international student movement. Although much rhetoric emphasized voluntary action as a means to break down barriers between students and communities outside colleges and universities, participation in voluntary action and the emergence of coordinating national and international student associations served to strengthen student identity and reinforce bonds between students. This was in part because of a strong desire to be seen to be undertaking social service, relief or campaigning as students—and indeed often to target aid at students elsewhere. With roots dating back before the First World War, by the late 1930s a broad-based student movement—which explicitly adopted a "popular front" approach to coordinate activities—had been forged through student social and political action on domestic and international issues.

Third, arguing that developments in student voluntarism have repeatedly set the pace for the wider volunteering movement, the book considers the evolution of volunteering in Britain since the late nineteenth century through detailed study of students' activities. It details student-led innovations in social service, social study and social action and shows that the contributions of students and universities to such causes as post–First World War reconstruction and famine relief, voluntary projects in the Depression and international development aid in the 1960s and 1970s are more significant to these wider movements than has hitherto been recognized. By the second half of the twentieth century, British students were seen as a reliable constituency of support and finance for a range of voluntary associations, causes and campaigns. A key feature of student voluntarism over time was the shift from "service" to "action" in practical activities as well as a change from participation in ameliorative measures to more wholesale questioning of the underlying causes of poverty and inequality. The book dates important changes in student attitudes and activities to a social service craze in the 1910s, the rise of a student social consciousness in the 1930s, and a shift to more politicized forms of community action in the 1970s.

SILENCES: LITERATURE ON VOLUNTARISM IN HIGHER EDUCATION

In his contribution to the new *Oxford History of England*, Brian Harrison identifies "the vitality of voluntarism" as one of five major themes of British history.[3] Although there has been renewed academic interest in the work of specific voluntary organizations since the 1990s, there are fewer accounts that explore volunteering as a phenomenon in its own right. Furthermore, despite recent research and policy interest in student volunteering as well as in the broader topic of how higher education institutions can improve their public engagement, the history of these related movements remain unexplored. In their 1997 book on students, Harold Silver and Pamela Silver called attention to the "silence" around student voluntarism and community action.[4] The experience of higher education students is still not yet a well-developed area of social or educational history, although it is a growing area of research.[5] In her 1994 book Reba Soffer noted that the informal side of student learning, and especially the role of student subcultures, had been almost entirely neglected by historians.[6] Scores of institutional accounts of universities, colleges and halls of residence have been consulted for this study, although such traditional histories are usually "commissioned, commemorative studies" with particular purposes to serve.[7] Only rarely do they reflect on wider social trends. However, newer institutional histories are beginning to place students center stage and to explore their experiences using oral history methods, notably in recent studies of the universities of Strathclyde and Winchester.[8]

Carol Dyhouse's research has added considerably to our knowledge of what it was like to attend university in England in the mid-twentieth century as has Keith Vernon's work on topics such as student health. Mike Day's ninetieth anniversary study of the National Union of Students (NUS) provides welcome insights into the changing lives of British students between 1922 and 2012, though it is primarily an institutional history of one organization.[9] While such studies have begun to address the student experience more broadly, the place of volunteering, social service or community action in students' lives remains under-researched. The excellent chapter on rags in Dyhouse's *Students: A Gendered History* is a notable exception and a recent journal article by Catriona Macdonald considers charitable fundraising as one activity among many through which students explored what it meant to be a citizen in early twentieth-century Scotland.[10] John Field looks at a hitherto neglected aspect of 1930s student voluntarism—student workcamps with unemployed men—as part of a wider study of the workcamp movement.[11] Jodi Burkett's book on post-Imperial Britain touches on the student contribution to radical causes including the Campaign for Nuclear Disarmament (CND) and the antiapartheid movement.[12] A number of histories of student organizations and networks including the SCM, European Student Relief and the WSCF were written in the first half of the twentieth century, usually by insiders who were themselves closely involved in these stories.[13] Internationally, scholars have begun to show new interest in such movements, and particularly in the intersection of gender, service and higher education, although there is as yet no academic history of the British Student Christian Movement.[14]

Historians' keen interest in student politics has meant other forms of student social action have been neglected. International student protest in the late 1960s, for instance, produced works seeking to shed light on the phenomenon through consideration of British students' social and political activities in earlier periods.[15] Of these, the fullest exposition is Eric Ashby and Mary Anderson's *Rise of the Student Estate*, which charts the growth of student representation in Britain.[16] The interwar period is the focus of historical work on students by Brian Simon, Arthur Marwick and more recently by David Fowler in his book *Youth Culture in Modern Britain*.[17] However, both Ashby and Anderson's book and Simon's 1987 paper underplay the importance of charitable activities in the forging of a broad-based student movement in the 1930s and neglect the coordinating role of groups like the SCM and ISS. The activities of left-wing and pacifist Oxford and Cambridge undergraduates during the 1930s have long exerted a strong pull for many scholars, while historians are now turning in larger numbers to the involvement of students in postwar New Left politics.[18] The Cambridge University Press's *History of the University in Europe* considers student engagement with social and political questions through a study of student movements and political activism on a European stage.[19] It understandably relies solely on the existing secondary studies—namely Simon, Marwick, Ashby and Anderson—to tell the story of student social action in Britain between the wars.

The one area that has received the most historical attention is the university-sponsored settlements, founded from the late nineteenth century in cities in Britain and elsewhere.[20] The focus of many of the books and PhD theses on the settlement movement has primarily been on the evolution of these institutions and the services provided to local communities, with graduate residents and paid staff members in the foreground overshadowing the student volunteers who supported settlements from a distance. Moreover, there has been a tendency of such histories to focus on the movement before 1939—and in many cases before 1914. Kate Bradley's 2009 book on London settlements does offer a much fuller picture of how settlements evolved in the post–Second World War period, but, apart from a useful chapter on living and volunteering at settlements, her focus is not on the student supporters of settlements.[21] In general historians have considered the provision of voluntary associations or activities *for* young people rather than volunteering undertaken *by* young people, with a strong focus on working-class youth as the recipients of philanthropic or statutory services.[22]

The focus on settlements, and the high-profile alumni they spawned, has arguably contributed to a skewed understanding of student engagement with local communities over time. Student groups themselves have contributed to this dislocation. Student memories are short and successive generations have sought to distance themselves from the models and methods of service undertaken by their predecessors. For example, in his 1943 indictment of the 1930s university system, former NUS president Brian Simon (1915–2002) claimed that the voluntary work of students undertaken during wartime was markedly different from the "condescension" of earlier forms of student voluntarism.[23] In the 1950s, students' new focus on postwar reconstruction and overseas volunteering meant they quickly forgot universities' interwar involvement with camps for the unemployed, and by the 1970s this episode had disappeared from student groups' accounts of their own past. Indeed in the 1970s students were keen to dismiss all previous student voluntary action as merely "middle-class do-gooding" and to present their model of SCA as a clean break. It is only in very recent years that student groups—such as the organization Student Hubs which was founded in 2007—have shown interest in the history of the movement.[24] This could be seen as part of a growing interest in young people's expressions of active citizenship and volunteering shown by both contemporary social researchers and historians. There is now greater interest in the American concept of "service learning" and in universities' engagement with the wider community as one aspect of the new research impact agenda in the United Kingdom and internationally. Moreover, since Lord Browne's 2010 review of higher education in England placed a premium on the "student experience," university leaders have a newfound interest in the extracurricular activities of students.

FROM SERVICE TO ACTION: CONCEPTUALIZING STUDENT VOLUNTEERING IN THE PAST

Student volunteering, social action and service took many different forms between 1880 and 1980. This book attempts to categorize different models under five headings: "support," "service," "social education," "self-help," and "social action." These categories do not correspond directly to chronological time-periods, although some forms are more associated with particular eras than others. These five categories are briefly defined here. Support encompassed not only raising funds and collecting gifts-in-kind but also students' work to raise awareness about particular causes and social institutions, such as settlements, refugee students or international development. Much of the voluntary action undertaken by students in the past falls into this category in part because residential universities and colleges often supported institutions located some distance away. Colleges and universities would appoint student secretaries or small committees to promote and channel students' support for each cause, appeal or institution. Notably students have always injected humor into their collections for even the most serious causes, for example, through rag collections for local hospitals and international relief campaigns.

In addition to such support students have also given practical service to a wide range of charities and individuals. In the pre-1945 period much voluntary service took place during vacations, when small numbers of students spent part of their vacation volunteering at a settlement, mission or camp. Students at nonresidential colleges were more likely to give regular term-time help to boys' and girls' clubs, settlements and other charities. There were also opportunities for longer periods of service at a settlement or as an overseas volunteer immediately after graduation. From the 1960s practical service channelled through university social service groups became a major form of student voluntarism. A third major theme running through the history of student voluntary action is social education. For effective service, students have needed to be able to locate practical activities in broader social context through study of social and international problems. Holding study circles, discussion groups and awareness-raising meetings would fall under a broad heading of social education.

Student self-help first emerged in Britain in the straightened times after the First World War, and included the provision of services, advice and material aid for students at home as well as internationally. The movement has roots in the *wirtschaftshilfe* movement, which emerged in Germany and Austria in the early 1920s. In the 1930s elements of this self-help movement were adopted in Britain where tough economic times combined with an increase in working-class and lower-middle-class students at the universities led to provision of facilities such as cooperative shops, employment bureaux and student healthcare. In time, such services became standard provision for colleges and students' unions. From the interwar period students across the world began to see themselves as part of a specific student class and hence support for students and universities in other countries was channelled through organizations like European Student Relief (later known as International Student Service) that emerged to meet this need. Self-help or mutual aid is an important category of voluntary action that is often neglected by historians, perhaps because it is usually considered to be a form of working-class charity. Sir William Beveridge's 1948 study *Voluntary Action*, for instance, indentified two main types of voluntary action which he defined as "philanthropy" and "mutual aid." Later historians of charity like Frank Prochaska have drawn attention to the fact that "in any study of organized charity, the contribution of the working classes is likely to be underplayed, for so much of it is informal and unrecorded, unostentatious and uncelebrated."[25] This book argues that the many manifestations of student self-help—and indeed the varied work of students' unions more broadly, usually ignored—should be considered as part of a broader study of voluntary action in higher education.

The final category social or community action is the name for a type of student voluntarism most closely associated with the late 1960s and 1970s, although in some cases seen earlier. The heading of "action" blends campaigning, protest, solidarity and boycott activities with fundraising and service. The term was first used in the 1930s and 1940s to describe the work of antifascist and antiwar student groups in their support for causes such as Republican Spain or the Chinese victims of Japanese aggression. In the 1960s it reemerged to signal dissatisfaction with student social service and rag fundraising. By the late 1960s, student volunteering societies were changing their name to SCA groups to signify a blending of practical service with more radical campaigning, social education and solidarity activities.

Dispensable Ephemera? Researching the History of Student Voluntary Action

Researching student voluntary action presents particular challenges because volunteers and students are both groups that are often hard to uncover in the historical record. As already noted, the resurgence of historical interest in voluntary action has tended to focus on specific voluntary organizations and exceptional individuals rather than on the phenomenon of voluntary service. There is a tendency to sideline the histories of ordinary volunteers as much as the beneficiaries of voluntary work.[26] The voices of volunteers are easily lost in the annual reports or publications through which historians generally approach the study of voluntary action. Students in Britain before the 1960s were always a small minority of their age group who in time were destined to become a ruling elite (albeit one which "actively rejected the concept of an elite" according to Brian Simon), so it is to be expected that many have left written accounts of their experiences, including published and unpublished autobiographies, papers, diaries and letters.[27] However, Oxbridge stories are unsurprisingly more prominent within these published accounts as are those of male politicians, writers and other public figures. This study has drawn on a far wider range of student testimony, including from women, from students who attended provincial universities and from those with minority religious or ethnic backgrounds.

Problems of both myth-making and memory loss occur in both oral and written historical accounts. Leta Jones—writing in old age of her experiences at Liverpool University in the 1930s—noted in the preface to her book, "These haphazard notes are distilled from pure memory: I kept no diaries...I plead to be excused my inaccuracies and the chores of research; time is too short for me now."[28] There is also a tendency for those involved in various types of social and political action as students to obscure, forget or mythologize these activities in memoirs written 40 or 50 years later. Arthur Clegg certainly believed that mention of the 1930s Aid China campaign had been deliberately omitted from the later memoirs and biographies of many of the left-wing intellectuals involved.[29] Likewise, one of Brian Simon's motivations in the 1980s for writing about the 1930s student movement was to dispel what he felt were misconceptions about its character and breadth.[30]

The challenge for this study has been to cross-reference later reflections, valuable as they are, with contemporaneous accounts of the student experience preserved in letters, diaries, reports of student activities, minutes of meetings and college magazines. The book draws on a rich vein of neglected materials produced by student groups and student leaders and preserved in a variety of repositories and private collections. Silver and Silver found in the 1990s that few university archive services had attempted to preserve students' union records— widely seen as "dispensable ephemera"—or had helped unions or student societies to do so.[31] My experience has been that university archives vary hugely in their preservation of the records of student clubs and societies, although excellent collections at the universities of Cambridge and Liverpool as well at several women's colleges have provided useful examples. I have been privileged to be granted access to several privately held collections including the papers of People and Planet (formerly Third World First) in Oxford, National Union of Students materials collected in the Edinburgh offices of NUS Scotland and the hitherto unused archive of the SCA movement dating from 1970.[32] In addition, much time has been spent tracking down papers of the English and Welsh branch of ISS in a variety of repositories.[33] Uniquely, this book makes extensive use of college magazines and newspapers, particularly those published by the civic universities across England, Wales and Scotland as well as national student newspapers. College magazines are perhaps more contentious than similar publications, forcing the researcher to assess how editorially independent they were from both the university authorities and the students' union or guild executive. In some ways, college magazines are trickier sources than publications such as the Communist-affiliated *Student Vanguard* (1932–1934), which in its own words made "no pretence at impartiality. It is written by students who are convinced that conditions in every section of social existence are more and more forcing a radical alternation in society."[34] As the test beds for the new approaches of successive cohorts of student journalists, college magazines are inconsistent publications over time and often exhibit a satirical and humorous bent. However, as Stephanie Spencer has argued about the value of school magazines for educational history, they can provide immediate insights into the priorities of a college or university.[35] Light has also been cast on student activities from unexpected sources such as special branch surveillance and Mass Observation reporters.[36]

The following chapters offer a history of student engagement with social, political and international questions from the late-nineteenth century to the late-twentieth century. The first two chapters show how the expansion of higher education in Britain and Ireland at the end of the nineteenth century engendered enthusiasm for social service and social study and set this in the context of an emergent Christian internationalist movement in which students played a key part. Chapter 4 looks at students' contribution to postwar reconstruction efforts in Europe and Russia, arguing that relief and reconstruction were important forces around which an incipient British student movement coalesced in the 1920s. Chapter 5 explores the shifting relationships between students and society in the 1920s and early 1930s through a discussion of the General Strike, student rags and the student self-help movement. Chapter 6 explores how students engaged with the widespread problems of the Depression and addresses the rise of a "student social consciousness." Chapter 7 discusses how antifascist relief effort combined traditional support activities with new forms of social action such as protest, boycott and campaigning. Collectively, these chapters on the interwar period show that a student "popular front" developed through cooperation of different groups in practical relief efforts. Chapter 8 looks at continuities and changes in student voluntary action during and in the period after the Second World War. The final two chapters consider postwar developments in student voluntarism, including the renegotiation of student volunteering in local communities, an upsurge of interest in questions of refugees and overseas aid and a shift to more politicized forms of community action in the 1970s.

CHAPTER 2

A New Era in Social Service? Student Associational Culture and the Settlement Movement

On his appointment as Bursar at Balliol College Oxford in 1883, Arthur Acland (1847–1926) noted that many of the undergraduates he met were "genuinely anxious to make themselves useful in work for the poor and others."[1] Similarly at the more recently established women's colleges, "we were all of us (or most of us) serious young women and thought we ought to do some good in the world" as Kathleen Courtney (1878–1974) later reflected.[2] From the 1880s students at universities and colleges in Britain and Ireland were increasingly receptive to the new ideas for practical social service that were being put forward by a range of writers and thinkers, and the universities emerged as important pools of volunteers for a range of new social institutions. The student social service movement drew on a varied set of intellectual and religious influences, streams that flowed together to raise the status of volunteering and make personal service at home or overseas incumbent on the educated classes. It is notable that significant developments did not begin until the expansion of higher education in the last quarter of the century, despite key advances in the theory and practice of charity in the late eighteenth and early nineteenth centuries. Through innovations like the creation of residential settlements in inner-city areas, British universities were central to what Clement Attlee (1883–1967) later described as a "new era in social service."[3] The developments in student social service that this book addresses form one facet of what we might call a "student associational culture," adapting a term used by a number of historians to refer to societies marked by the strength and vigour of their clubs, societies and voluntary associations. The chapter begins with a discussion of the expansion of higher education and the emergence of a distinct student culture, before exploring the place of the university settlement movement in the lives of undergraduates of the late Victorian and Edwardian eras.

ALL OUR TRADITIONS HAVE TO BE MADE: STUDENT CULTURE BEFORE 1914

To receive higher education before 1914 was a privilege reserved for a tiny minority in Britain, engendering a strong ethic of service among students. This service ethic drew on a variety of influences, one of which was Idealism and its core concept of "active citizenship."[4] Although citizenship was and remains a disputed and amorphous concept, in the last quarter of the nineteenth century the term was increasingly used in public debate to describe "duties that individuals owed to their communities, the nation and the Empire."[5] A new generation of politicians and writers who "spoke and wrote the language of citizenship" pictured a division of duties and responsibilities between citizen and state, and were strongly influenced by the ideas of British Idealism emanating from the universities.[6] Indeed, Jose Harris has argued that Idealism exerted as pervasive an influence on the socially aware middle classes as evangelicalism had earlier in the nineteenth century.[7] Idealist philosophers such as T. H. Green (1836–1882), Edward Caird (1835–1908), Bernard Bosanquet (1848–1923) and F. H. Bradley (1846–1924) held a vision of a well-ordered society built on active citizenship and public spirit.[8] The Idealist understanding of citizenship emphasized the need for active participation in the life of local communities and Green's own example of involvement with social and educational schemes in Oxford was long-remembered by generations of undergraduates.[9] The Idealists also placed emphasis on maintaining the unity of society in the face of challenges posed by modern social and industrial conditions. Caird argued that students should remain conscious of "those ethical bonds which unite us to our fellow citizens...[for] it is only such an ideal of social service that can really purify our lives."[10] Caird's students at Glasgow and Oxford were made aware that they had a twin responsibility to the "the poor and weak" in British society and to members of "less civilised races" under British rule.[11]

This late Victorian and Edwardian concern with making good, active citizens was often couched in the language of "character building." Building character came to be seen as the "great object of education" in Britain and the wider British world.[12] Stefan Collini has suggested that character was "an expression of a very deeply ingrained perception of the qualities needed to cope with life."[13] Character could be developed through a variety of techniques—such as competitive sports—as part of both formal and informal education, but instilling young people with an ethic of service was central to this wider project. As Gary McCulloch has argued, a Platonic version of "education for leadership" in which character training, communal living and service were key elements attained particular currency.[14] The service ideal therefore drew on the Platonic notion of "guardianship," an idea that exerted strong influence on educators who sought to prepare young people for future public service at home and overseas. [15] Social service enthusiasts also found in Aristotle's concept of continual self-development the idea that the cultivation of an individual's highest nature or best self was possible only though service for others.[16]

Before 1860 the only universities in England were the medieval foundations of Oxford and Cambridge and the more recent universities of Durham (1832) and London (1836, University College founded in 1826). Scotland had four universities (St Andrew's, Aberdeen, Glasgow and Edinburgh) and Wales had a university with degree awarding powers at Lampeter (1822). In Ireland, the sixteenth-century Trinity College in Dublin was joined by three colleges of a new Queen's University at Belfast, Cork and Galway established by Act of Parliament in 1845. In the last quarter of the century there was significant growth in student numbers through expansion of these existing institutions as well as the foundation of several new universities and university colleges. Owen's College, Manchester—which had begun to give university-level instruction as early as 1850—formed the first college of the new Victoria University in 1881 and was later joined by Yorkshire College at Leeds (1874) and Liverpool University College (1881).[17] In England, new university colleges were established to prepare students for degrees of the University of London, including Mason College, Birmingham (1875); Bristol (1876); Firth College, Sheffield (1879); Nottingham (1881); Reading (1892) and Exeter (1893). Most university colleges also founded affiliated Day Training Colleges to train elementary school teachers, and these developed over time into university teacher training departments. In 1893, the University of Wales was founded, formed of three colleges at Bangor, Cardiff and Aberystwyth. Queen's University was reorganized into the Royal University of Ireland in 1880 and in 1909 Belfast College became an independent university known as Queen's University Belfast. Growing state support for higher education led to the new universities and colleges receiving government grants from the 1880s. By 1900, then, there were around 20,000 university students in Britain as a whole.[18] Two thirds of higher education students in England were studying in institutions other than Oxford or Cambridge.

Before 1914 higher education was heavily restricted on grounds of class and gender. The scarcity of scholarships and the lack of government grants for fees or maintenance meant that although the new county grammar schools that opened after 1902 helped supply better educated recruits for universities and colleges, working-class male students in England could generally only enrol on part-time evening courses. The Scottish universities had greater numbers of working-class students and from 1901 the Carnegie Trust for the Universities of Scotland, established by philanthropist Andrew Carnegie, paid the tuition fees of students either born or educated in Scotland. On average 3,600 students benefited from this arrangement each year from 1901 to 1925.[19] Women remained a minority in higher education, despite making important advances during the last quarter of the nineteenth century. Colleges for women were opened at Cambridge (Girton, 1869, and Newnham, 1871), Oxford (for example Somerville and Lady Margaret Hall both 1879), London (including Westfield, 1882), Ireland (Alexandra College Dublin, 1866, and Victoria College Belfast, 1859), and Scotland (Queen Margaret College, Glasgow, 1883). From 1878 London University degrees were opened to women and most provincial university colleges began to admit women on the same grounds as men, albeit with separate women's unions, common rooms, tutorial positions and hostels to cater for their pastoral needs. The provincial universities also attracted women from a more diverse range of backgrounds than the residential colleges.[20] In 1900, women formed 16 percent of university students in Britain, although the proportion was higher in Wales than in either England or Scotland.[21] By 1914 higher education had opened up to a wider range of individuals than before, an expansion that offered new ways of promoting the concept "education for leadership" by drawing graduates of civic universities and university women into the national elite.[22]

Ever since John Henry Newman (1801–1890) judged individual development to be the most valuable aspect of a university education, the educational value of a corporate culture at universities and colleges had been strongly urged. Organized games were an important aspect of this culture and have received historical attention elsewhere, even if most of the focus is on Oxbridge traditions.[23] Although remaining largely nonresidential before 1914, many of the new university colleges developed sporting facilities and opened common rooms and unions to provide recreational spaces on campuses. Athletics associations were formed at Liverpool, Manchester and University College in the 1880s.[24] A second feature of the ideal corporate culture was residence; despite the fact that numbers in university accommodation remained low before the Second World War. Only a small number of hostels were opened at provincial colleges before 1914, and in the first instance this was by voluntary effort without formal university recognition. Some of the earliest halls of residence were founded for students of Owen's College, for instance, where Dalton Hall was founded by the Society of Friends in 1876 and the Anglican Hulme Hall opened in 1886. In 1887 sociologist Patrick Geddes (1854–1932) opened University Hall in Edinburgh as the first hall of residence in Scotland and encouraged early residents to become involved with social projects in nearby slum areas.[25] However, the Scottish model of a self-governing hall without a warden did not catch on in England, where the Oxbridge pattern of collegiate residence was hugely influential.[26] Many women's hostels were opened in the 1880s and 1890s including College Hall in London, Alexandra Hall in Aberystwyth, Ashburne Hall in Manchester and University Hall in Liverpool. These new halls of residence began to develop their own associational cultures, with sports teams, magazines and old students' associations as well as regular social functions such as dances and "at homes." Residence was routinely cited as an essential precondition for the development of a corporate life, and the regular appearance of the topic on the agenda at the interuniversity congresses held between 1904 and 1913 shows it was a question to which undergraduates were alive.

A third aspect of the student corporate culture was the formation of university clubs and societies. Some of the earliest expressions of voluntary action in the universities lie in the religious societies formed during the eighteenth and nineteenth centuries. Perhaps the best-known example is John Wesley's (1703–1791) "Holy Club" at Oxford in the 1730s, which encouraged its members to visit sick people and prisoners.[27] Edinburgh students also founded a number of theological, discussion and medical societies in the late eighteenth century, which in the 1830s developed into a body known as the Associated Societies, the forerunner of the Edinburgh Students Representative Council (SRC).[28] From the early nineteenth century Christian missions working both at home and overseas were supported by missionary associations and prayer societies formed by university students and tutors.[29] Further religious awakenings in the 1860s and 1870s resulted in a new wave of evangelical student associations and prayer unions. Toward the end of the century, the older universities as well as newer institutions including Manchester, Leeds and Liverpool started literary, scientific or historical societies, debating clubs and unions or model parliaments as well as editorial committees to run college magazines. As one of the few scholars to have studied these organizations, Reba Soffer argues that extracurricular historical societies at Oxford, Cambridge, Manchester and University College were "proving grounds for future leaders," where the emphasis was less on the historical content than on the possibilities for insights into the world of politics, diplomacy and human nature.[30] As the universities at this date had relatively small numbers, it was not uncommon for students to remain members of university societies for several years after graduation, and even to take on leadership positions. Manchester University student William Fletcher Shaw (1878–1961), for example, remembered that in the early 1900s the chairs of the Men's Union, the medical society and the debating society were all graduates.[31]

Extracurricular clubs and societies were most fully developed in residential colleges, but by 1914 most university colleges could boast a debating society, an engineering or scientific society, a literary society and magazine committee as well as a branch of the Student Christian Movement (SCM). At Birmingham University there were on average three society meetings or special lectures each night in the Edwardian period.[32] The largely nonresidential nature of the civic universities meant that there was often a small core of students very active in college life. Student life centered on separate men's and women's common rooms and unions, but social occasions, dances, mixed debates, magazine editorial boards and some mixed societies provided more opportunities for mixing between the sexes than at the residential colleges. According to Julie Gilbert, women students "were active participants and often leaders" in the social and extracurricular activities of civic universities and often exerted an influence out of proportion to their numbers.[33] At the women's colleges society meetings, reading groups, working parties and socials were organized every night of the week.[34] For women students, such societies were valued for the unique opportunities they provided to hone arguments in stimulating yet private all-female spaces. Kathleen Courtney recalled the excitement of discussing "all the fundamental questions of life as though we were the first to venture upon them."[35] It is worth noting that at this date students often identified more closely with their faculty, particularly in medicine, arts or engineering, than with the university as a whole. University magazines began to be promoted as a means of encouraging the "spirit of fraternity, or unity of purpose, without which the students as a body can never hope to attain their purpose," as an editorial in Birmingham's newly founded *Mermaid* put it in 1904.[36]

Specialist clubs with an emphasis on social questions were also formed at several universities in the 1880s and 1890s, reflecting the increased priority accorded to such topics in national discourse. In Britain, the interlinked problems of urban poverty, poor housing, unemployment and industrial unrest were emerging as national concerns, and attention was being drawn to social conditions through research by investigative journalists, clergymen and social reformers. In the 1880s the Charity Organisation Society *Reporter* noted, "books on the poor, poverty, social questions, slums and the like subjects rush fast and furious from the press."[37] In 1883, the famous *The Bitter Cry of Outcast London* and the series of "How the Poor Live" illustrated articles published in *The Pictorial World* had an immediate impact in the universities. Although the incipient Labour movement advocated different approaches, many social investigators and reformers considered the solution to urban poverty was to be found in bridging class divides and strengthening communities through new expressions of active citizenship—a powerful message taken up by many university students and recent graduates. In the Edwardian period, suffrage societies also became popular at women's colleges and in the women's unions. For example, the Women's Suffrage Society at Royal Holloway College (affiliated to the Nation Union of Women's Suffrage Societies) counted half the 150 students as members in 1910, while at Bedford College a Society for the Study of Women's Franchise admitted members "of all shades of opinion."[38]

From the 1890s religious societies at the universities enjoyed an increase in popularity under the new emphasis on the social responsibilities of Christianity that cut across all denominations. Reflecting shifts toward a new incarnational theology that gave greater emphasis to the fatherhood of God and its corollary in the brotherhood of man, there was a stronger recognition of the ethical imperatives of Christ's teaching.[39] A new generation of Anglo-Catholics, led by the "Holy Party" of Charles Gore (1853–1932) and Henry Scott Holland (1847–1918), began to embrace a high church brand of Christian Socialism, growing out of the incarnational theology expressed in their collection of essays *Lux Mundi*.[40] Leading Cambridge theologian Brooke Foss Westcott (1825–1901) argued for a focus on society rather than the individual.[41] The formation of the Christian Social Union in 1889, with Westcott as President, was one sign of this new social awareness. Branches were active at several colleges and universities in England, particularly at Oxford, where the tradition of

Anglo-Catholic social concern enjoyed a long life. In Ireland, student philanthropic and religious societies flourished in the Catholic colleges, and in women's colleges the Sodalities of the Children of Mary became a significant part of student life.[42]

The long-standing evangelical tradition at English and Scottish universities also received new impetus under the influence of a distinctive spirituality inspired by visiting American evangelists and nurtured by the Keswick convention. The Keswick convention, held annually in the Lake District from 1876, was the focal point of the holiness teaching of the late nineteenth century, which urged evangelical Christians to aim for a second decisive experience after conversion known as "sanctification."[43] Anglo-American revivalist preachers taught that conversion entailed a commitment to active Christian service.[44] The Keswick call "to entire dedication of body, soul and spirit to the service of the Lord" was a powerful impetus for social and missionary service and especially attractive to the newly expanded middle class.[45] Despite mainly attracting middle-class evangelical Anglicans, some high-profile non conformists, such as the Baptist leader Frederick Meyer (1847–1929), were drawn to Keswick's spirituality which they too combined with a strong social message.[46] In the 1890s Keswick was the natural launch-pad for an important new student organization, the SCM, which will be addressed in detail in the next chapter.

Student rag developed as a distinctive aspect of student culture in the decades before the First World War, initially at universities in Scotland, Ireland and the north of England as high-spirited celebrations linked to holidays or theater trips and, as the tradition spread to other universities, evolved into carnivals.[47] In 1887, students at Manchester introduced the idea of a torchlight fancy dress procession as a tradition apparently borrowed from German universities.[48] By the mid-1890s this had developed into a custom of costumed procession through Manchester to the pantomime on Shrove Tuesday. At Queen's College Belfast the yearly "Students' Night" of entertainments at the theater also began to feature a costumed procession of students carrying Chinese lanterns and acquiring various "trophies" on route.[49] Some women's unions did take part but festivities were largely male-dominated and the average parade featured a considerable number of male students dressed as female stock characters such as nurses, titled ladies and suffragettes. Although an increasingly important part of male student culture, it was not until after the First World War that rag celebrations became synonymous with charitable collections.

The final aspect of the British "student associational culture" was student representation. Here it was the Scottish universities, not Oxbridge, that provided the most influential model. Edinburgh's Students' Representative Council had been formed in 1883 with three core functions of representing students, providing an official channel of communication between students and university authorities and developing social and academic life. [50] The Edinburgh council was quickly followed by the formation of SRCs in the other Scottish universities and in the 1890s at Liverpool, Leeds, Durham, Belfast, University College and Birmingham.[51] In 1905, an SRC was formed for the University of London to strengthen links between students at the various colleges, and several intercollegiate clubs and societies followed.[52] Developing out of these experiments in self-government was a limited attempt to forge a national student movement before the First World War. In Scotland, the four SRCs had formed a consortium in 1888 but it was not until 1904 that English and Welsh students met at the first Inter-University Students' Congress at Manchester University. This first conference attracted 40 men and women student delegates representing every university in England and Wales. The congress met annually at different universities until 1913. The meetings were attended largely by officers of students' representative councils and guilds and, from 1905, included delegates from colleges across England, Scotland, Wales and Ireland. Matters discussed at the early congresses included residence, organization of degree courses, external degrees, medical training, publication of a students' song book and development of university employment registers. [53]

These intervarsity congresses provided student delegates with a valuable education in university traditions. Keen to show off their university or colleges to the visitors, organizing committees planned congress sessions to allow delegates to experience occasions such as foundation celebrations, degree ceremonies and sports days as well as arranging special social functions including concerts, dances, garden parties and at home gatherings in women's unions.[54] Delegates were welcomed at receptions hosted by university vice chancellors and local dignitaries. Optional tours of sites of local interest such as Chatsworth and Durham Cathedral usually ended the program. Compared to other prewar student gatherings such as the annual conferences of the SCM, meetings were small-scale affairs that were not very representative of the wider field of higher education. Yet at a time when students at the civic universities were acutely aware of the need to invent their own traditions, such opportunities to compare the institutions and practices of other students' unions, to meet students from all parts of the United Kingdom and to begin to forge a common student movement were hugely valuable. Attending the congress at Edinburgh University in 1906, for example, a delegate from Manchester reported his surprise at the far greater importance of the Scottish SRCs compared to the English ones.[55] In their book on the student estate Ashby and Anderson dismiss these congresses as agreeable social occasions and suggest that the growing disenchantment with the congresses reflects the fact that "there were, in those years, no issues on which students, as students, felt passionately."[56] However, this analysis rests on Ashby and Anderson's narrow focus on representative student politics—the overwhelming concern of universities at the time of writing in the late 1960s—rather than an interest in student associational culture more broadly. Ashby and Anderson's neglect of a wider range of student organizations, including the SCM and other clubs and societies, also underplays the significant contribution of women students to the formation of a student culture before 1914. It is to what was to become a central element in an emergent student movement—social service and social study—that we now turn.

A GREAT VOLUNTARY MOVEMENT: UNIVERSITY SETTLEMENTS

The growing interest in social problems in the universities entailed the creation of new models of service for students and recent graduates. Supportive tutors endeavored to open up new outlets for students' desire to serve, including as volunteers on the various programs for university "extension" developed from the late 1860s or on experimental projects like John Ruskin's road-building scheme in 1874–1875. The most influential and long-lasting model of service, however, developed out of the idea that upper- and middle-class volunteers could give the best service by living in, rather than just visiting, poor areas of major cities—and in 1883 the university settlement movement was born. From 1875 the Reverend Samuel Barnett (1844–1913) and his wife Henrietta (1851–1936) had been encouraging undergraduates to volunteer in their parish of St Jude's in Whitechapel, sometimes staying for a few days or weeks.[57] Students helped out at men's clubs, at parish parties, boys' boxing clubs or visited homes for the Charity Organisation Society and Children's Country Holiday Fund. The most famous of these early "settlers" was Arnold Toynbee who spent a few weeks in the long vacation of 1875 living in Whitechapel. The novel idea of the residence of educated men in working-class districts was further popularized by the publication of several editions of Edward Denison's letters between 1871 and 1884.[58] Son of the Bishop of Salisbury and nephew of the Speaker of the House of Commons, Denison (1840–1870) had lived in Mile End for eight months in 1867–1868 and involved himself in work for the poor in the parish of the Reverend J. R. Green (1837–1883).[59] Denison believed that the real problem of East London was the lack of middle-class residents and suggested that his plan of living in the East End was "the only really practicable one, and as I have both means, time, and inclination, I should be a thief and a murderer if I withheld what I so evidently owe."[60] The possibility of expanding this scheme had been discussed at a meeting called by Ruskin in 1868, although Denison's early death prevented it being taken forward.[61]

University settlements also owed a debt to the school mission. Indeed to understand the growth of social service in universities and colleges, we should first briefly consider the ways in which schools built on familiar practices of giving established in early childhood. Children in Britain, as in America and elsewhere, were routinely trained to set aside a small portion of their pocket money for the Church plate, the mission box or for a charity's youth "auxiliary" such as the Royal Society for the Prevention of Cruelty to Animals Band of Mercy or the National Society for the Prevention of Cruelty's League of Pity.[62] Schools developed techniques to sustain interest in charitable causes through encouragement of charitable donations, fundraising activities and practical service. This was in part a response to recurrent criticism that educational institutions for the upper classes isolated their pupils from reality and thus failed to turn out good citizens.[63] Emerging out of this concern to teach pupils to think of others was an influential model of service known as the "school mission." From the 1820s overseas mission initiatives had inspired the Church of England to create a network of home missions to supply additional clergy and lay volunteers for rapidly growing urban parishes. Headmaster Edward Thring (1821–1887) and senior pupils at Uppingham founded the first school mission in 1869 when they raised money to sponsor a missionary curate in South London. The plan was widely copied by other boys' schools in the 1870s and 1880s. School missions adopted a section of a poor parish and a clergyman—usually an old boy of the sponsoring institution—was employed as missioner with his salary raised through chapel collections. An initial focus on London reflected the late nineteenth-century belief that the city at the "heart of the Empire" had unique social needs and problems. Activities organized by missions might include mothers' meetings, boys' and girls' clubs, savings banks, gymnasia, sports teams and later Scout or Guide troops. From small beginnings in rented buildings, many missions were converted into full parishes with considerable institutional presence.[64] From the 1880s several Oxford and Cambridge colleges began to start missions along similar lines.

With the expansion of schooling for middle-class girls in the last quarter of the century, womanly "traditions" of service were formalized and received new impetus in school-based societies.[65] While middle- and upper-class girls had long been trained in charity, the channelling of such activities through social service leagues was a new phenomenon.[66] Since few could finance social work on the scale of the school or college missions, working collaboratively became an important feature of the social service developed by girls' schools and women's colleges alike. In 1896, 12 schools formed the United Girls' School Mission in South London, which later opened the Peckham Settlement.[67] Most secondary schools did not find it viable to finance social service solely through pupils' subscriptions, so various methods of raising money were introduced. Moreover, drawing on local civic pride, fundraising for voluntary hospitals through the technique of sponsoring a cot or a nurse's salary became common in many schools after the 1890s.[68] The mobility of teachers across the British imperial world meant that international connections were frequently forged between schools through the efforts of former staff or pupils. Although fundraising was always important, many teachers preferred to encourage pupils to give time rather than money, reflecting both a desire to promote active citizenship and late Victorian concern about indiscriminate giving.

Building on all these earlier initiatives, in November 1883 Samuel Barnett formally proposed starting a "university settlement." Barnett advised undergraduates from St John's College Cambridge who had written to him for advice on developing university social work to drop the mission model. Although a St John's College Mission did in fact go ahead, starting work in Walworth in January 1884, there was also strong interest in Barnett's alternative settlement idea.[69] Committees of tutors and undergraduates were formed in both Oxford and Cambridge to raise money and oversee the progress of his scheme. Barnett's plan was that graduate residents would "do citizen's duty," as he called it, while living in poor parishes among a supportive community of fellow volunteers. By the end of 1884 a settlement named after the recently deceased Arnold Toynbee (Toynbee Hall) had opened in Whitechapel, along with a high church settlement called Oxford House, which was located in Bethnal Green. The idea spread rapidly and by 1911, 45 settlements had opened across the United Kingdom, although a much smaller number could properly be called "university settlements."[70] Unlike the college missions, settlements were rarely located in the very poorest districts or "slums," because the clubs and educational classes they offered were targeted at the respectable working and lower-middle classes. Yet despite the publicity accorded to the settlement movement, college missions continued to attract undergraduate support, particularly in Cambridge. By 1892 there were six Cambridge missions in South London as well as two supported by Oxford colleges.[71] South London was said to "bristle with Cambridge enterprises."[72] Some colleges began to develop alternative forms of social work rather than adopting a section of a parish, such as a nonreligious settlement, Cambridge House, which developed out of the Trinity College Mission in 1896.[73]

Enthusiasm for social service spread beyond the Oxbridge colleges most commonly associated with university missions and settlements. Although excluded from the first settlements, university women were quick to become involved. In 1889, women at Manchester University felt they should become involved with some form of social work because similar work was being done "by all other colleges of any kind of standing."[74] Student help at a girls' club in the city therefore preceded the formation of the Ancoats University Settlement in 1895. The interuniversity Women's University Settlement (WUS) opened in Blackfriars, South London, in 1887 and Oxford's Lady Margaret Hall Settlement in 1897. As historians including Martha Vicinus have pointed out, women's settlements, like colleges, provided new forms of residential community for independent, educated women. For residents they "combined familiar structures from college with new public freedoms."[75] In 1905, Hilda Cashmore—a tutor at the women's teacher training college affiliated to University College, Bristol—started a Social Service Guild which proved so popular that 105 out of 120 students became members.[76] Cashmore's successful encouragement of social service among her students led in part to the formation of the Bristol University Settlement, of which she became the first warden in 1911. Significantly, Bristol had just received its university charter, and the settlement was hailed as an important feature of the new university and a means of the university enriching the life of the city.[77] Cashmore based the daily life of the Bristol settlement on her own experiences as a student at Somerville College. In Scotland, however, where there was no tradition of students living away from home, the residential model was less successful and Queen Margaret Settlement, Glasgow, opened in 1897, struggled to recruit suitable residents.[78]

With the opening of the first settlements Walter Besant (1836–1901) declared that a "great voluntary movement" was just beginning.[79] The settlement movement immediately generated strong interest from social reformers overseas, especially in the USA and Japan.[80] This interest was fuelled by conferences, international exchanges and publications such as Robert Woods' *English Social Movements,* largely written during a six month stay at Toynbee Hall in 1890.[81] In 1895, a large conference was held at Toynbee Hall to promote the idea of university settlements.[82] Speaking at Glasgow University in 1893 Sir John Gorst (1835–1916), Conservative Vice-President of the Committee of the Council on Education, suggested young people held a "conviction that the only life worth living is one in which the talents and capacities of the individual are spent in the service of mankind."[83] Therefore older forms of charity could not satisfy their desires because students longed "to come into personal contact with human suffering."[84] Settlements linked to universities were started in cities across Britain, including Toynbee House (1886) and the University Students Settlement (1889) both in Glasgow, Edinburgh University Settlement (1905) and Liverpool University Settlement (1907).[85] At Liverpool, plans to develop a settlement began in 1903 after a group of students had attended a World Student Missionary Conference in Edinburgh. It was felt that members of a university established in a "great city" were under special responsibilities to the community and that "what has been done elsewhere for enabling students, past and present, to share in social work" ought to be attempted in Liverpool.[86] Thus possession of a settlement came to be seen as a hallmark of a provincial university with ambitions for civic and regional influence, even though, as Jenny Harrow notes, settlements usually lacked "formal legal, administrative or financial relationships with the universities, whose names they used."[87]

The settlement and college mission models were also adapted and modified by a wider range of educational institutions than has previously been recognized, both in Britain and overseas. As one example of many, the Blackheath Kindergarten and Training College adopted a kindergarten in a poor parish of Woolwich as its "mission" in the first years of the twentieth century.[88] Oxford's nonconformist Mansfield College opened its own settlement in 1890, while the Christian Social Union, with several well-supported university branches, was able to start a settlement called Maurice Hostel in Hoxton in 1898. [89] University settlements were the subject of a long debate at the first students' Inter-University Congress in 1904. A motion approving of settlements was proposed by Henry Lygon of

Oxford, with contributions from students at Birmingham, London and Manchester. The motion was eventually carried unanimously by all 40 delegates, reflecting widespread student interest and consensus on the topic, as few other motions were so-well supported.[90]

Double Duties: Contacts between Students and Settlements

Much has been written elsewhere about the wide range of social, welfare and educational activities developed by the university settlements, particularly in the period 1884–1914.[91] Historians have also tended to focus on leaders and staff of settlements and their highest profile residents.[92] My interest here is in the changing relationships between settlements and missions and the universities and colleges that supported and funded them, and particularly in the place of settlements in the lives of undergraduates. Students were usually excluded from involvement in governance and long-term residents were usually recent graduates, but settlements did open up new opportunities for undergraduates as student secretaries, regular volunteers and short-term residents. A pattern developed where one or more secretaries would be selected from among undergraduates or junior tutors to represent each social institution supported by a particular college or university.[93] These secretaries or small committees would arrange meetings and speakers, collect funds and subscriptions, recruit volunteers and raise awareness of the institution's work.[94] In addition to raising money, colleges regularly collected and sent gifts-in-kind such as clothing, flowers, toys and Christmas presents to the institutions they supported.[95]

University settlements and college missions served a dual role providing social and religious services to local communities and acting as educational centers for student volunteers. From the 1890s many involved in settlement work in Britain began emphasizing the need to study the origins of social problems and to develop training for volunteers.[96] Women's colleges were quick to see the potential of the settlements as training grounds for their students, with a view to equipping graduates for new paid and unpaid roles in health and social welfare work thatwere opening up to women. The first residents at the WUS declared they had a "double duty" to combine social work with social service training for women volunteers.[97] From its early days the WUS arranged meetings of volunteers and organized courses of lectures and study sessions on a wide range of social questions such as housing, health, child welfare and education.[98] In view of these attempts, the Principal of Somerville College welcomed the settlement as "a school for young workers."[99] With such small numbers of women attending university, in practice, however, university women actually formed a minority of the settlement's residents before 1914.[100]

In 1894, the WUS started a more formal training course, sending out trainees as paid or voluntary workers for the Charity Organisation Society and settlements elsewhere.[101] Several colleges began to develop structured social service training courses, again aimed mainly at women volunteers, beginning a strong tradition of university social work training in partnership with settlements.[102] At Birmingham, a one-year course was started in 1908 for both paid and voluntary workers, described as a happy "combination of Settlement and University life" which would be a "splendid finish to the education of girls."[103] By 1912 six universities in Britain and Ireland offered some form of theoretical instruction in combination with practical experience of social work at a settlement.[104] Trained students commanded salaries of not less than £100 a year for work as organizers of clubs, secretaries of relief societies and care committee organizers, although many continued to take unpaid roles. Alongside these formal diploma courses, settlements also developed shorter programs to tap into the growing enthusiasm for "social study" in the Edwardian period that will be discussed in the next chapter. For instance, Birmingham Women's Settlement organized annual three-day vacation schools of social study for women students at the university; 50 students attended the course in Easter 1910.[105]

As part of the core function of settlements to provide social education, welcoming successive parties of visiting students became a common aspect of the work of settlement wardens. From the outset students were strongly encouraged to visit missions and settlements and such visits were always recorded and reported in annual reports or settlement journals. As the Dean of St John's College Cambridge reflected, "the visits of members of a College make the College Mission."[106] At Easter 1887, for example, more than 50 undergraduates visited the newly opened Trinity College (Cambridge) Mission in Camberwell.[107] Visits were encouraged by the design of the first settlements as familiar-looking establishments, arranged "as far as possible to suggest an English college" with a central quad "so dear always to the heart of a university man" as Woods wrote of Toynbee Hall.[108] Although not built to accommodate permanent residents, most college missions were also usually able to provide a few rooms for visiting students who helped with both religious and social work in the vacations. In the 1890s Pembroke College (Cambridge) Mission, for instance, had around 15 undergraduates in residence at any one time during the vacations, according to its former missioner C. F. Andrews (1871–1940).[109]

Such short visits to settlements and missions—as well as hospitals, workhouses or boys' and girls' clubs—should be seen as part of a wider passion for "slumming" in the late Victorian and Edwardian period. After the 1880s the "slums" of major cities across the world became popular destinations for journalists, tourists and students as well as social reformers and social servants.[110] Mary Bhore, an Indian studying in Britain in 1901, was forcibly struck by the interest of her British friends in slumming.[111] The educative value of visits to poor districts, however, may have been questionable since students approached the slums with ideas about what they might encounter already shaped by others' accounts.[112] Although the height of the fashionable mania for slumming was the 1880s and 1890s, in the early twentieth century the SCM and other organizations urged that visits to specific social institutions could be of educational value. The SCM judged that a couple of visits to a settlement or other social institution comprised the "minimum contact with social service" that every student should experience as part of his or her education.[113] The Salvation Army, for example, welcomed visitors to its social service institutions in London for tours that were "sure to be educative in the highest degree."[114] Westfield College Social Club started to arrange daytime visits for students to see soup kitchens and "children's dinners."[115] Such visits were important glimpses of other worlds for men and women students alike but they could generate unrealistic expectations on both sides. On the other hand, short visits could sometimes have the effect of challenging of what students themselves described as "habitual and half-unconscious class superiority."[116] One former member of the Westfield Social Club noted "it gave us a chance to come into contact with conditions of life far different from our own and awakened our sympathy with the poor and crippled and unfortunate."[117] Increasingly educationists recognized that the value of a visit to a settlement or a talk on slum life depended on how well students had been prepared in advance through social study.[118]

A second important point of contact between students and settlements was through the visits to colleges arranged for groups from the settlement or missions. Such visits evolved into annual "treats," often Whit Monday or August Bank Holiday outings where student volunteers would entertain parties from the settlement clubs in college grounds, as well as Christmas entertainments organized by groups of students at the settlements.[119] For men students, annual sports fixtures between boys' and men's clubs and a college team were a popular part of such visits. Joint debates and talks were also held between settlement clubs and university clubs.[120] For women, the treats often involved weeks of advance preparation: making toys and clothes to give as gifts, practising musical or theatrical entertainments and decorating Christmas trees. Arranging these treats became an annual tradition passed down from one generation of students to the next, with seemingly little variation in form or content until the interwar period. Involvement was hugely enjoyable and satisfying for students as well as providing valuable red letter days for beneficiaries. However, for many student volunteers, interactions with working-class men, women and children were thus limited to what were artificial and stage-managed affairs, exacerbating the difficulties of bridging divides of class and understanding. Commenting on entertaining parties of factory girls one woman student suggested "they were as much of a mystery to us as we to them."[121] Misunderstandings could arise when students expecting "slum dwellers" to visit their college were met by "prosperous" looking working-class people in their Sunday best and had to be informed that "the poorest will almost always on occasion produce a decent suit of clothes."[122] What these working-class visitors thought of their trips to the colleges is harder to establish, though unsurprisingly they are generally reported as having enjoyed themselves thoroughly. However, missioners and wardens were not above recording the "humorous mistakes" relating to college life made by the visitors.[123]

In addition to short visits, settlements did provide new opportunities for regular volunteering for small numbers of students. Student volunteers helped the permanent residents and paid staff of college missions and settlements to keep the clubs, classes and programs of visiting running. At Manchester, students were recruited to help with activities such as evening socials and children's concerts and in Glasgow women students were relied on to help with Saturday games for children at the Queen Margaret Settlement.[124] Bristol students helped tutor local residents, supported a play center and organized sports at the annual Settlement May Festival.[125] As settlements developed specialist services such as the "poor man's lawyer," settlements also recruited student and graduate volunteers keen to use their professional skills giving *pro bono* legal advice or providing free medical or dental services.[126] London-based settlements and missions could rely on fewer local volunteers but students were particularly valued in supporting vacation-time activities such as summer camps.[127] Groups of Oxford students, particularly from Balliol, helped regularly at the

Oxford Medical Mission's summer camps.[128] Some undergraduates also became involved in the surveys of local need and social provision that formed part of the settlement movement's contribution to social research and social reform.

However, only relatively small numbers of students became involved in practical social service activities with settlements. College missions and university settlements failed to attract as many student volunteers, supporters or donors as they wanted or needed. In 1911 the Head of Cambridge House N. B. Kent reported a feeling among some undergraduates that the college mission existed to "exact tribute from them, and is therefore regarded as a thing to be avoided if possible."[129] Rather than a wholesale rejection by students, Jenny Harrow argues that there was a "gradual distancing" of settlements from universities over the period 1884–1914 through which potential constituencies of support believed that others associated with the universities were helping out.[130] Women students were always the most active volunteers at settlements. Manchester University Settlement, for instance, repeatedly appealed in vain for greater involvement of male students to support club work or lead social surveys in Manchester and Salford.[131] Before 1914 women students constituted between a quarter and one-third of the student population at the provincial universities but their involvement in social service was out of proportion to these numbers. Data collected by the SCM in the Edwardian period confirms that the women's student unions and colleges developed stronger traditions of social service and supported a more varied range of social institutions than men's.[132]

The greatest impact of service with settlements was on arguably on students themselves. Educationists attached greater value to the educative function than to the results of social service. Indeed the idea that through social service volunteers could achieve self-fulfilment and happiness was repeatedly put forward.[133] Miss White, Principal of Alexandra College Dublin, for instance, urged young women to take up social service, because it would "make your own lives far fuller and happier, for nothing impoverishes life so much as the narrowing of sympathies by concentrating them on ourselves."[134] Reminiscences recognized that the main advantages of settlements accrued to residents, and volunteers' reports indicate that they derived much personal satisfaction, fulfilment and enjoyment from involvement. Social service was also a way for students to develop valuable organizational and secretarial skills in fundraising, keeping minutes and accounts and putting on events as well as public speaking and writing articles or reports.[135] For both men and women, therefore, participation in social service at college could be an important stage in a voluntary "career" and might lead to paid or unpaid roles as full-time social workers, secretaries, missionaries or political activists. Gladys Page-Wood, a student at the Bristol Day Training College, later recalled membership of the Social Service Guild was for her and for many of her peers "the beginning of a life-long interest in social service."[136] Importantly, the potential benefits of involvement in social service as a student were greater for women than for men, who already had more secure routes of entry to established professions in the Church, law or the home and overseas civil service.

CONCLUSIONS

The expansion of higher education in Britain and Ireland coincided with a new enthusiasm for social service and social study among undergraduates who recognized that the privileges of education carried social obligations. Interest in social service spread far outside Oxbridge colleges, as the university settlement or college mission model was extensively adapted and modified in Britain and internationally. The settlement movement influenced models of student service in the USA, Japan and Finland and inspired a number of "hybrid" social service and missionary organizations such as the Missionary Settlement of University Women in Bombay, discussed in the next chapter. Involvement was highly significant for the students who did take part. Voluntary work experience at settlements provided male graduates with new routes into traditional careers in politics and public administration, and led to some shaping new fields of work in adult education, youth work or prison reform. For women it was both a valuable activity in itself and a way into wholly new careers in social welfare and public service. Although representative student politics was in its infancy, social service and social study were central to the emergence of a vibrant associational culture at universities and colleges before 1914. While relatively small numbers of students actually took part in practical activities at a settlement and student social service before 1914 was unsurprisingly heavily gendered, there was wider support for the ideals of university settlements and pride in the possession of one. Looking at student social service channelled through branches of the SCM, college social clubs or settlement associations broadens our understanding of what it was like to be a student before 1914, and reveals that women students played a significant role in this extracurricular arena.

Developments at the universities and colleges also helped forge a wider social service culture in Britain before 1914. From the 1880s educationists welcomed the embrace of social service by the universities and sought to extend such activities to others through the formation of associations in which service was a central component. It was recognized that taking up some definite volunteering might be harder for those "do not happen to move in circles where social service is a familiar habit."[137] A particular target group were the lower-middle classes, for whom a range of young people's guilds were formed. These leagues were multisided organizations which aimed to organize members' recreation, channel Christian social service and encourage mutual improvement.[138] As Geoffrey Crossick has argued, voluntary associations which embraced different levels of the middle class were central to the process of incorporating the lower-middle classes into a bourgeois ideological world.[139] The Edwardian period was marked by a search for new outlets for national and social service on the part of the British elite in response to growing levels of industrial unrest and working-class discontent. This was stirred up by the constitutional crisis brought about by the House of Lords rejection of the "People's Budget" in 1909 and the "peers versus the people" election of 1910. In 1912, the *Daily Mail* published a series of articles on Labour unrest by H. G. Wells (1866–1946), which provoked a stream of responses that were later published as a book.[140] The writer John Galsworthy (1867–1933) contributed a paper condemning British public schools but several educationists sought to counter these claims, asserting that public schools and universities had never done more "to train men in the sense of responsibility of wealth and culture."[141] Several new social service leagues were formed in response to this criticism— including the Agenda Club and the Cavendish Association—and owed a strong debt to college missions and university settlements, although their formation was also testament to the failure of these models to inspire lasting ideals of social service.[142] The Cavendish Association, founded in the week of King George V's coronation in 1911, justified its appeal to educated young men on patriotic grounds because the nation needed the service of those who had "privileges of position, education and opportunity."[143]

Speakers at a 1911 meeting in Oxford urged that settlements were still offering the best opportunities for educated men and women to make contact with the urban poor and suggested that it was through continued support that universities could play a real part in the life of the nation.[144] The Edwardian period was marked by such repeated— if often unsuccessful—efforts to promote the settlement movement to new generations of students. However, if the links between universities and settlements were weakening as Jenny Harrow asserts, there were new openings for students interested in social service. In 1911, N. B. Kent recorded with satisfaction the "increasing desire to serve which is so widespread at the present."[145] Indeed, in the later Edwardian period social service became a unifying force among students of different religious and social backgrounds, and it was in part its active promotion of service and study that secured the SCM a voice as a national student association, as we shall see in the next chapter. Moreover, through international organizations such as the World's Student Christian Federation British students were to carve out roles for themselves in the wider movement of Christian internationalism.

CHAPTER 3

Christian Internationalism, Social Study and the Universities Before 1914

In 1908, missionary educationist C. F. Andrews considered that "one of the most striking developments of the present century has been the growing connection between students in Colleges and social work among the poor" and noted that the "East is rapidly taking up the new social movement."[1] In the late Victorian and Edwardian periods global networks of educationists, missionaries and social workers ensured that developments in student social service and social study in Britain did not develop in a vacuum, but shaped and were shaped in turn by wider trends. A key conduit for exchange of ideas and practices on social topics was the global student Christian movement, which this chapter addresses. The British Student Christian Movement (SCM) encouraged support for overseas causes alongside local social work, motivated by the belief that British students had a leading role to play in an emergent Christian internationalist movement. Since the late eighteenth century the British had prided themselves on a philanthropic and humanitarian tradition that embraced overseas causes alongside domestic concerns. The idea of empire as a place for charitable aid and voluntary service fed into the British self-image as benevolent rulers since concern for "fellow subjects" overseas was at the core of British imperial ideology.[2] The chapter argues that social service also served an important function as a relatively uncontroversial common point of contact between British students and students internationally, in North America, Australia, New Zealand, as well as in India, China and Japan. Social service and social study became one of the most popular topics addressed at international student gatherings and in this way models and methods developed in one country spread rapidly to others.

The Solidarity of the Student World: The International Student Christian Movement

The British SCM emerged out of the late nineteenth-century trans-atlantic missionary revival which had spread quickly throughout university and college-educated young people in the United States. At a Keswick convention in July 1891 Robert Wilder, founding member of the American Student Volunteer Movement, issued a strong appeal to British university and college students to offer themselves for Christian service overseas.[3] After a follow-up tour by Wilder to universities in England and Scotland, the British Student Volunteer Missionary Union (SVMU) was formed by representatives from eight universities meeting in Edinburgh in April 1892. Like its American counterpart, the SVMU acted as a recruiting agency for Protestant mission societies by encouraging students to pledge themselves to missionary service and helping them sustain this resolve through study circles and annual conventions. Around one-in-ten of all students in Britain and Ireland joined the SVMU before 1914, 80 percent of whom subsequently made a formal offer of service to a missionary society. The SVMU appealed most strongly to students whose concern was for the whole person, body and soul, and initially its largest body of volunteers were medical students.[4] The optimism and Anglo-Saxon confidence of this first generation of university-educated missionary volunteers was encapsulated in their infamous watchword, "the evangelisation of the world in this generation." Overseas service came to be seen by many evangelical Christians in the universities as the highest form of service to mankind and to God.[5] In 1900 Eugene Stock (1836–1928), secretary and historian of the Church Missionary Society, paid tribute to the movement's work in inspiring students to take "up a cause just as men take up a political cause or a social cause."[6]

It was in order to strengthen this overseas work that in 1893 20 college Christian unions came together to form the Inter-University Christian Union, which by the turn of the century was known as the SCM of Great Britain and Ireland.[7] Unlike the North American movement, which was divided on lines of gender into college Young Men's Christian Association (YMCA) or Young Women's Christian Association (YWCA) work, the British SCM was coeducational from the start, although at college level activities were usually arranged through separate women's and men's branches. Grassroots student enthusiasm combined with effective national organization led to the SCM's rapid growth. Employing travelling secretaries to develop the movement outside the founding colleges, by 1908 the SCM had

130 branches across Britain and Ireland with a membership of more than five-thousand students.[8] Ruth Rouse (1872–1956), a graduate of both Bedford College and Girton College, served as one of the first travelling secretaries and helped to form a large number of branches. Rouse's later work for the Student Volunteer Movement and College YWCA in the USA and Canada, the Missionary Settlement of University Women in Bombay and the World's Student Christian Federation (WSCF) gave her unrivalled opportunities for fostering international student friendship and spreading the gospel of social service.[9]

Starting initially among evangelical Anglicans and nonconformists, SCM leaders in Britain pursued a policy of inclusion, seeking to broaden the basis of membership and attract students from other Christian traditions including those at high church theological colleges. A second important part of this work was the extension of SCM into teacher training colleges, an organizational innovation Rouse ascribed to the influence of women students.[10] The average student, the SCM considered, was far more likely to be influenced on religious and social matters by a college society than by the churches, and as university was a time of transition for young people, it was important that a specifically Christian organization should exist to safeguard students amid the temptations of city life.[11] A typical college branch before 1914 ran a series of bible circles, missionary bands and social study circles for members as well as holding daily or weekly prayer meetings and organizing occasional general meetings with outside speakers. There was often considerable overlap in membership of the college SCM with that of other student societies and many SCM members were also involved in the students' guild or union. By the Edwardian period SCM annual summer conferences may be seen as broadly representative of the British student population, consisting of hundreds of male and female students and recent graduates drawn from universities, university colleges, theological and training colleges across Britain and Ireland. However, it was a movement in which women played a role out of proportion to their numbers in the universities and colleges. The 1906 gathering, for example, included 500 men and 350 women students.[12]

In the Edwardian period the SCM, with an increasingly sophisticated organization of paid secretaries and volunteer-led branches, began to see itself as a national student body with responsibility for the wider social education of students. Despite some earlier local efforts, it was not until a summer conference in Matlock in 1903 that SCM members seriously discussed social problems and social service.[13] They concluded that college Christian unions should begin social study groups and actively cooperate with fellow students in voluntary social work.[14] This shift in emphasis from missionary to social service reflected waning evangelical influence in the SCM, as the movement embraced a wider spectrum of student religious opinion. Most branches embraced an increasingly liberal theology alongside the new concern with social problems, while the growing influence of women was decisive in the raising of the SCM's social consciousness.[15] In 1909, SCM formed a Social Service Committee and appointed a paid Social Service Secretary, whose job it was to visit colleges and set up meetings between local social workers, university staff and students. College branches were encouraged to elect a student secretary to act as a focus for social service and to liaise with other societies and local social workers.[16] At national level, the Social Service Committee published textbooks, provided study outlines, developed training and issued advice pamphlets to student secretaries.[17] Involvement in social work was described as a way to "rally hundreds of students in the British Colleges who stand aloof from Christian work, but are fully alive to the necessity of doing something for the alleviation of social wrongs."[18]

In 1895, the British SCM was one of the founder members of an international federation of national student Christian groups known as the World's Student Christian Federation. Before 1919, the WSCF was the only international student organization in existence and played an important role in fostering international networks, particularly among university women, as several historians have now begun to recognize. Renate Howe, for example, shows that for Australian students, attendance at a WSCF conference could provide important links into global women's networks and counter the sense of isolation they experienced at small Australian universities.[19] By 1900 better travel and communication links meant that rapid exchange of ideas was possible across the student world through participation in conferences, visits and tours of student delegations. The visits of WSCF travelling secretary Ruth Rouse to universities in Australia, New Zealand or India, for example, were important in stimulating women's greater involvement in their national SCMs and also in provoking new interest in social service. The large quadrennial conferences of the WSCF provided similar opportunities for fostering international fellowship. Like the British SCM, the WSCF was moving toward a more ecumenical stance toward non-Protestant denominations and world religions.[20] One aspect of this was the changing nature of conference talks and discussions from personal salvation and evangelism at early international conferences in the 1870s and

1880s to problems of race, immigration, poverty and labor reform at WSCF meetings in the 1900s.[21]

The WSCF saw non-Christian students as "strategic points" in the world's evangelization.[22] Therefore India, China and Japan, where there were large numbers of young people receiving higher education by the late nineteenth century, presented key opportunities for university-based mission work. Although it was not an exclusively imperial movement, many within the British SCM saw India as arguably the most important locus of overseas service. India was already the location of several high church missionary brotherhoods including the Cambridge Mission to Delhi (1877), Oxford Mission to Calcutta (1880) and Dublin University Mission to Chota Nagpur (1891). As university-sponsored missions, these Anglican brotherhoods placed great emphasis on dialogue with the student classes of India, for example, supporting institutions including St Stephen's College, Delhi and the Oxford Mission Hostel in Calcutta. One Oxford women's college, Lady Margaret Hall, developed strong links with the Community of the Epiphany, a lay sisterhood attached to the Oxford Mission to Calcutta.[23]

The international student Christian movement also gave rise to hybrid institutions such as the Missionary Settlement of University Women in Bombay. This settlement was started in 1896 by pioneer British student leaders Agnes de Selincourt (1872–1917) and Ruth Rouse, who noted the strong pull of the settlement movement on university-educated women and saw the model as a way to gain support for missionary work among educated Indian women.[24] They looked to leading women missionaries and social workers in Britain for advice and support in setting up the new venture.[25] In Bombay, the women settlers made links with the small but growing numbers of women students at the colleges of Bombay University and in 1906 the settlement opened a hostel. As an international venture, the Missionary Settlement drew on the support of women's colleges in Australia and New Zealand as well as in Britain. Another hybrid social institution was the work started in 1900 by Anglican members of the SVMU, led by Willie Holland, among the students of Allahabad in North India.[26] Originally this initiative was intended as sort of missionary settlement for male students at Allahabad University, but the work eventually became more focussed on running a men's hall known as the Oxford and Cambridge Hostel.[27]

Educational institutions like those in India and elsewhere in China, Japan and Ceylon (Sri Lanka) provided opportunities for university-educated volunteers to offer Christian-inspired service outside their home countries. Importantly, the encouragement of lay involvement in the international SCM allowed for greater involvement of women. The WSCF, YWCA and YMCA offered a new type of missionary role in ecumenical and interracial organizations, often recruiting young people to work among young people. Well-known missionary advocates such as J. H. Oldham (1874–1969) and J. N. Farquhar (1861–1929) began their careers as YMCA student secretaries in India. Such secretaries were appointed for definite terms of service rather than the lifetime commitment of traditional missionaries. Key mission institutions such as Trinity College, Kandy, the Oxford and Cambridge Hostel, Allahabad, St Stephen's College, Delhi and Forman Christian College, Lahore, also came to rely on similar "short-service" volunteers. The Church Missionary Society (CMS) short-service scheme recruited new graduates to serve in English-language schools and colleges in India for postings of between one and five years.[28] Short-service workers were successful in developing student societies, introducing organized games and promoting social service ideals among Indian students.[29] Principal Rudra at St Stephen's noted that "the life brought into the College by these young workers has been invaluable."[30] C. F. Andrews was a leading promoter of short-service because he felt that the national awakening and interest taken by Indians in social service after 1907 signalled a need for more "young earnest men" to come from Britain as volunteers.[31] The MSUW welcomed short-service workers for periods as short as six months because their help in raising awareness of the settlement at women's colleges on their return to Britain, Australia and New Zealand was greatly valued.[32]

An Acceptable and Universally Appreciated Contribution? Toward a Global Student Social Consciousness

In an age of increasing unease with colonial rule on the part of students and missionary educators alike, social service emerged as a topic that was one of the most "acceptable and universally appreciated contributions" from the West, as Forman professor Daniel Fleming (1877–1969) put it.[33] American-born Fleming was one of a number of strong advocates of student social service working in India. Like Andrews he had been impressed by what he saw as the "marked development of [a] social consciousness among students" in the West and the subsequent take-up of the idea in Asia.[34] Ideas on social service spread rapidly through the global student Christian movement through conference discussions as well as the many speeches and writings of enthusiasts for social service. In 1909, the WSCF's quadrennial conference was held in Oxford and, reflecting the concerns of the British organizers, was marked by a strong emphasis on "the social problem."[35] Following the conference student Christian organizations in the USA, Australia, Germany and elsewhere established social service departments. For example, Australian student Christian leader Stanley Addison (1880–1972) returned home from Oxford determined to foster "a growth of social consciousness" among students, a message he reinforced by helping to organize six-week speaking tour of Australian universities and colleges by Christian socialist William Temple (1881–1944).[36] A key player in both the SCM's 1909 Matlock conference and the WSCF Oxford conference, Temple was then a recently ordained school teacher, actively involved in the settlement movement and serving as President of the Worker's Educational Association (WEA), founded in 1903. The Australian Student Christian Union appointed a Social Service Committee in 1913 and published study guides and information on social service, but Renate Howe argues that attempts to establish much practical social service on settlement lines were largely a failure. In New Zealand's universities, the social question was also the subject of several SCM discussions, meetings and conferences in the years 1910–1914 and students at several colleges formed branches of a Social Service League in which Christian and secular groups came together.[37] As at British universities and colleges, it seems that while social service topics were widely discussed in Australasia, practical social service was less widespread and limited to certain colleges—often women's colleges—which developed a particular tradition in this area.

In the so-called mission lands of Asia including India, China, Burma, Korea and Japan, ideas of social service were also circulating among students in the first two decades of the century, particularly among the large proportion of students being educated at Christian higher education colleges or in contact with the YMCA secretaries. In China, for example, social service was developed in a number of university centers including Tientsin (Tianjin), Peking (Bejing), Shanghai and Canton (Guangzhou) under the leadership of YMCA secretary and Princeton graduate John Stewart Burgess and colleagues including R. M. Hersey.[38] In 1912, students from three government and three missionary colleges formed the Peking Students Social Service Club, which had a membership of six hundred mainly non-Christian students by 1915. Its members were engaged on a range of projects including free night schools, children's playgrounds, surveys of rickshaw pullers and public lectures.[39]

In India social service emerged as a safe and constructive expression of patriotism for students.[40] Although the international SCM was important here too, it was not the only influence. In 1904–1905 lecturers in Indian colleges began to report a growth in student patriotism connected to the Japanese victory over Russia and discussions over Lord Curzon's proposed partition of Bengal.[41] For example, Moderate politician and educationist G. K. Gokhale (1866–1915) called for the "service of motherland" to become "with us as overmastering a passion as it is in Japan."[42] Local politics played a part. The controversial Risley Circular, issued by the Government of India in May 1907, attempted to suppress student political activism by prohibiting discussion of politics in schools or colleges. Henceforth, encouraging social service became a method to channel and direct students' growing patriotism into constructive outlets away from direct involvement in politics.[43] The period of national awakening in India was seen as an opportunity by missionary educationalists who saw themselves contributing to the leavening of Indian society rather than immediate conversion of students. [44] Many were guided by a fulfilment theology which allowed for relatively positive and sympathetic engagement with Indian religions.[45] As politics became the overriding interest of many Indian students, so too did missionary educators pay more attention.[46] The many social service brotherhoods and leagues which they helped found harnessed students' loyalty to their college or hostel as well as drawing on wider patriotic, religious and communal sympathies. Thus an important unlooked for impact of the social service movement in India, as in Britain, was in strengthening group solidarity among the educated elite. One student at Wilson College, Bombay, noted that through participation in influenza relief work, "a new link was forged between student and student...that will not be easily broken."[47] There was also a high degree of co-operation in social service between members of different communities, particularly between high caste Hindus and Europeans.[48]

However, social service in India was not confined to Christian-sponsored educational institutions. Indeed the social service movement as it developed in India – and elsewhere in Asia – represented a fusion of Western or Christian traditions and techniques with indigenous understandings of charity and service. Drawing on Christian methods and ideals of service, the Servants of India Society, founded by Gokhale in 1905, had a significant influence on the development of the social service movement in Indian higher education. Christian and non-Christian propagandists concerned to spread the "gospel of social service" across India drew heavily on Gokhale's rhetoric of "servants of India" and "servants of the nation."[49] This interplay of ideas makes it difficult to establish who was reacting to whom, as *The Times's* correspondent in India Valentine Chirol acknowledged in 1910, noting that the Servants of India Society "exemplifies the cross currents that are often so perplexing."[50] At the colleges, social service secretaries appealed to new students by reminding them of their responsibilities and duties to their college, to their city and to India. The Students' Brotherhood at Madras Christian College, for instance, held annual tea parties where students were told they were "preparing to become servants of India and of humanity."[51] Yet, in their attempts at cross-class or cross-caste social service Indian students came up against a number of barriers, which they identified as fatalism, superstition, ignorance and indifference on the part of villagers or urban slum dwellers. Rarely having mixed with these social groups before, student social servants reported great difficulties in communication with the lower classes. As one student reported, "to talk to them on any topic, whether social or political, is very tiresome".[52] Suspicion and misunderstanding could turn to outright hostility as one Forman student who tried to deliver a lecture on sanitation in a Sikh village discovered, "They [villagers] ran after me, and I do not know what would have become of me, had I not at once got upon my cycle and shrunk away."[53]

The interest in social service taken by students in Asia was widely discussed among students in the West, and a market for books on the unrest in India and "the East" emerged.[54] For example, in his role as WCSF travelling secretary, Sherwood Eddy was responsible for spreading ideas about social service between students.[55] Eddy told American students meeting in Kansas about the "new conception" of brotherhood and social service he had noted among Indian students.[56] Ceylon-based educationist Alek Fraser spoke at several universities in Britain and Australia describing social service as a notable feature of the national movement in India.[57] Eleanor McDougall described her experiences of a study tour in 1912–1913 in a series of talks to Westfield College students with such vividness that "India seems to have come nearer to us."[58] Moreover, G. K. Gokhale's repeated trips to Britain between 1905 and 1915 gave him numerous opportunities to publicize the work of the Servants of India Society. In August 1913, for example, he addressed a large meeting of British and Indian students at the Caxton Hall in London.[59]

Thus in the early twentieth century, and especially between 1909 and 1914, social service was a topic very high on the agenda of the global SCM. Developments in student social service and social study

were forged in and across national boundaries through a mobile network of educationists, missionaries and students and at international
conferences. Social service was taken up so strongly by the SCM
because it was a means of getting access to large number of students
and of engaging with non-Christian students. While many national
student Christian organizations in the West adopted a strong educational approach, with emphasis on reading, discussion and talks from
experts rather than student involvement in practical social service,
in Asia students had greater opportunities to make a contribution
to such causes as health promotion, famine relief and educational
projects. Many advocates of social service felt that the pressing social
welfare needs in Asia called students to involvement in social service
even more than in Britain or America, while others argued that interest among students in Asia was evidence of the success of Christian
leavening and justified ongoing commitment to Christian colleges,
hostels and YMCA or YWCA work.[60] Yet in India and China as elsewhere, student social service was often frustrated by the gulfs of experience and understanding between students and the impoverished
groups of people they tried to help.[61] In many cases social service
did more to establish connections and strengthen solidarity between
students of different nationalities, than between students and people
of lower classes or castes in their own countries.

The First Rung on the Ladder of Service: Social Service, Social Study and the Beginnings of a Student Movement in Britain?

Back in Britain, the SCM recognized that the capacity of students
to become involved in much practical social service was limited and
thus its goals in promoting student social service were largely educational. This represented a shift of emphasis from the social service
and settlement enthusiasts of the 1880s and 1890s, and reflected
wider changes to what was described as the "now highly specialised
world of social service" in which few students could hope to have
time or training to play much part. [62] In fact, the SCM advised student groups against assuming sole responsibility for a piece of social
work since "continuity in policy, regularity in service, experience
in oversight and sufficiency of funds are all difficult for students
to provide."[63] However, publicity produced by the Social Service
Committee strongly encouraged students to make personal contact

with the poor through limited practical volunteering and regular visits to settlements or other social institutions. As part of its self-appointed educational mission, the SCM widely promoted the "study circle" as an ideal model for learning about social problems, social legislation and social service.[64] A study circle was a small group—six to ten members were considered ideal—which met regularly to study a specific textbook. Around half of SCM branches were organizing some form of social study in 1910. These ranged from study circles to one-off meetings or talks, which might have a very general title such as "Social Service" or "The Social Problem," but which would attract a wider audience of students. Statistics collected by the SCM between 1909 and 1912 show that study circles were far more popular among women than men, excluding theological students, with around 60 active circles run by women's colleges and women's unions compared to just a handful of groups for men.[65] Other voluntary organizations shared this mission of social education for university students. From 1908 the recently formed British Institute of Social Service offered to support the SCM by arranging talks, providing students with careers advice in the field of social service and allowing members access to its Westminster-based social service library.[66] The strong interest of students in social problems was illustrated by the popularity of a course of special lectures on poverty and social service delivered in 1907–1908 by leading social workers such as Samuel Barnett and Percy Alden, which attracted more than five hundred students from the University of London.[67]

Student interest in social study was one expression of growing popular interest in politics and should be seen in the context of the changing role of the state in the era of New Liberalism.[68] The study circle was a model also recommended for working-class associations such as Adult Schools or various denominational organizations like the Catholic Social Guild.[69] Likewise social study summer schools organized as part of a program of university extension became increasingly popular in the mid-Edwardian period. Study circles were one response to the desire to understand the new social legislation and the increasingly complex workings of local government. After the long-running Royal Commission on the Poor Laws issued its famous majority and minority reports in 1909, easy-to-understand digests of these reports became some of the most widely read textbooks. Popular SCM textbooks reflected the twin interest in social conditions at home and overseas. In 1912–1913, the best-selling study circle book was Barclay Baron's 1911 *The Growing Generation: A Study of Working Boys and Girls in Our Cities,* while C. F. Andrews' *Renaissance in India,* with its focus on national awakening and student life in India was also widely used.[70]

The SCM push for student social service and organized social study coincided with the opening up of new opportunities for volunteers as part of the expansion of state welfare services after 1906.[71] Commentators like Cecile Matheson (1870–1950), warden of Birmingham Women's Settlement, wrote of an "insistent call for social servants" in this period.[72] An early article on the Guild of Help movement reflected that "personal service and not almsgiving is the highest form of charity."[73] Volunteers were recruited to serve on children's care committees, patient after care committees and in burgeoning maternal and child welfare and health services.[74] For example, 5,000 volunteers came forward to serve on London care committees and Birmingham's had 1,600.[75] Although some older social workers, mainly associated with the Charity Organisation Society, protested against the extension of state welfare, such views were increasingly held to represent the attitudes of the previous generation.[76] New associations that emerged to channel these volunteers were committed to working closely with the state, including the Guilds of Help, Councils of Social Welfare and the Personal Service Association as well as many youth service leagues. Growing interest by students in social service and social study before 1914 was therefore a small part of a wider movement, but it was one in which the British SCM—and particularly its publishing arm—played an influential role.

Enthusiasm for social service among British students was demonstrated by the growth of clubs and societies that aimed to channel service and social study, the popularity of study-circles, lecture courses and books on social service, and content of discussions at national and international student conferences. The extensive cooperation and sharing of ideas between organizations such as the British Institute of Social Service, the SCM, university settlements as well as denominational social service unions indicate the importance of social service as a channel through which to encourage cooperation, promote unity and engender "nation building." In their use of chivalric rhetoric which depicted student and graduate volunteers as "modern knights" and "young Templars," social service advocates sought to rework patriotic idiom to link social service with nation-building.[77] Before 1918 most higher education students could not vote in parliamentary elections, but participation in volunteering was seen as a valid expression of citizenship that might rank alongside military or other forms of public service. Although student levels of interest and commitment fluctuated greatly over the period 1884–1914, a university-sponsored settlement or college mission remained a powerful symbol, routinely invoked by those seeking to demonstrate the social awareness of the educated elite.

Despite the rhetoric around bridging class divides, it was rare that one-off contacts between students and those who, say, used a settlement's services overcame the many barriers of communication and understanding. In contrast, social service and social study had the effect of strengthening group solidarity among students. For minority groups such as Jewish and Catholic students—as well as for students at provincial university colleges—participation in social service could also be an effective means of integration into the emergent student culture and the national elite. For instance, the Jewish Lads' Brigade (JLB), which by 1914 had around four thousand members, is well-known for its emphasis on anglicizing and befriending young immigrants.[78] However, the JLB also provided valuable opportunities for the middle-class young men, many of them university students and recent graduates, who volunteered as its officers.[79] Similarly the Catholic Social Guild, founded in 1909, aimed to bring middle-class Catholics into full citizenship through social service, particularly among poor fellow-Catholics.[80] As part of this shift Catholic schools as well as Catholic university students began to support boys' and girls' clubs, the Catholic Boys' Brigade and settlement work, particularly in London and Liverpool.[81] For students and staff at the new universities, taking a lead in settlement or other forms of social work locally could demonstrate civic leadership as well as enabling participants to stake a claim to membership of the national elite.

Enthusiasm for social study and social service became a unifying element among students of different backgrounds in the years before and during the First World War.[82] Bristol University tutor George Hare Leonard, for instance, recognized that there was no better way of making friends than by joining together in social service.[83] In a series of important articles published in *Student Movement* in 1903, Leonard and others argued that those involved in the SCM needed to show sympathy with the social and charitable work of other students and to become involved with settlements. SCM leaders began to draw on the popularity of social service as a way to make contact with and evangelize students, since they argued that "involvement in social work often leads those who take part in it to a new revelation."[84] It is significant that the students most involved in social service were actively cooperating with students from a range of religious traditions and social backgrounds. Several universities and colleges formed social service committees that brought together SCM groups, Christian Social Union branches, Fabian societies, social study groups and women's suffrage societies.[85] At Leeds, Manchester and Aberdeen, for example, there was strong cooperation on the subject of social study between members of the SCM branch and the university sociological societies.[86] In other cases other college societies such as the Howard Club at Goldsmith's Training College, the Agenda Club at Girton and the Social Reform Leagues at Homerton College and Aberystwyth Women's Union took a lead on social study, often in partnership with the SCM.[87] In 1912, SCM leaders successfully appealed to the interests of a broad swath of the student population through its conference in Liverpool on the theme of "Christ and Social Need," which attracted two thousand students and was accompanied by a touring exhibition.[88] However, despite widespread interest, the actual practical service undertaken by students in this period was often limited to vacation volunteering or short visits to the slums and rarely encouraged cross-class dialogue. Therefore social service before 1914 provided more opportunities for strengthening links between different groups of students than between students and wider society.

CONCLUSIONS

In a 1917 handbook on students and citizenship, the SCM's Hugh Martin considered that during wartime students had become further "awakened to the nation's need and eager to serve her."[89] The First World War depleted British universities and colleges of male students but women's colleges and women's unions ramped up their involvement in practical social service through working parties to make comforts for troops, aid for Belgian refugees and Red Cross work. As in the wider population, students were involved in extensive fundraising for war charities. The war also gave women students more opportunities for leadership in college societies and SRC or union committees, with the effect that social concerns featured more on the agenda of such organizations.[90] For the SCM, publication of its 1917 citizenship handbook marked the culmination of a decade's work promoting social service and social study among students in colleges across Britain and Ireland. Written as the act enfranchising some women (including graduates of British universities aged over 30), passed through parliament and explicitly employing the term citizenship for the first time, the handbook was prepared by well-known suffragist Cecile Matheson with advice from Marion Rutherford of Queen Margaret Settlement to make it relevant to students in the Scottish colleges. In one sense it was a standard-issue SCM social study text-book but the widely reviewed volume also registered the disappoint-ment that despite support from a range of educationists, social service and social study remained extracurricular activities organized by stu-dents themselves. Martin recorded that "no student society can deal adequately with the situation but in the almost complete absence of other provision, the SCM is trying to do what it can."[91] Reluctance on the part of university authorities to take a lead in this area prompted the SCM to call for their greater involvement:

> Ought not some training in Citizenship to form part of the college course of every student. Should not the training of all professional men and women include instruction on their place in the national life, the opportunities and obligations of service presented to them by their calling?[92]

Although university and college authorities eschewed such respon-sibilities, before 1914 university settlements, college missions and related institutions were important centres of social education, some-thing often overlooked in settlement historiography. They provided thorough training for small numbers of students and recent graduates preparing for careers as social workers, teachers, clergymen or mission-aries while at the same time providing a more limited introduction to social problems and social service to larger numbers of students. Thus social study constituted what we might describe as early form of citizenship education in many colleges and universities. Women were central to the development of social service in the universities, and the intersection of gender, higher education and service is a topic that will be explored in more detail in the succeeding chapters.

Students in Britain were part of an upsurge of interest in social service across the student world, connected by global networks of educationists, missionaries and social workers, who ensured that developments in Britain did not develop in a vacuum. International causes inspired many forms of student voluntary action before 1914, while there was increasing interest from students and recent graduates in undertaking a period of overseas service. These valued openings for responsibility, service and adventure on the part of the British student classes were fully recognized only when such outlets were threatened by decolonization in the 1950s and 1960s, and new programs such as Voluntary Service Overseas were developed in response. Social ser-vice also provided a common point of contact between British stu-dents and students internationally, particularly in North America,

Australia, New Zealand as well as India, China and elsewhere in Asia. In the West, social service was widely interpreted as a positive aspect of a wider "awakening" across many Asian societies, notably in the heated political atmosphere of early twentieth-century India. Social service was seized upon as an acceptable alternative to involvement in politics and a field in which students in Asia were prepared to accept help and guidance from Western educationists.

Discussion of social problems, social service and social study were important to the emergence of a student associational culture at individual universities and colleges before 1914. Moreover, although we should not overstate the extent to which higher education students in Britain saw themselves as part of a distinct student class or "student movement," in this period, student social service and social study, particularly as shaped by the SCM, played an important part in the beginnings of this movement. Although actual volunteering was a minority activity for students before 1914, after the devastation wrecked by the First World War on universities and student culture across Europe, it was to be around international relief, social service and self-help that a broad-based student movement, perhaps even a "student popular front," was to emerge in the interwar period, as we shall see in the succeeding chapters.

CHAPTER 4

The Student Chapter in
Postwar Reconstruction,
1920–1926

In February 1920 Ruth Rouse, travelling secretary of the World's Student Christian Federation (WSCF), was on a postwar tour of central Europe when she came across women students in Vienna who were facing extreme hardship and near famine conditions. Rouse and her secretary Eleanora Iredale immediately realized that the condition of these students—many of whom were surviving on one meal a day in unheated rooms in the middle of a harsh European winter—necessitated international relief. Rouse and Iredale put out an urgent call for aid through the WSCF, still the only world-wide student organization then in existence.[1] The appeal generated an almost immediate response from student groups across Europe as well as in the United States, India and South Africa. In Britain, £2,000 was raised during the summer term of 1920 after a "lightning campaign" led by students involved with the Society of Friends and the Student Christian Movement (SCM).[2] This chapter explores the involvement of British students in this international movement to ease student hardship in Europe and Russia and in so doing allows insights into the changing student experience after the First World War. International relief and reconstruction were important forces around which an incipient British student movement coalesced in the early 1920s. Relief activities were closely bound up with the emergence of student internationalism through the formation of new organizations like the National Union of Students (NUS) in Britain and the *Confédération Internationale des Étudiants* (CIE) internationally.

HALF THE STUDENT WORLD IN RUINS: THE UNIVERSITIES' COMMITTEE AND EUROPEAN STUDENT RELIEF

In the years following the 1918 Armistice, Central Europe was subject to an Allied-led blockade that caused famine conditions. In Britain, as elsewhere in Europe and America, a number of relief efforts led by both existing agencies and new organizations emerged in response, including by the recently formed League of Nations. In 1919, the Fight the Famine Council was formed to protest about the British government's part in the blockade and sisters Eglantyne Jebb and Dorothy Buxton started the Save the Children Fund (SCF) as an off-shoot of this body. In March 1920, a new national appeal for funds known as the Imperial War Relief Fund was launched at Lambeth Palace.[3] Chaired by Conservative politician Lord Robert Cecil, the Imperial Fund channelled funds to existing organizations including Save the Children, the Friends' Emergency and War Victims Relief Committee, the British Red Cross and dozens of smaller groups.[4] A special effort on behalf of British universities was part of these wider developments. At Ruth Rouse's instigation a Universities' Committee was set up as a sub-committee of the Imperial Fund, with Sir William Beveridge (1879–1963), one year into his term as Director of the London School of Economics, as its rather reluctant chair.[5] At its first meeting staff and student representatives agreed that the appeal to British universities and colleges should be for the needs of European students and professors specifically, "as from class to class," rather than for more general suffering.[6] The committee judged there was no point in trying to duplicate the efforts of the many general relief agencies. In British universities and colleges groups of interested students and staff members set up local relief committees in the summer and autumn term of 1920.[7] The work of these college groups was coordinated by the Universities' Committee that met regularly and was attended by student representatives able to travel to its London meetings as well as senior university figures. Eleanora Iredale became the committee's active secretary, working to produce publicity materials and issue fundraising advice to student groups. She travelled extensively and spoke regularly at university meetings across England, Wales and Scotland.

This Universities' Committee is historically important as it was the first fundraising body set up by a coalition of British universities and colleges and provided a precedent for later collaborations such as the Universities' Committee on Camps for the Unemployed in the 1930s and relief for student refugees from Hungary in 1956. It is also a demonstration of the relative strength of British universities and colleges after the war compared with their counterparts in mainland Europe. In Britain, the universities' intake was boosted by large numbers of ex-servicemen on government scholarships, whose numbers peaked at 11,512 in 1920–1921.[8] David Fowler has described this as a "staggering social transformation in the British university system that has never been properly investigated."[9] I show here that this generation of ex-servicemen was central to a number of key developments in student social service in the 1920s, and thus important in the forging of a national student movement. Their enrolment was part of a wider postwar expansion of higher education. By 1922 the numbers of university students had doubled from their prewar figures and the social origins of students were broadening as new funding arrangements allowed more young people to attend university, notably the State Scholarship scheme that covered fees and maintenance for several hundred of the highest performing school leavers in England and Wales.[10] It is also worth noting that the Universities' Committee predates the establishment of the NUS by two years. Starting with the formation of the Universities' Committee, the 1920s were to be marked by a strong push for intervarsity endeavor. Its early success was largely determined by the support of the Student Christian Movement, which retained its position as the leading national student organization and was at the height of its influence during the immediate postwar years, as well as the involvement of broad range of British universities and colleges (Figure 4.1).

The flow of money and goods-in-kind to Geneva in response to Rouse and Iredale's appeal raised the question of who was to administer this relief in the field. Accordingly when the central committee of the WSCF met in August 1920 they voted unanimously to set up a new scheme known as European Student Relief (ESR). British SCM leader Tissington Tatlow later recalled that the meeting was urged not to forget "the fact that famine, disease and death were stalking abroad in Central and Eastern Europe."[11] ESR was empowered to organize the supply of food, fuel, clothing and student supplies; to provide lodgings and rooms for study; to give medical aid; to offer training, equipment and facilities for promoting self-help; and to help repatriate students.[12] Aid was to be administered impartially without regard to race, nationality or religion and, importantly, the concept of "self-help" was to be central. European Student Relief was established as a special committee of the WSCF with its headquarters in Geneva.

Figure 4.1 Front cover of Ruth Rouse's personal history of European Student Relief, 1925.

Dr Conrad Hoffman, a former American YMCA worker fresh from service in German prisoner of war camps, was appointed its General Secretary. Hoffman oversaw the work of a central staff in Geneva, field representatives for each relief area and over a hundred international volunteers.[13]

The special student relief effort made a substantial contribution to the broader postwar aid movement. Over the period 1920–1925 about 12 million Swiss Frances (about £500,000 or roughly £14 million in today's money) in cash and kind was raised from 42 countries and spent on relief projects in more than 120 universities over 21 countries. By March 1921 ESR had organized relief programs in Hungary, Czechoslovakia, Estonia, Latvia, Poland and Turkey and was feeding 20,000 students daily in Germany.[14] ESR also set up a Health Department to care for students suffering from TB, cholera and typhus.[15] In the following years, ESR broadened its work to support student groups affected by famine in Russia from 1921, the refugee crisis in 1922–1923 after the Greco-Turkish war and the collapse of the German mark in spring 1923.

As well as providing emergency aid, from the outset ESR encouraged schemes of student self-help or *wirtschaftshilfe* designed to make students self-supporting.[16] Help for students was not to be considered charity and each country receiving aid had to appoint representative groups of students to administer funds, distribute food and clothing and develop self-help initiatives. In all the countries of Central and Eastern Europe these ESR committees were "unique in containing members of staff and students, nationalists and socialists, majorities and minorities."[17] From June 1922 students in Austria and Germany began to form self-help groups to develop student-run industries, cooperative buying schemes and subsidized *mensa* (canteens). At Vienna Technical College, for example, students operated a printing press and book binding shop for collective profit while art students undertook commissions. At the University of Leoben a hostel for 60 students was built by student volunteers' own labor and included a garden that helped supply the hostel kitchen with food. Items such as coal and wood, drawing paper and writing paper were bought wholesale and sold cheaply to students. At this date, most self-help schemes operated on traditional gender lines. In student canteens women cooked food grown by male students, women mended clothes while the men cobbled.

Maintaining neutrality in relief in postwar Europe was a strain for ESR, with Russian famine relief in particular presenting major challenges and dominating discussion of relief at international student gatherings in the early 1920s.[18] ESR sent two field workers to Russia in 1922, including Donald Grant under the wing of the Nansen Mission.[19] ESR's neutrality was severely tested in 1922 and 1923 when it was feeding thousands of Russian refugee students in university towns across Europe as well as up to 30,000 students a day inside the newly created Soviet Union.[20] Faced with increasing Soviet government interference in relief efforts, the International Section of ESR eventually withdrew from Russia in May 1924 and the American section in April 1925. However appeals to students' "friendship and plain humanitarian sympathy" for five thousand Russian refugee students continued in the mid-1920s.[21]

A New, Vital and Really Thrilling World of Adventure and Thought: Fundraising and Volunteering for ESR

Despite some reluctance among the student body to fundraise for former enemies, British universities and colleges raised significant donations and gifts-in-kind amounting to around £30,000 a year in the early 1920s.[22] This was a not inconsiderable sum for the small university and college sector to find. In a 1926 report, Eleanora Iredale reflected that much of impetus behind fundraising came from ex-servicemen students who felt that to oppose relief would be to fail those who had not come back from the trenches.[23] Robert Mackie recalled Iredale speaking at a meeting in the autumn of 1920 when he was a student at Glasgow University, "the main issue for us was whether men who had come home from the war should help students in ex-enemy countries. It was a tough argument, and ESR won a victory, not only in financial response, but in moving men's minds."[24] Although by summer 1922 ESR had begun to reduce aid to Germany, renewed efforts were launched after the collapse of the mark in January 1923. This prompted a wave of protest that resulted in the committee circulating a letter from the Archbishop of Canterbury roundly condemning the "prejudice which exists in some quarters" toward the relief of German students.[25] Ruth Rouse urged aid for German students as "the salvation of the intellectual life of the European universities."[26]

Student fundraising for Russia and Europe drew on a range of old and new techniques. Records of the Universities' Committee show that concerts, plays and other performances were common ways to raise money, as were sales of work, while there was extensive collection of clothes and other gifts-in-kind. At Newnham College students collected small items such as soap, needles and cotton. At Leeds, textile students gave up two weeks of their Christmas vacation to weave cloth as a gift for the students of Vienna.[27] SOAS lecturers delivered a course of talks to raise money. Students with relatives in manufacturing appealed for gifts-in-kind. For instance, at the very start of the appeal in March 1920 George Cadbury donated a ton of cocoa at the request of his niece Helen Fox.[28] Fundraising also tapped into the renewed desire among students for fun and entertainment after the privations of war, through methods such as putting a small "tax" on entertainment and dance tickets. It also harnessed student delight in pranks, practical jokes and "ragging" to raise money. After the First World War the fancy dress processions, which had become features of prewar student theater nights or "rags," were legitimized as fundraising activities, and over time were turned to the support of local hospitals. At Glasgow University, for instance, although a "theatre night" was resurrected after the war in 1920, the following year this had turned into a fancy dress "infirmaries parade," which aimed to "extort" money from the town's population.[29] Students dressed as red Indians, Pierrots, golliwogs, Salvation Army lasses and Charlie Chaplins raised £4,000 from the parade, in which a wide range of groups of students participated.[30] Birmingham University's rag also started in 1921 when male medical students organized a University Hospital Carnival at short notice, raising around £2,000 through a street collection.[31] ESR was one of the earliest beneficiaries of this new student fundraising trend. In March 1921, for example, six London colleges cooperated in a special rag day during which students collected money at West End hotels and theaters. It raised £363 in aid of ESR.[32] In the long vacation of 1921 a money-raising tour of Oxford and London undergraduates "raided" hotels in Switzerland, raising £287.[33]

Like the emerging rag tradition, the Universities' Committee sought to foster friendly rivalry between universities and colleges in order to spur the local groups on to collect more money. At a meeting in November 1921 both Glasgow and Liverpool universities were praised for the energy, organization and success of their local appeals.[34] By the middle of 1922 Queen's University Belfast and Bradford Technical College were also being singled out for special praise.[35] Notes of how other colleges were raising money were circulated by Iredale to inspire students elsewhere. Suggestions from Holloway College included a room-to-room collection in which students were recommended to "stand at the door till you get something" and University College representatives suggested passing around collecting boxes at college meetings but warned "Do not do it too often!"[36] Interestingly, Armistice week emerged as an important occasion for student collections for ESR.[37] The more famous Armistice fundraising—the British Legion's scheme of selling poppies in aid of the Earl Haig's Fund for ex-servicemen—began as an experiment in November 1921 before being rolled out more widely after 1922.

Rather contradicting Iredale's claims about ex-servicemen students, it appears that women students at women's colleges and mixed universities alike were at the forefront of fundraising efforts. By summer 1922, for instance, Girton and Newnham had each independently raised as much money for ESR as the rest of Cambridge University put together.[38] Notably, many of the student representatives who attended the Universities' Committee's London meetings—and ran the local appeals—were women students who found an outlet in ESR for their latent leadership and organizational talents. One such was Kitty Lewis (1898–1984), an Aberystwyth graduate and daughter of Sir Herbert Lewis (1958–1933), MP for the University of Wales. Kitty was praised in committee minutes for her full-time volunteer service in organizing the University of Wales appeal, where she used family connections to interest friends of the university in the cause and organized a sale of work by Austrian students in her own home.[39] In addition to fundraising efforts at the universities and colleges, dozens of British students gave up part or all of their vacations to volunteer with ESR relief efforts in central Europe at their own expense.[40] Ben Greene—a cousin of the novelist Graham—was so strongly influenced by one of Dr Nansen's talks on Russian famine relief at Oxford that he signed up to spend his summer vacation on relief work with the Friends' Foreign Relief Service. Back at university Greene became convinced that "the academic life at Oxford was too remote from the realities of the world."[41] Instead of completing his final year at Wadham College, in spring 1923 Greene set out to Russia with the Friends' Famine Relief Fund. Such prolonged participation could have lasting impacts. Students who had played a leading role in the ESR movement at universities and colleges went to on enter the diplomatic service, business, foreign correspondence and other professions. As Iredale summed up, involvement in the relief campaign opened up "a new, vital and really thrilling world of adventure and thought...I tremble to think how far our net has been spread."[42]

More Than Emergency Rescue: Relief, International Understanding and the Universities in the 1920s

The originators of ESR had from the beginning seen "in student relief more than mere emergency rescue."[43] The conclusion of delegates to the first ESR conference held in Turnov, Czechoslovakia, in 1922 was that relief work should lay the foundation of renewed international student fellowship.[44] As various articles noted, had the university system in war-torn Europe collapsed because of student privation, European culture itself would have been under threat.[45] Thus ESR was conceptualized by its leaders as not merely as giving of alms, but as a "really magnificent contribution to international education and the cause of peace."[46] One practical approach was to organize a series of annual ESR conferences to bring students together. In 1922, the Universities' Committee sent Harold Abrahams (1899–1978), a Jewish student at Cambridge who was to win gold at the 1924 Paris Olympics, to represent British students at the first ESR conference in Turnov.[47] Abrahams, later immortalized in the film *Chariots of Fire*, was a canny choice as the first action of this conference was to defuse national tensions by organizing athletic contests and team games.[48] Links were also strengthened by a number of exchange visits. In summer 1922, Balliol student Carlos Blacker led a party of Oxford students on a visit to six universities in Germany, Austria, Hungary, Poland and Czechoslovakia. Blacker's report was so well received by the Universities' Committee that its treasurer, banker Cecil Baring, paid for a printed copy to be sent to each member of the House of Commons and the House of Lords.[49] Robert Mackie was a member of a student party that visited Germany during the currency crisis of summer 1923, recalling "I then got my first impression of the suffering of fellow students. For me, as for hundreds of others in Britain, ESR was the beginning of international consciousness."[50]

There is ample evidence that students involved in ESR supported these ideals of international understanding and transmitted them back to universities and colleges.[51] In the summer of 1924, James Parkes attended both the ESR conference in Schloss Elmau in Bavaria and the CIE conference in Bad Saarow in Prussia. While the ESR conference he found to be "intensely serious and realistic," the business of the CIE conference was frustrated by ongoing central-European politics.[52] After attending the 1925 conference in Gex near Geneva, one Manchester student reported "we have made friends with students from all over the world, we have learnt to see their point of view, to understand that we all have the same ideals."[53] The minutes of the Universities' Committee record several instances where college fundraising was boosted by the return of a student from an ESR conference.[54] After meeting Russian refugee students who had served in the White Army at the conference in Karlovci, Yugoslavia in 1926, a Bristol student came back determined to put their case and to assure would-be donors that they were both "deserving" of relief and "profoundly grateful" for it.[55] Despite a strong desire not to depict student-to-student relief as "charity," such terminology reflects a long-standing need to be able to depict recipients of food aid as "deserving" in order to generate donations. Such tactics had been integral to the success of earlier international relief campaigns like the series of appeals for famine aid in India in the 1890s, as to other charitable ventures in Britain.[56]

In the early 1920s, then, student relief efforts went hand-in-hand with strong interest in international cultural cooperation and the universities were hailed as more "consciously international than they had been even in the middle ages."[57] Support for ESR was part of the postwar revival of extracurricular activities and the period was marked by the formation of new societies for learning and discussion about world problems, seen mostly notably in the rapid expansion of university branches of the League of Nations Union (LNU). The LNU was an independent voluntary organization formed in 1918 to champion the League of Nations among the British public. Helen McCarthy's recent study conceptualizes the LNU as a "major presence within the wider political culture" of interwar Britain, enjoying popular support across the political spectrum.[58] It certainly had a strong following at the universities where students took part in debates and discussions, attended meetings outlining the work of the LNU and joined the LNU summer schools that were often held on university premises.[59] By the end of 1920 there were active LNU branches at many universities and colleges including Cardiff, Cambridge, Oxford, Manchester, Liverpool, Bangor, Aberystwyth, Sheffield, Armstrong College, Newcastle and colleges of the University of London.[60] Indeed, LNU's journal *Headway* optimistically took this university interest as "probably the most hopeful indication of the ultimate success of the League of Nations."[61]

Like LNU branches among the wider population, college branches organized regular programs of talks, discussions and study circles but were also closely involved in raising money through the Universities' Committee. Topics such as "Disarmament," "Arbitration" and "The Colour Problem" were studied over consecutive terms.[62] At Oxford, ex-serviceman student James Parkes had been a founding member of one of the first university branches during the academic year 1919–1920. As university LNU secretary he set up a mock League of Nations Assembly that met three times a term at the Oxford Union. It was modelled on a prewar trend for mock parliaments and reported in *Headway* as a valuable experiment.[63] Parkes later recalled that because his student generation of ex-servicemen was "exceptionally mature" he was able to set a high standard of debate and discussion that made this Assembly the most popular regular meeting in the university at the time.[64] In some areas, university staff and students were at the forefront of the push to spread the message wider.[65] Parkes, for example, organized a program of talks by students in towns and villages surrounding Oxford.

Internationalism also underpinned the formation of the *Confédération Internationale des Étudiants*. Work to develop this international student association began immediately at the end of the war
on French initiative, with a meeting in the University of Strasbourg
in 1919.[66] The first official meeting of the CIE was held in Prague
in March 1921 with English delegates attending on behalf of two
student groups: the Inter-Varsity Association and the International
Students Bureau. The students who took a lead in forming the
NUS in 1922—again largely drawn from the body of ex-servicemen
students—realized the need for one organization to speak on behalf
of all students in England and Wales (Scottish students were already
represented by a body for its student representative councils formed
in 1889).[67] The first meeting of the newly formed NUS was held
in February 1922 with representatives from 27 universities and colleges. Since the Oxford and Cambridge Unions were private debating clubs rather than representative student bodies, NUS allowed
individual college junior common rooms (JCRs) to affiliate and individual students' unions of the University of London colleges as well
as the University of London Union. At the same period reforms to
students' unions or representative councils, such as direct election
of Union officials and the formation of mixed unions, were taking
place at several universities. At Leeds, for example, ex-servicemen students were closely involved in the drafting of a new union constitution in 1922.[68]

The formation of the NUS was a direct outcome of the postwar
movement for cooperation and reconstruction: "the spirit of service pervades the movement," as its first president Ivison Macadam
noted.[69] Unsurprisingly, then, much of its initial work focused on
international affairs; a publicity pamphlet noted "the first and most
vital need for the various nations is to understand one another."[70]
To this end the NUS established a Travel Department to organize
student tours overseas, exchange visits and place au pairs. It worked
closely with the German Students' Union to set up tours of Germany
as early as July 1922.[71] The Travel Department grew rapidly with
an aim of bringing "the educational benefits of travel within reach
of almost every student."[72] Such a goal was always going to be difficult and the university magazines of colleges such as Cardiff and
Armstrong College, Newcastle, record constant griping that the
excursion fees were too high for their students.

From the mid-1920s the NUS sought to establish itself as a
national organization which would act as a link between different
universities and colleges and "develop and express the corporate life

of the students."[73] This required an active publicity campaign and the tireless work of enthusiastic volunteers. In the academic year 1925–1926 founder Ivison Macadam, now styled "Honorary Organising Secretary," spoke at 57 different meetings at colleges, unions and hostels. A regular stream of articles in college magazines sought to explain the goals and activities of NUS to "the general body of students."[74] However, a typical college magazine editorial might reflect that the NUS was mostly known to students as a body "continually requiring money."[75] From 1925 NUS began holding an annual Universities Congress, not for making policy, which was then decided at council meetings of union representatives, but as social events and holidays. The congresses nevertheless attracted high-profile speakers and offered opportunities for debate and discussion among students from different universities. As an indication of the interests of this student generation, the first conference included a number of sessions on international matters and relief efforts, including a talk from Eglantyne Jebb on the Save the Children Fund and a film screening of the work of ESR in Russia and Europe introduced by Eleanora Iredale.[76] From 1922 the NUS had been particularly keen to cooperate with the Universities' Committee because it represented such a range of university opinion. For example, at Macadam's invitation Iredale gave a presentation to one of the very first meetings of the NUS executive committee in October 1922.[77]

The Universities' Committee was dissolved in 1924, and NUS deferred to the Student Christian Movement as the only student organization in a position to assume responsibility for ensuring continued British support for ESR.[78] The immediate postwar period marked "the great days of the SCM" when conference platforms were "crowded with national figures in Church and state" as Parkes later recalled.[79] The *Manchester Guardian*, for example, hailed the SCM as a significant movement and "another League of Nations."[80] In the mid-1920s SCM membership totalled 17 percent of day students at universities and colleges and when in 1923 Parkes was employed by SCM as International Study Secretary, he joined a body of staff 40 strong, including a wide range of specialist secretaries for universities as well as for the training, theological and technical colleges and for foreign students.[81] Alongside spiritual work, SCM continued its prewar program of social education through residential social study conferences that combined talks and lectures with visits to schools, factories and welfare centers as well as arranging talks at local branches by social workers as well as "rank and file working men and women."[82] The SCM annual summer conferences at Swanwick in Derbyshire were well attended and the model was increasingly being copied by other student groups.[83] As well as NUS, the SCM cooperated closely with the other national student organizations that were emerging after the war such as the British Universities League of Nations Societies. Wherever one was concerned with political or social progress, Parkes wrote, "one would find members of the SCM in on the ground floor."[84]

By 1925 the need for student relief in Europe had all but disappeared apart from continuing aid for the hundreds of Russian refugee students scattered through France, Belgium, Germany, Czechoslovakia and Yugoslavia. As the immediate crisis passed, then, European Student Relief sought a larger role within the international student movement. In 1925, it changed its name to International Student Service (ISS) to reflect a shift from relief toward cultural cooperation and self-help, as well as the growing internationalism of the organization. A liaison officer between ISS and the CIE was appointed to promote cooperation and at the seventh Council meeting of the CIE in Copenhagen in 1925 a commission on "Student Service" led to a formal scheme of cooperation on social service.[85] In an increasingly secular age, ESR also sought to move away from its roots in Christian internationalism and in 1931 ISS dropped its affiliation with the WSCF entirely. Such changes to the ISS program gave rise to some disquiet among British students about the continued need to send money to Geneva. Despite strong earlier support, the NUS launched an inquiry into how the money was allocated because it was now so long since the war "that conditions ought to have returned to normal and students in various countries should have learnt to meet their own difficulties."[86] However, despite the shift to cultural cooperation, new relief programs continued to be coordinated by ISS in the years before the Second World War.[87]

CONCLUSIONS

Although the work of European Student Relief has been almost entirely neglected by historians, it deserves a bigger part in the story of the postwar emergence of an international student movement as well as in accounts of the student experience in Britain. As a sub-committee of the Imperial War Relief Committee, the Universities' Committee enjoyed national-level establishment support but also managed to successfully mobilize grassroots enthusiasm. Although the largest sums were raised at Oxford, Cambridge and the London colleges, committee accounts reveal support for

ESR from universities and colleges across England, Wales, Scotland and Ireland. Eleanora Iredale's efficient organization helped ensure that Britain was the largest donor (other than the United States) to ESR in the early 1920s. Faced with not inconsiderable challenges of raising money for former enemies, students involved with the campaign sought to depict relief as a work of international cooperation, allied to other forms of international understanding and cultural exchange. Interestingly, the success of fundraising campaigns at individual colleges was often correlated to the involvement of students with direct experience of relief work overseas or participation in the ESR conferences. Indeed, student travel and exchange emerged as central to fostering international understanding for a number of different student organizations in this period. For students to travel and learn about other cultures first hand was described in Blacker's 1922 pamphlet as more "important for the welfare of the world" than academic study.[88]

Studying the work of the Universities' Committee provides insights into the changing dynamics of the postwar British student movement. Participation in relief for a common cause was a way to strengthen an emergent student identity in what remained a fragmented higher education system. Harold Silver notes that undergraduates at Oxford and Cambridge remained largely ignorant of their fellow students at the so-called modern universities in the 1920s and 1930s.[89] In turn, students at the provincial universities had little knowledge of Oxbridge students other than a set of stereotypes and prejudices.[90] However, the Universities' Committee provided an important meeting place for student leaders from Oxbridge, the London colleges and the civic universities. Initial fundraising success relied on existing networks of students mobilized through the Student Christian Movement. Although the more recently founded NUS and its leader Ivison Macadam emerged as key players on the Universities' Committee, in 1924 only the SCM was in a position to take over its work until independent ISS committees were established after 1931.[91] There was considerable overlap in personnel between the Universities' Committee, the SCM, the NUS and the British Universities League of Nations Societies with the result that a certain common thinking emerged around the need for greater cooperation across the student world, both nationally and internationally. From the end of the Great War students were made aware of international events such as the Russian Famine as much through the work of ESR as the activities of the so-called representative student bodies NUS and CIE. A further important legacy of the postwar relief effort for European universities was the emergence of a student self-help movement which by the late 1920s was making its influence felt in British universities and colleges and was one indication of the changing relationship between students and society in the interwar period, which we will now address.

CHAPTER 5

No Longer the Privilege of the Well-to-Do? Student Culture, Strikes and Self-Help, 1926–1932

A 1930 publication summing up seven years of progress of the National Union of Students (NUS) pointed out that in Britain there had not yet been a "self-conscious or articulate Self-help movement" on the lines of that in continental Europe.[1] This was because the necessity for such a scheme had been delayed by the period of prosperity immediately following the war and because "it is not in the British psychology to create a national 'movement' when a situation may be met at least partially by individual or local effort." Though there may not have been a movement on European lines, ideas of self-help were certainly under discussion in British universities in the late 1920s and early 1930s. The idea of *wirtschaftshilfe* or work fellowship and self-help had emerged in Germany and Austria as a way of alleviating student hardship in the early 1920s.[2] By 1926 students in Germany and Austria were in a position to share their experiences with students of other nations including those in "fairly normal economic conditions" and set up an office in Dresden to provide information and advice on hostels, restaurants and "self government activities of all kinds."[3] Students' union shops and bars and the provision of student discounts by private companies are so taken for granted today that they seem obvious solutions to the problem of student hardship, but these were new ideas for the British student movement in the 1920s and 1930s. It was only as the social background of students broadened in the interwar years and as economic downturn at the end of the 1920s began to affect the universities, that such methods were contemplated. This chapter discusses a range of interwar student social service activities—including General Strike volunteering, the rise of charity rags and the emergence of a self-help movement—in order to explore changes in student culture and identity as well as the shifting relationships between students and society.

OUTSIDE THE LECTURE ROOM: THE UNIVERSITIES AND STUDENT CULTURE IN THE 1920S AND 1930S

Harold Silver described the British university landscape of the inter-war period as having evolved into if not yet a national system of higher education, at least into a "proto-system."[4] Continued expansion of student numbers in the 1920s and 1930s was fuelled by the spread of secondary education as well as changes to university funding, resulting in the foundation of new university colleges, including at Swansea (1920) and Hull (1928) and the continued evolution of university colleges into independent universities such as Reading (1926). However, all British universities and colleges remained very small by modern standards. Even the largest civic universities such as Leeds, Manchester and Birmingham counted less than two thousand students each, while most were considerably smaller. For example, Exeter had 318 students, Nottingham 486 students and Reading 573 students in 1922–1923. The new Hull University College opened with just 39 students, reaching 100 full-time students by 1931.[5] Excluding overseas students who made up around 10 percent of the total intake, by 1930–1931 there were 33,669 full-time university students in England, 2,868 in Wales and 11,150 in Scotland and just under a third of them (27%) were women. The above figures include a significant proportion of both men and women students training to be teachers in university training departments (6,029 students in 1929–1930), while in that same year there were an additional 12,406 students taking a two-year course at teacher training colleges, which would enable them to teach in elementary schools. There were also more postgraduate students than before the war—2,237 in 1930. Access to university in the 1920s and 1930s was by passing the national Matriculation examination, although some colleges imposed additional entrance tests or scholarship examinations.

However, the period saw greater advances for men than for women. At Manchester, for example, the number of women students rose to a postwar peak in 1923–1924, but then fell back to an average of 690 women out of 3,000 students.[6] Strong advances in medical education for women gained during the First World War were reversed as student numbers fell during the 1920s, but women did began to take a wider range of courses such as in engineering, theology and architecture. Moreover, women continued to play an important part in university life at the civic universities through their own unions, mixed social activities and the Student Christian Movement (SCM). Joan Webbe, editor of Leeds University's magazine, pointed out in 1936 that it was curious that the pioneers of women's education "have not kept their place in the front in University life. Neither at Oxford nor at Cambridge, have women achieved anything like the equality with the men that they have at other universities."[7] Women were excluded from much of these universities' extracurricular provision, although they made up for this with a strong college-based corporate life. Women were able to receive University of Oxford degrees from 1920, although at Cambridge this privilege was not granted until 1948.

Popular images of the varsity men who were part of a wider "Bright Young Things" culture in the 1920s masked changes to the profile of students at British universities and colleges in the interwar period. An important report into student poverty published by Doreen Whiteley in 1933 revealed that a university education was no longer "the privilege of the well-to-do" and estimated that around half of university students received some form of financial assistance.[8] Phoebe Sheavyn, Senior Tutor for women students at Manchester, reported that women from "aristocratic or wealthy parentage" did not as yet go to university, and argued that most women students in the 1920s were from homes of limited means intending to earn their living.[9] In his *A Student's View of the Universities* Brian Simon pointed to a "vivid contrast" between poorer students, usually at the civic universities, and the comparatively wealthy students of Oxford and Cambridge.[10] The higher costs of studying at Oxford, Cambridge and London often deterred poorer students from taking up scholarships at these institutions. Simon further noted that only 1 in 150 of the pupils at an elementary school ever reached a university, compared to one in eight from public schools.[11] Later research into interwar student finances in England reveals how students funded themselves through a patchwork of state scholarships, local authority awards and loans, school or charitable grants and contributions from parents, other relations and even supportive teachers.[12]

Students' choice of degree subject and subsequent profession remained largely determined by social background in the interwar period. Often the only way for students from poorer backgrounds to access higher education was to "pledge to teach," an arrangement by which students received Board of Education grants for a three-year degree course and a postgraduate training year if they enrolled as teachers for a set period after graduation, regardless of their personal

inclinations. Of students intending to become teachers at Queen
Mary College in 1938, for example, 8 percent in Science faculties and
16 percent in Arts reported that they did not want to teach but could
find no other way to get a degree.[13] In contrast, medical students
often came from wealthier backgrounds. At King's College Medical
School, for instance, the background of new students in 1938 was
solidly middle class.[14] It appears that during the interwar period many
university and college students in Britain—and certainly those outside Oxford and Cambridge—experienced significant hardship and
found the high costs of travel to and from university, food, books
and healthcare difficult to meet. Leta Jones, a Liverpool University
student of Welsh origins whose father was a bank manager, described
how she survived on "a cheap lunch" of brawn, lettuce leaves, bread
margarine and tea followed by chips, bread and camp coffee for sup-
per. She noted that:

> Students came to the red brick universities not on scholarships but
> on repayable and inadequate loans...The average woman in hostel
> lived on a pound per week (twenty shillings or two hundred and forty
> pence). A quarter would be spent on meagre lunches and coffees; the
> rest covered books, undies and shoe repairs, lipstick and cigarettes.[15]

There were differences too between students from different parts
of Britain. The Carnegie Trust for the Universities of Scotland continued to pay all or part of the tuition fees of a high proportion of
students in Scotland, although increases in numbers of students and
fees required the introduction of a means test in 1927.[16] Around half
of students entering Glasgow University were thus supported in the
interwar period.[17] Parents of students in Wales included high numbers of farmers or smallholders, colliers, shopkeepers and craftsmen.[18]
Fifty-five percent of students at the colleges of the University of
Wales had previously attended a state elementary school, compared to
18 percent at English universities. Lack of employment opportunities
elsewhere contributed to a rise in university intake during the 1930s,
particularly in depressed regions like South Wales.[19] Student numbers
at the four Welsh colleges peaked in the academic year 1933–1934
at 3,518 full-time students, leading to a consequent rise in graduate
unemployment.[20] Writing of the University of Wales in 1936, Cardiff
student W. Moelwyn Merchant (1913–1997) identified the "paradox
of a University which has thrived on depression," but also argued that
this increase in the number of students during times of unemployment

was the traditional response to hardship in Wales.[21] Even Cambridge and Oxford were not entirely immune from hardship. Around half of students responding to a survey at Oxford reported economizing on food for financial reasons in the late 1930s.[22] Kenneth Sinclair Loutit (1913–2003) went up to Cambridge in October 1931 at the height of the Depression and noted that although his contemporaries were "mostly the children of prosperous families" he did know one or two students who dropped out because their parents could not continue to finance their studies, commenting "I had never before been led to question the stability of the society into which I had been born."[23]

Despite these demographic changes in the student body, associational culture at many universities and colleges continued to develop along lines laid down before the First World War. The 1920s and 1930s were marked by a strong push to develop the "corporate" life of universities and colleges that came from students themselves as well as from the then higher education funding body, the Universities Grants Committee (UGC), which had been set up in 1919.[24] In the 1930s the government contributed just over a third (36%) of universities' income in England and Wales, with the remainder coming from student fees, local authority funding and endowments and donations.[25] Keith Vernon notes that the UGC's vision of university education was one which encouraged "the development of students' humane and civic sensibilities, acquired and honed through social integration and engagement."[26] Such a vision was out-of-kilter with the reality. Most universities and colleges remained nonresidential with few activities on campus after lectures. Excluding Oxford and Cambridge, in 1929–1930 just 18 percent of full-time university students in England lived in colleges or halls of residence.[27] In Scotland, around 7 percent were in residence.[28] David Daiches (1915–2005) who entered Edinburgh University in 1930 recalled that most men students lived at home, although there were a few university-run hostels for women.[29] The few colleges that did have a majority of students in residence tended to be located in the south of England, and included Royal Holloway, Reading, Exeter University College and Southampton University College. Excluding Oxford and Cambridge, universities and colleges drew most of their students from the local area, a radius of between 30 and 50 miles.[30] Yet the ideal of residence remained a key goal of many educationists and it was one which students themselves shared.[31] At the largely nonresidential Armstrong College, Newcastle, the Students Representative Council (SRC) played a key role in lobbying for the opening of the first men's hostel.

Students surveyed at the end of the 1930s at many colleges noted widespread awareness of the "advantages of university residence" and a desire to live-in if they could possibly afford to do so.[32] The activities of halls of residence were routinely reported in college magazines along with articles urging greater participation in clubs, societies and student politics.

Part of the push for residence was based on the notion that it was the long daily commute many students experienced, which hampered the development of extracurricular activities on campus. A report on the waning fortunes of the Liverpool Scout Club, for example, which ceased to exist in 1924 after its president had gone down, ascribed its decline to being a nonresidential university: "Everyone rushes home or to 'digs' after lectures or evening meetings, and only a visit of the Chief [Scout] would bring them back."[33] Indeed a standard college magazine editorial in the 1920s and 1930s was a piece complaining about student apathy and lack of interest in the doings of the college or university. An editorial in the *New University* pointed out that "nine out of every ten University magazines talks of apathy and the apathetic student" and suggested it was in the nature of magazine editors to thus criticize their peers. [34] The article then went on to roundly condemn student apathy, apparently without irony. There was some backlash to this continued assault on "apathetic" students. "Tantalus," an anonymous student at Armstrong, wrote in frustration to ask "why all this fuss about inducing people like myself to take part in 'College Life' or 'Social Activities' or 'College Sports'? My job while in Armstrong is to get a degree."[35] Tantalus took an hour and 15 minutes to get home and if he missed the 5 p.m. train home from Newcastle, he would not get home until after 9 p.m. As he noted, this journey "somewhat damps my ardour for the society meetings I occasionally feel inclined to attend."[36]

As part of the UGC's commitment to promote corporate culture it made funds available for the development of students' unions, sports facilities and halls of residence. Universities also sought funding for buildings works from local philanthropists and students themselves raised money for union buildings, sports fields and other student facilities. In Scotland, the Carnegie Trust contributed considerable sums toward building hostels and students' unions.[37] In England and Wales, students were involved in raising money for the "NUS Establishment Fund Appeal," launched to help the NUS buy its own London headquarters.[38] After several years in temporary accommodation, in 1925 the new NUS premises at Endsleigh Street were formally opened and offered a club room where students could take tea.[39]

By the end of the 1930s, then, there was a wide range of social activities available to students, including regular "hops" (dances), musical recitals, rag festivities, drama groups and literary clubs and access to a broad range of sports and athletics as well as the chance to attend talks, debates, study circles and political meetings. Although lacking the institutions of hall dinner, members of nonresidential colleges pointed out the college refectories provided ideal places for discussion and that despite students being widely scattered in homes and lodgings "what is surprising is not that societies get so little support; the surprise is that they do."[40] David Daiches, the son of a rabbi, found the "great variety of social and intellectual life outside the lecture room" at Edinburgh University to be "intoxicating."[41] Such programs of activities were sustained by greater mixing of the sexes at the universities between the wars. At the civic universities advances made during the First World War on equal access to refectories and common rooms were often maintained. However, both women's halls of residence and women's colleges retained strict rules on male visitors and "gate hours." At Oxford and Cambridge the first mixed-sex student societies were allowed in the interwar period and rules on chaperonage were relaxed.[42] Moreover, students in college were more closely monitored than at nonresidential universities. David Daiches was unprepared for the total difference in atmosphere between Edinburgh University (where he had taken his undergraduate degree) and Oxford, which he entered in 1934, where even as a postgraduate research student he felt he was treated as a child.[43] Similarly, although a student at Cambridge, Eric Hobsbawm (1917–2012) spent vacations at the London School of Economics (LSE) in the 1930s, which he felt confirmed more to his view of what a "real" university should be.[44]

The regular cries about student apathy in the 1920s and 1930s often failed to consider that students might prefer to continue their involvement in leisure, political, religious or sporting activities in their home communities. "Tantalus," for example, was involved in the Amateur Dramatic Society in his home town and liked to watch football locally on Saturday afternoons. One article on Birmingham University by SCM Secretary David Paton did recognize that many students had commitments to churches, boys' clubs, Girl Guides and cultural associations at home, but rather snobbishly argued that the reading choice of students—picture papers and local newspapers— "point to the inadvisability of hoping too much from the home interests and activities of these students."[45] In the interwar era there was also a rapid growth in the range of commercial leisure activities available to students. Like other young people, students were particularly attracted by the cinema and dancing, activities which often unfortunately clashed with Wednesday afternoon and Saturday evening activities or meetings at students' unions. Yet maintaining such local links were important and deliberate strategies for students trying to reduce the dislocation from family and friends which receiving a higher education often entailed in the mid-twentieth century.

A WATERSHED MOMENT? THE UNIVERSITIES AND THE GENERAL STRIKE

In their history of the student estate Ashby and Anderson noted that the only event to "break the surface of student" life between the First World War and the depression was the General Strike.[46] In contrast, I have already shown that international affairs such as postwar reconstruction and Russian famine relief did attract considerable student attention and activity. Yet the General Strike of May 1926 has become inextricably linked with our view of interwar university students because of the prevalence of images of upper-class student strike breakers in accounts of the period. Historians writing on the General Strike have perpetuated the familiar story of undergraduates gleefully—and ineptly—driving trains and buses. Such images were readily disseminated by the press during and after the strike and while they reflect the reality that large numbers of students did volunteer their services they also mask two crucial facts. Firstly such images perpetrate the myth that all or most General Strike volunteers were upper-class university students and secondly, they reinforce a mistaken idea that all students held the same attitudes to the General Strike.

Rachelle Hope Saltzman's 2012 *A Lark for the Sake of Their Country* is the first book-length account of the General Strike volunteers and uses oral history data collected in the mid-1980s.[47] Saltzman argues that while most volunteers were neither undergraduates nor came from upper-class backgrounds, students were often the most visible and newsworthy of volunteers. On the railways, for example, while the majority of volunteers were actually retired railway workers, men employed in related industries or in nonunion grades, undergraduates were given low-skill but highly visible roles as porters. The Fair Isle sweaters, plus fours and new-style "Oxford bags" worn by Oxford and Cambridge undergraduates marked them out as volunteers and attracted widespread comment and attention. Similarly, amusing tales of privileged student drivers rerouting buses or not knowing how to stop a train made for better headlines than did similar stories where the protagonist was a clerk or shopkeeper. The actual numbers of student volunteers are unclear, although students appear to have been a significant and highly visible minority who received press coverage out of proportion to their actual numbers. In one of the earliest histories of the General Strike published in 1957 Julian Symons argued that the importance of undergraduates to the government in maintaining the supply and transport service throughout the country "can hardly be overestimated."[48] In Scotland, university students made up around 3,500–4,000 of the total 25,000 volunteers who were enrolled.[49] Thus a proportion of around 20 percent, or slightly higher, might not be unreasonable for England as well.

Given that the majority of strikers were not university students, what was the university response to the General Strike? It is clear that thousands of students did take part as "volunteers"—some of whom were paid for their labor, others receiving nothing more than free meals and cigarettes—during May 1926. University authorities adopted different attitudes, with strong encouragement for volunteering at Exeter, Edinburgh, Oxford, Cambridge and University College, London. For example, examinations at some universities were postponed and students were given leave of absence to volunteer. An American student at Oxford recalled the master of his college calling a special meeting in which he urged undergraduates to do their part in the national crisis, the only requirement being to tell the Head Porter where they were going.[50] A majority of students at the universities of St Andrews, Oxford and Cambridge enrolled as volunteers. At Glasgow, however, only a few hundred students out of a total student body of 4,489 volunteered, partly because the authorities did not offer such concessions and partly because of the differing social makeup and political sympathies of Glasgow students.[51] Undergraduates were deployed in a range of roles during the strike including as tube, train and tram drivers, bus conductors and special constables. Large numbers of students, both locally sourced and arriving from Oxford and Cambridge, were used to load and unload ships at Liverpool, Grimsby, Hull, Bristol and London dockyards. However, not all those who volunteered saw active service. At Edinburgh, half of the student body of four thousand volunteered but only one thousand were actually given any work to do. Male students had many more opportunities for volunteering than women students did, although many university women did wish to take part. Press reports about women volunteers tended to dwell on older society women or "glamorous debutantes" rather than women students.

As early as May 1926 Ernest Barker pointed out that while universities other than Oxford and Cambridge had supplied volunteers, the press coverage would not have led one to believe this was the case.[52] Although Symons did record that the red-brick universities provided their fare share of volunteers, few later scholars have looked in any detail at the motivations or activities of student volunteers across the provincial universities.[53] Saltzman argues that scholars have taken at face-value "the frame that university volunteers themselves and much of the contemporary media insisted on imposing around their acts," thereby providing a rationale to dismiss rather to examine students as among the central actors in the strike.[54] However, the only university publications even Saltzman consulted were those published by Oxford and Cambridge. Ashby and Anderson reported that "nearly all those students who took any interest at all helped to break the strike; the handful of students who sympathised with the workers found themselves cold shouldered by their friends."[55]

Such representations do need to be questioned as an accurate portrayal of national student opinion. A closer look reveals that many students were unsure about what their response to the strike should be. In June 1926, the editor of *The Northerner*, Armstrong College's magazine, felt that many people had "too hastily formed opinions of what was the Students' attitude to the National Emergency" and published a range of student opinion he believed to be fairly "representative."[56] In her book Saltzman sums up the motives underlying people's decision to volunteer, as ranging from "feelings of duty and patriotism to a desire not to miss the fun, from a fondness for larks to a desire to earn some money."[57] Symons argued that the undergraduates, like other volunteers, considered the strike to be "a lark, an agreeable change from everyday work."[58] Evidence from the *Northerner* confirms this mixed picture of motives applies to students in Newcastle, at least, where the outstanding feature of the strike appears to have been "the utter lack of cohesion and leadership" among the students and only a minority with strong political opinions had made up their minds one way or another.[59] One, for example, argued that because the college was supported by public money, students should have refrained from taking any one side in industrial disputes.[60]

Many of the respondents to Saltzman's enquiries in the 1980s who had been students in 1926 recorded that they didn't see volunteering as "strike breaking" but merely as national service. Taking part was a rare opportunity to "do something more practical than Academic studies, and at the same time to win social approval, not usually available" as a Newnham student Sylvia Makower expressed it.[61] Similarly, writing to Brian Simon in the 1980s Kit Meredith remembered that strike breaking by students was portrayed at the time as being in the interests of the community and acknowledged that participation was also seen widely as a bit of fun.[62] Volunteering was presented as evidence that students could contribute during periods of national emergency and could work hard at "disagreeable tasks."[63] An editorial in *University College Magazine* went so far as to claim students' service during the crisis was a "vindication of higher education," albeit in the tongue-in-cheek fashion that characterized most student writing on the strike.[64] Birmingham University issued an emergency edition of its journal during the strike, typed and duplicated rather than printed, informing students of the University Senate's decision not to defer university examinations. Its editorial stated that students who chose to volunteer ought to do so as private individuals not as university students, however ended with an appeal to students that tapped into both civic and national pride:

> The city badly needs all the help it can get, and University Students are the most free to help. They have the least essential demand upon their time; they can give up a week to volunteer service without hardship. We should make every effort to help our city and our country at such a time of crisis.[65]

At this date, provincial students' identities were often more bound up with home, family and their local town or city than with their college or university, the more so because a majority lived at home and commuted to lectures. Therefore parental influence was likely to have been a decisive influence on students' choices about involvement in the General Strike. One Armstrong student claimed he volunteered in the interests not of the capitalists or coal owners, but of the "classes, which in normal times are just able to eke out an existence," people who needed to travel long distances to their work and who might lose their jobs if they couldn't get there by public transport.[66] However the strike could also divide families. Jack Gaster (1907–2007)—recently down from the LSE—was radicalized by the strike, and horrified that his brother Francis served as a student "blackleg" bus driver.[67] Students at the residential colleges were far more likely to become involved as volunteers because of the powerful effect of not wanting to be left out, even if their own political inclinations may have erred on the side of the strikers. Margaret Cole, wife of Labour-supporting Oxford Don G. D. H. Cole, remembered that unless some worthwhile occupation was quickly found for the small group of socialist students the Coles had been nurturing at Oxford "they would be away driving buses and trains for the Government out of sheer boredom."[68] The Coles became involved in a University Strike Committee set up to liaise with the Trade Union Congress in London and spread knowledge about the strike in the university and nearby villages. At Balliol, Principal A. D. Lindsay "gently discouraged" students from volunteering to break the strike with the result that several students, led by Walter Oakshott (1903–1987) and John R. Hicks (1904–1989), moved to London during the strike and produced a conciliatory newspaper called the *British Independent*.[69] During the strike normal newspaper publication was suspended and a number of special strike papers produced, notably the government organ, Winston Churchill's *British Gazette* and the Trade Union Congress's *British Worker*. The student-run *British Independent* first appeared toward the end of the strike to give a voice to what it called the "growing body of moderate opinion" and to promote the Archbishop of Canterbury's three-point reconciliation plan which the BBC had been pressured into not broadcasting.[70] Its first editorial stated:

> This paper is being run by a body of Oxford undergraduates who are convinced of the need for such an undertaking. We are thus a purely voluntary organisation, and hope that our lack of political connections or entanglements, if it is in many ways a handicap to us may enable us to pursue a policy of peace with more impartiality than might be possible for some others.[71]

The notable exceptions of the *British Independent* and the *Northerner* aside, analysis of college magazines and newspapers shows that those reporting seriously on the strike were in a minority. Most did not mention the strike at all. The only mention in Sheffield's journal *Floreamus* was to regret that the strike had led to cancellation of a popular annual union debate with American students and an inter-varsity meeting of biological societies from Northern colleges.[72] Several published humorous illustrations, sketches and poetry about the strike, mainly lampooning student volunteers. Such a response was in tune with the tone of undergraduate publications more generally in the 1920s. The NUS journal, *New University*, did not mention the events of May 1926, and Mike Day suggests this was because NUS was prevented by its constitution for expressing any view. In their 1968 article on student politics, A. H. Halsey and Stephen

Marks considered that there was no evidence that students who volunteered viewed their actions as a "distinctively student intervention"[73] Yet student writing does hint that the strike prompted some at least to question "the undergraduate's conception of realities, his relations to the outside world."[74] It is perhaps no coincidence that from the late 1920s student organizations began to reflect on students' place—as a class—in wider British society. Writers of the late 1920s could assert seemingly without challenge that the "student class of this country is well-known for its apathy to social, political and religious matters."[75] Things were changing, albeit slowly. In fact, an NUS executive meeting held just before the General Strike in February 1926 had discussed "the part that NUS should take in social service" and had also considered a proposal to institute a loan scheme for students.[76] The following year NUS appointed a Special Enquiries Secretary—Richard Pyke—to begin to investigate issues such as student hardship and possible solutions in the form of loan schemes, vacation employment and European models of self-help. In 1927 Pyke was one of a five strong English and Welsh delegation that attended the first Dresden conference on student self-help.[77] The high profile involvement of student volunteers against the trade unions was to have later repercussions in the form of hostility to various schemes to organize vacation work for students requiring financial assistance during the 1930s as well as to some student-led social service for unemployed men.[78] Despite the lack of a coherent student response at the time, the General Strike became a significant watershed moment for later student generations who sought to contrast student social concern and solidarity with the unemployed with the activities of May 1926.

WIRTSCHAFTSHILFE IN WALES: THE BEGINNINGS OF STUDENT SELF-HELP

Demographic changes in the student body in the interwar period had consequences for the types of voluntary activities students became involved with. By the late 1920s the topic of student self-help was under discussion in British universities. Strongly promoted by International Student Service (ISS), the message was spread in part through regular visits of ISS leaders to British universities and colleges.[79] Self-help conferences in Dresden 1927 and 1929 attracted over one hundred students from 20 countries, with strong delegations coming from Britain, France and Spain.[80] It was in Wales, where the coal crisis of the late 1920s was causing widespread distress, that student self-help really took off in Britain. Students from Cardiff and Aberystwyth were involved in local relief efforts such as collecting toys or arranging entertainments for children in the South Wales valleys, but there was also growing hardship among students themselves.[81] In 1927, three Welsh students returned from Dresden determined "to put the word 'self-help' into the vocabulary of their fellow students."[82] Self-help committees were formed at the four colleges of the University of Wales and students at Cardiff and Aberystwyth began experimenting with cooperative buying schemes.[83] This work was developed in the academic year 1928–1929 and was also taken up at Swansea and Bangor.

The situation in the Welsh colleges gained the attention of International Student Service, thanks to the efforts of the new General Secretary Dr Walter Kotschnig (1901–1985) and his Welsh wife Elined Prys Kotschnig (1895–1983).[84] A graduate of the University of Wales with experience of relief work in Romania after the war, Elined met Austrian-born Walter at the Quaker educational settlement Woodbrooke and they married in 1924. In March 1929 Kotschnig secured a £100 grant from the ISS assembly for promoting self-help in Wales, a relatively small sum of money that was less important than the knowledge, interest and contacts of ISS leaders in Geneva and Dresden. In 1929, a Self-Help Council for Wales was set up and Kitty Lewis, previously lead organizer of the European Student Relief campaign at the University of Wales, became its volunteer secretary.[85] At the first meeting of the Council three main functions were identified: promotion and coordination of self-help activities in Welsh Colleges; raising of an educational loan fund and emergency fund; and spreading of knowledge about international self-help in Welsh Colleges.[86] One of its first moves was to appeal for a share of the money flowing in to the Lord Mayor's Fund for the newly designated "Distressed Areas," which raised £1.75 million— including a substantial government donation—between April 1928 and April 1929.[87] Kitty's request was rejected on the grounds that the fund was intended only for basic relief such as provision of food, boots and clothing and not for educational purposes. This was a big blow to the Council, which nonetheless proceeded to build up a small emergency relief fund, largely through significant donations from Kitty's parents. Although the fund was unable to deal with most of the pitiful requests for help pouring in, it did make a series of small grants to students who would otherwise not be able to continue their university course because of family poverty. Hundreds of these begging letters survive at the National Library of Wales and provide strong evidence of student hardship in Wales as well as extensive details of students' coping strategies. In at least one case Kitty herself made a private grant to a student, appealing to him not to inform the Council she had done so, and in another she offered a student some employment writing letters for her.

Plans were also developed for more permanent loan scheme in partnership with other agencies, notably the NUS. NUS Special Inquiries Secretary Pyke had been researching the whole issue of scholarships, loan schemes, employment and student insurance for two years. His work paid off in 1928 when the NUS received a grant of £1,000 from the Cassel Educational Trust to set up a loan scheme in which university-sourced funds would be matched by Cassel/NUS funds.[88] Support and guidance was sought from the student self-help office in Dresden in setting up this scheme, which eventually operated in Cardiff, Swansea, Armstrong College in Newcastle and at Manchester women's union. A key principle of the program was that applications for loans should be considered by mixed committees of students and staff. As a 1930 NUS report tried to suggest, this work fell under the umbrella of student self-help: it was a "plan with educative value and without any air of charity."[89] Unfortunately, the scheme cannot be considered a success. It failed to expand beyond the four colleges mentioned earlier and was abandoned in Newcastle as early as the mid-1930s.[90] In 1936, Sheffield University published a report critical of the NUS in which it identified the loan scheme as one of several "schemes of value which gave been brought forward and subsequently dropped."[91] The NUS responded that limited resources prevented it being developed further. Mike Day agrees that the scheme was unsuccessful, but argues its creation demonstrated "just how quickly the organisation had moved away from the sentiments of meetings in 1922."[92]

During the late 1920s and early 1930s a number of other self-help ideas were trialed in universities and colleges mainly in Northern England and Wales. One method popular on the continent was vacation work for students. Armstrong College in Newcastle prided itself on being "*the* pioneer" of such work in Britain after arranging an archeological excavation at Newminster Abbey, home of local shipbuilder turned landowner Sir George Renwick, during the summer vacation of 1928.[93] However, Armstrong's vacation work committee failed to capitalize on this success.[94] Unlike in the USA and elsewhere, vacation work for students was not a British tradition and it was made more difficult by the fact that there was already high unemployment owing to industrial depression and the fact that "the idea of vacation work for university men not yet taken shape in the mind of the British employer."[95] In 1929, NUS Secretary Ralph Nunn May made appealed in vain to potential employers via the letter columns of *The Times*, suggesting that roles might be found for needy students as laborers, shop assistants, waiters, governesses and laboratory assistants.[96] In Wales the Self-help Council's attempts to find vacation work for students were also only partially successful.[97] An article in NUS organ *New University* concluded that the chances of students obtaining paid work over summer 1932 were "very small indeed."[98] Carol Dyhouse's research confirms this picture; very few of her respondents at university between the wars were able to secure paid employment during vacations. Most, she noted, responded to her question with incredulity.[99] A key problem was that trade unions were opposed to the employment of students as casual labor, the more so as memories of the General Strike were still very sharp.[100] There were isolated examples of success such as Christmas 1937, when around three hundred Birmingham University students worked as temporary sorters at the Birmingham General Post Office, but this was controversial enough to prompt a question in the House of Commons by veteran trade unionist and Labour MP Will Thorne.[101] While trade unionists were suspicious, students hailed a workable scheme that could be rolled out to other universities, but it was not to be.

Owing to the failure of methods to increase the income of students through loans or vacation work, the emphasis in the British self-help movement fell largely on schemes to reduce living costs. At the Dresden conferences students learned that the three main methods included securing discounts from private enterprises such as railways or theaters; cooperative buying of food, drawing materials and books; and opening a student-run shop. Such a shop would sell necessities as cheaply as possible but offer small luxuries such as sweets, pictures, room furnishings and gifts to make a profit. Dresden delegates learned that these self-help enterprises should be run by student volunteers and received advice about recruiting and retaining volunteers, as well as warnings about assigning "responsibilities beyond the capacity of the student volunteer." [102] Moreover, the educative value of student self-help was urged because such "practical experience is of real value to the student in rounding out his personality and is giving him valuable human experience quite apart from his university study."[103] By 1930 there were cooperative buying schemes in place at colleges including Aberystwyth, Cardiff, Sheffield and Manchester.[104] The Self-Help Council for Wales issued a handbook enabling students to obtain reductions from local firms and organized the cooperative sale of scarves, ties and exercise books.[105] The Student Representative Council (SRC) of Armstrong College operated a volunteer-run student shop selling textbooks and stationery successfully into the 1930s.[106]

One of the greatest expenditures for students in the interwar period was textbooks. As Brian Simon's research in the later 1930s discovered, very few students were able to afford to purchase course books. In addition, libraries at many provincial universities were often poorly resourced which meant that only a small proportion of students on a course would have access to the books recommended by the lecturers. This lack of books actually dictated the style of teaching in many colleges. Lecturers found themselves having to take the place of books, and writing up and studying their lecture notes became the main activity of many students. Simon's report quoted a new lecturer at a civic university as saying "all my theories [on teaching] had assumed the facilities of the older and richer universities; without them they didn't apply. I had to turn myself into a textbook."[107] There were some efforts to address this problem. In 1925, NUS established a textbook supply scheme with the bookseller Foyles in which students sold textbooks back to Foyles to be sold second hand to other students.[108] In its first year 1,500 students took advantage of the scheme.[109] The NUS also worked to obtain student concessions on newspapers and rail fares. Travelling in Europe to attend an ISS conference in 1926, a Reading student was surprised that the railways gave students half-fares, and asked rhetorically in his write-up of the trip "why is England the only country in the world where no special reduction is given to students?"[110] Although railway companies were reluctant, except for large group travel, by the mid-1930s *The Times*, *The Manchester Guardian*, *The Spectator* and *The World Review* all offered a concession to students.[111] Although these were small victories, the principle of student discounts established by voluntary effort in the 1920s was to be built on after the Second World War.

PRACTICALLY EVERYONE RECOGNIZES THE PUBLIC UTILITY OF CHARITY RAGS

In the 1920s student rag emerged as a "standard feature of University life" according to one article which concluded that "practically everyone recognises the public utility of Charity Rags."[112] In the 1920s longstanding student traditions of an evening of licensed misrule as part of a visit to a play or panto were legitimized as fundraising activities. The invented tradition of rag day spread rapidly across the

university world and by the late 1920s was raising significant funds
for local hospitals and medical charities. Carol Dyhouse has argued
that studying student rag can throw light on "gender relations and
shifts in student culture and identity, as well as the changing relationships between students and society during this period."[113] Student
rags were a visible demonstration of university presence in a town or
city, and one of the few occasions on which the public would encounter students as a body. The main feature of a university rag was a costumed procession or carnival at which students collected money from
the public. The potentially large fundraising potential of this idea
whetted the appetite of hospital treasurers and stirred the ambitions
of student organizers, according to Nunn May.[114] By the early 1930s
the Birmingham rag, for example, had grown into a huge organizational and logistical effort with several dances, a large street procession and a public raffle in which the top prize was a Triumph Super
Seven car.[115] In 1929, the rag raised £6,701 for the city's hospitals
and there was much soul searching when the 1930 rag failed to set a
new record at £6,520.[116]

New fundraising techniques spread rapidly between colleges and
included balls, revues and concerts; publication of "rag mags" with
humorous articles, jokes and cartoons; and sales of "immunity badges,"
protecting the wearer from hassle once they had made a donation.
Rivalry was an important aspect of rags, with students from different
faculties or colleges competing to raise the most money.[117] The festivities included kidnapping of college mascots and even fights between
groups of rival students deploying such weapons as rotten fruit and
flour bombs. T. E. Lawrenson, a student at Manchester in the 1930s
and Senior Tutor of a Manchester Hall of Residence in the years after
the war, argued that the student rag was an inevitable, recreational
outburst from day-to-day student life.[118] Since funds in the 1930s
were usually dedicated to the support of local hospitals, it was medical
students who often initiated rags and were the most active in collecting. The Liverpool Panto, for example, allocated all its money to the
city's hospitals. Other causes did sometimes get a look in, for example, in 1931 Sheffield University donated 10 percent of takings to the
British Universities Fund for the International Student Sanatorium.[119]
However, with the rise of such extensive fundraising for local hospitals
it seems likely that earlier student causes such as university settlements
may have been among the losers, although at some universities rag collections did raise money for the settlement. At Edinburgh, for example, most of the money raised in the 1930s was shared by Edinburgh
University Settlement and the Royal Infirmary.[120]

In 1928, Hugh Herklots, a member of an NUS committee on the problem of universities though writing in an independent capacity, considered rags to be an important aspect of student culture in the "new universities."[121] This observation seems to fit with the very extensive coverage of rags in college magazines. Rags brought students at what were still mainly nonresidential universities together for a common purpose and could attract credit to the university as a source of financial support for local charities and hospitals.[122] One article in *The University* considered that rags had raised around £160,000 for charity between 1921–1929, a "social service of no small importance."[123] It further suggested that instead of holding a variety of rags "of local character and appeal, dotted all over the calendar of the university year," students should cooperate to hold one annual Universities' Hospitals Day and sell one standard rag mag. Yet it was this very local character which was so important to the success of rag fundraising. Rags were also important as an area of cooperation between different groups of students particularly at a time when men's and women's activities were usually highly segregated.[124] In *A Student's View of the Universities*, for instance, Simon concluded that rags were the one occasion when the majority of students were united.[125] At Birmingham around two thirds of students reported taking part in the annual Carnival, compared to a much smaller percentage who were actively involved with other student activities.[126] At Liverpool, Leta Jones perhaps too fondly remembered the annual Panto Day as the "big spree of the year" where women dressed in gowns and mortarboards and students "rattled collecting tins, trespassing happily into offices, warehouses and shops among the good-natured Liverpudlians."[127]

By 1932 the expansion of rag activity had come to the attention of the NUS which discussed rags at its January executive meeting, concluding that rags should be scaled back because they placed an "intolerable burden of work on the shoulders of the students organising them."[128] Such warnings fell on deaf ears and did not prevent the movement's continuation in the years before the Second World War. One indication of this was the December 1937 conference of organizers of "University Carnivals in aid of Hospitals" convened by the NUS in Liverpool in order to facilitate exchange of ideas and methods.[129] Suggestions in the early 1930s that students were growing disillusioned with rag collections because over organization had made what began as a lark into an increasingly difficult business proved premature.[130] Throughout the 1920s and 1930s the student rag grew in importance as a route for students to develop local patriotism and foster a corporate culture at civic universities. Indeed, rag has proved to be one of the most resilient forms of student charitable activity.

CONCLUSIONS

While our abiding image of the interwar undergraduate may have been shaped by the "Bright Young Things" of Oxford and Cambridge and the General Strike volunteers in their Fair Isle sweaters, a closer look at what the wider body of students across Britain were actually doing, writing and thinking challenges this stereotype. By the 1930s the changing social profile of university and college students led to student investigation and activity in areas such as self-help, financial assistance, health and graduate unemployment that would have been "unthinkable" in an earlier period.[131] Considering this diversity of student activities also calls into question assumptions of widespread student "apathy" voiced by commentators at the time and afterwards. High unemployment and economic depression produced an incipient movement for organized economy and relief among the student community in the north of England and in Wales which gradually evolved after the Second World War into the many of the most recognizable activities of students' unions of the late twentieth century. Following an initial interest in international affairs, by the time of the General Strike in 1926 the NUS had begun to pay greater attention to domestic issues affecting students, although much of this work owed more to local initiative than national policy. Students' attitudes to social and political questions such as the General Strike were more heterogeneous than writers at the time or since have allowed, although the carnivalesque tended to dominate in student magazines and the press. Similarly by the end of the 1920s charity rags had emerged as a notable aspect of student culture at the civic universities, worthy of debate and discussion at national level, as well as attempts at coordinated activity. However, despite its valuable role in strengthening student identity, calls for reform of rag that would have greater impact on local hospitals or charities went unheeded because rag was essentially viewed as an annual expression of student high spirits; pranks and petty vandalism were legitimized by the significant charitable receipts. While most international relief efforts placed British students in the role of donors, after 1929 student communities in the "depressed areas" of South Wales became a focus for the international support of International Student Service. Like earlier emergency relief efforts, experiments with student self-help provided further opportunities for cooperation and joint action between existing the national student organizations NUS and SCM together with the newly constituted English and Welsh branches of ISS. Self-help therefore contributed to the strengthening of a student movement. Although practical self-help activities had only limited success nationally, for those students involved it was a valuable training in cooperative action and played a small part in alleviating student hardship. Moreover self-help fed into wider debates about student health, welfare and self-government in higher education that were to resurface after the Second World War.

CHAPTER 6

Digging with the Unemployed: The Rise of a Student Social Consciousness? 1932–1939

An article in the University of London Magazine identified the academic year 1932–1933 as marked by "a rapid growth of a new student attitude, chiefly characterised by an awakening to social problems" and the resultant widening of activities of student organizations such as the National Union of Students (NUS) and the Student Christian Movement (SCM).[1] Similarly, a 1932 conference of representatives of International Student Organizations meeting in Paris chose "The University and Social Service" to be its main topic because it was a "major problem" facing universities worldwide.[2] Such sentiments were echoed in many other student publications of the early 1930s, while Brian Simon later pinpointed 1933 as a key date for understanding the whole student movement of the interwar period.[3] This chapter discusses the ways in which students in Britain engaged with the widespread problems of the Depression in order to explore the shifting relationships between students and society. The student response to unemployment included a renewed interested in social study, offering material aid and moral support to Hunger Marchers, participation in experimental workcamp projects and organizing residential camps for the unemployed in the 1930s. Such changes may be seen as one outcome of the heightened political consciousness that marked universities and the rise of a student social conscience in the interwar period.

Young Minds for Old? Student Politics and Social Concern in the 1930s

In the 1930s, British university students made their voices heard as never before on a wide range of social and political topics. Students of the 1930s were keen to distance themselves from the perceived escapism of the Bright Young Things generation and the decade was marked by "a determination to do something," manifest through increased student social and political activity.[4] Growing numbers in the universities, the changing social profile of students and more effective national student organization combined with external factors such as the Depression and the rise of fascism led to the growth of what has been called a student social consciousness.[5] As in previous generations, ideas spread rapidly through the university world and facilitated the emergence of a "student popular front" by the late 1930s. Particularly noticeable was an increase in party political activity—and particularly left-wing action—on university campuses (as indeed in some public schools). Following the formation of the National Government in 1931—widely seen on the left as a betrayal of socialist principles—a number of Marxist student societies were founded as direct competitors to the older University Labour Federation (ULF), including the October Club at Oxford, the Gower Socialist Society at University College and others at the London School of Economics (LSE), Cambridge, Bristol, Durham, Leeds, Manchester and Reading. The first groups were formed independently of the Communist Party of Great Britain (CPGB) but soon made contact, and some students became party members.[6] The Socialist Club at Cambridge numbered one thousand by the mid-1930s, of whom one in four was also a CP member.[7] However such high membership at Oxford and Cambridge was in part because it was necessary to belong to a society to attend its meetings—and many students were also members of other political groups, including the Conservative party.

In 1932 the CPGB formed a secret Student Bureau and became strongly committed to the recruitment of university students after abandoning its earlier policy of distrusting middle-class intellectuals.[8] Central to the success of the Communist movement among students in the 1930s was the work of organizers including Frank Strauss Meyer (1909–1972), Jack Cohen (1905–1982) and James Klugman (1912–1977).[9] Meyer, an American student who studied at Oxford and LSE, was described by an Oxford contemporary turned MI5 source as "the founder of the student CP movement" in Britain.[10] Klugman was part of the Trinity Communist cell from which the notorious "Cambridge Spies" were recruited by Moscow. Other important activities of the CPGB Student Bureau were the newspaper *Student Vanguard* and the Federation of Student Societies (FSS) formed in 1933 to coordinate and mobilize Communists in the universities.[11] Although it may have missed the Cambridge Spies, British Security Service MI5 was aware of the secret political work among students and from the late 1930s closely monitored the movements of the student organizers, socialist clubs and the NUS. The FSS program committed members to anti-war and antifascist protest, solidarity with the unemployed, agitation against university staff serving as union officials and promotion of the achievements of Soviet Russia and China.[12] Organizations for Indians studying in Britain—of which there were large numbers at Oxford, Cambridge, London and some other universities in the 1930s—also came under increasing Communist influence. In 1937, several such groups affiliated to a new Federation of Indian Students' Societies led by Cambridge students Rajni Patel and Mohan Kumaramangalam (1916–1973). Communists were also infiltrating Labour clubs and, pushing a "united front" approach, the FSS repeatedly sought affiliation with the ULF, a merger that eventually occurred in 1936, with John Cornford (1915–1936) becoming first student Vice-President.[13] Reflecting on this merger, Reginald Smith of Birmingham University noted that while many socialist students still felt uncomfortable with the more extreme "mumbo-jumbo" elements of Communism, they had a strong enough bond and enough of a shared philosophy, particularly in antiwar work, to support a united front, despite the disapproval of older members of the Labour Party.[14]

The rise in CPGB membership to around 18,000 by the end of the 1930s was largely due to an influx of middle-class recruits including both students and white collar workers.[15] Many students arrived at university from school ripe for recruitment to the Communist cause, while for others triggers included contact with Hunger Marchers and direct experience of fascism.[16] Philip Toynbee (1916–1981) acknowledged that membership of the CP—which he joined in his first term at Oxford in 1935—was partly about the thrill of belonging to a semi-secret society. He later reflected, "In our hunger for an earthly paradise we grossly deceived ourselves about Stalin's Russia and foolishly accepted the harsh and cynical methods of our own party."[17] However, although socialist societies had been formed at most colleges and universities by the mid-1930s, outside Oxford, Cambridge and London, the fortunes of such groups were usually dependent on a small number of committed students. The University College of the South West (Exeter) started a Socialist Society in 1933 but failed to maintain interest in succeeding years, struggling by with just 15 members out of over 300 students. Its secretary lamented Exeter students' "regrettable lack of political consciousness."[18] Similarly, at Hull University College the Socialist Society did not survive the departure of its founder member.[19] At most universities there remained a large

Figure 6.1 NUS Vice-President George Bean speaking at a meeting of the *Rassemblement Mondial des Etudiants* [World Student Association] in Paris in 1938 or 1939. James Klugman is on the platform, and Eric Hobsbawm is sitting in the front, looking up at Bean.

Source: Image from the Brian Simon Archive (Ref: SIM/4/5/1/49) held at the Institute of Education Archive.

number of students who saw the business of coming to university as that of getting a degree, and could "safely be relied upon to keep away from all the most interesting meetings where political, social and moral problems are discussed," as Lucy Crewe Chambers of Liverpool University put it in a 1936 collection of essays edited by NUS President Lincoln Ralphs called *Young Minds for Old*.[20]

Moreover, though powerful, socialism was not the only driving force behind the rise of a student social consciousness in the 1930s. The longstanding tradition of Christian social concern in the universities received new life under the influence of William Temple as Archbishop of York from 1929 and the national leadership of the SCM turned increasingly to social and political concerns in the 1930s. Although by the 1930s the SCM had lost its preeminence as alternative avenues of social and political organization opened up, it remained influential within the national student movement.[21] In his survey of the universities Brian Simon identified the SCM as one of the best organized and active student societies, although he reported that "there is a definite tendency for its members to separate themselves off from the rest of the student community." [22] In 1986, Kit Meredith suggested that Simon should have put more emphasis on the contribution of SCM in his account of the student movement of the 1930s, and argued that student Christian organizations "constituted, along with the CP/YCL [Communist Party/Young Communist League] the most effective link between the students and the rest of the youth movement."[23]

A further factor behind increased interest in social and political questions on campus was that students themselves were not immune from the effects of the Depression. This was particularly the case at colleges located in Wales, the North (especially Liverpool, Durham and Newcastle) and some parts of Scotland, where unemployment was highest and where students were more likely to live at home and remain in close touch with communities. Cardiff student W. Moelwyn Merchant argued in his chapter for *Young Minds for Old* that the response of Welsh students to the Depression was less to turn to extreme socialist politics than to become involved in social service. Merchant argued that most Welsh students came from homes in which one or more family members were unemployed and a "vital connection is maintained with the effects of continued want and deprivation." [24] This desire for connection with the unemployed on the part of students who could not claim such close links was a driving force behind the camps for the unemployed which formed a major student response to unemployment. In addition to the student hardship detailed in the preceding chapter, in the 1930s concerns for many were the high rates of graduate unemployment and underemployment. It was not uncommon for students to seek work for several years after graduation, giving them direct experience of the dole. The experience of a London science graduate writing to the NUS journal *New University* may not be untypical. In 1933, he had been unemployed for two years and he was living with his school teacher mother but had just been deprived of benefits by the imposition of a new means test. Of 50 jobs applied for, only 16 had responded and just two had offered him an interview.[25]

A Mediating Part

Like other voluntary associations in the early 1930s, student organizations began to recognize that the scale of unemployment was unprecedented—there were 2.8 million insured workers on the unemployment registers by 1931—and that the universities and colleges needed to make a response. As historians including Bernard Harris have shown, despite expansion of state welfare services to deal with the crisis such services were subject to considerable limitations.[26] Thus in the 1930s government came to rely heavily on voluntary effort, further strengthening the "unique partnership" between the state and the voluntary sector that social worker Elizabeth Macadam (1871–1948) identified as the "new philanthropy."[27] Voluntary responses to the unemployment crisis ranged from relief of immediate material distress to more radical and political proposals for social and economic change. In coordinating charitable responses to unemployment the key body was the National Council for Social Service (NCSS), which sought to tread, as its historian Margaret Brasnett noted, "a cautious middle course between soup kitchen and revolution."[28] In fact it might be argued that the Depression secured the long-term future of the NCSS (which later became known as the National Council for Voluntary Organisations). Between 1932 and 1939 the Ministry of Labour channelled considerable sums of money for relief through NCSS, which allocated grants to a range of schemes including educational settlements, clubs and camps. From 1934 the government also supported land settlement schemes, allotment projects and industrial societies through a Special Areas Fund, which again passed through NCSS to grassroots projects.[29]

In addition to appeals for financial aid there was also a new call for volunteers that is important in understanding the student response to the 1930s unemployment crisis. The NCSS enlisted its Patron—the then Prince of Wales—to launch a campaign for "the youth of the nation to take up social service" for the unemployed with a broadcast appeal from the Albert Hall in January 1932.[30] Reinforcing this call A. D. Lindsay, Master of Balliol and a Vice President of NCSS, urged conciliation as he had in 1926, arguing that "voluntary service from those who are not unemployed must play the mediating part between the Government and the unemployed."[31] The Prince's appeal resulted in the launching of hundreds of new voluntary initiatives for the unemployed; by the autumn NCSS was in touch with seven hundred schemes.[32] Much of this voluntary welfare work was small-scale, poorly organized and failed to benefit large numbers of the unemployed.[33] Nevertheless, this new call to national service was relayed by students themselves and personal service became an important student expression of sympathy and solidarity with the unemployed. Organizations and publications representing students from diverse social and religious backgrounds called on students to take up voluntary service.[34] Such appeals for service recalled those of 50 years earlier, perhaps unsurprising given that many leading public figures of the interwar period had cut their teeth in the late Victorian settlement movement. Such parallels were not lost on the new student generation. A report on the Paris conference of International Student Societies noted there was increasing recognition that "those kinds of service which might be called philanthropic" were outdated, yet continued:

> But there is no less need for that "enthusiasm of humanity" which inspired the founders of the University Settlements, though these days enthusiasm must be tempered and controlled by knowledge, skill and scientific method.[35]

Although not receiving the public attention of the 1880s and 1890s, settlements in the 1930s continued to be busy offering a wide range of services to local communities, particularly through boys' and girls' clubs. Yet the university link was no longer seen as central and Jenny Harrow argues that by the 1930s settlements were "estranged from their universities."[36] Settlements retained a relatively low level of support from sponsoring universities and colleges. A 1921 *Nonesuch* article reflected "it is somewhat sad, yet nevertheless true, that many [Bristol] students have not the slightest idea why the Settlement exists, what it is or what it is doing."[37] Growing professionalism in social welfare and youth work meant that the undergraduate contribution was necessarily more restricted than before the war. In some cases, it seems, university settlements did not know what to do with student volunteers. Gwendolen Freeman, at Girton in the late 1920s, volunteered to help at the Women's University Settlement during her Christmas vacation, but was dashed at the "chilly reception" she received, and realized that her "Victorian idea" that a student could "come in on odd days and provide important services was out of date."[38] In the 1930s, too, public concern for the poor of inner cities, and London in particular, was gradually being replaced with new interest in and sympathy with the unemployed workers of the "depressed areas" in Wales and the North. Not surprisingly, this new social concern was where students sought to direct most volunteering and fundraising efforts in the 1930s.

Such low level of support was not in reality very different from prewar years as voluntary service had always been restricted to a small number of committed students. In the 1920s and 1930s Bristol students helped residents run the Barton Hill Settlement's annual program of activities including play centers, lads' and girls' clubs and a Mother's School.[39] At Queen Margaret Settlement a new boys' club was opened in 1928 and run almost entirely by male Glasgow University students.[40] At Manchester small numbers of women students volunteered on the Ancoats Settlement After-Care Committee, visiting the homes of pupils who had just left local schools.[41] Students from many women's colleges continued the tradition of arranging Christmas parties and summer outings for groups of mothers and babies or children from the Women's University Settlement throughout the 1920s and into the 1930s.[42] At Oxford in the 1930s a "Below Bridges Club" brought together students and tutors with an interest in raising money and finding volunteers to support the many men's and boys' clubs linked to Oxford House and the Oxford and Bermondsey mission clubs in South London.[43] Interestingly, Liverpool University Settlement began to report a change in the social class of student volunteers and residents, as greater numbers of students entered the university from elementary schools, thus reducing the "gulf" between volunteers and settlement service users.[44]

From the early 1930s students began to engage with the new and pressing issues of unemployment through a renewed interest in social study, a trend fostered and encouraged by the settlements. Continuing their prewar role as educational and training centers for students, residents organized tours and short stays for students, while wardens continued to pay regular term-time visits to supporting colleges and universities.[45] The SCM and others were now of the opinion that student social study was more effective when undertaken as part of a specialist residential conference than in a part-time study circle on the prewar pattern.[46] Study weeks offered by the British Association of Residential Settlements (BARS) and SCM grew in popularity in the 1930s, and combined residence in a settlement, talks and lectures with visits to housing areas and factories.[47] Questions of unemployment and poverty were also discussed at SCM meetings, political societies, International Student Service (ISS) groups and at specially organized conferences. At Leeds University, for example, the students' union created a new Social Service Committee that held a conference in November 1932 and began recruiting volunteers for practical service schemes such as workcamps.[48] In April 1935, an ISS conference at Cardiff on "The Problems of a Depressed Industrial Area" inspired similar conferences elsewhere, including at the universities of Liverpool and Birmingham.[49] Connections between settlements and university social work training programs were also formalized and extended in the interwar period. Several universities offered a two-year postgraduate Social Study diploma which often involved a period of compulsory residence at a settlement.[50]

A further practical expression of a growing social consciousness in the universities was the support some students provided to the Hunger Marchers in the early 1930s. In October 1932 and February 1934 students provided food, first aid and accommodation to contingents of marchers as they passed through university towns on their way to London.[51] The Hunger Marches were organized by the militant National Unemployed Workers Movement (under Communist leadership) as a means of drawing attention to their plight and protesting about specific measures such as the imposition of the means test. The marches were not officially endorsed by either the Trades Union Congress or the Labour Party, although many union activists and Labour Party members supported marchers. At Cambridge in 1934, for example, students met the marchers a few miles outside the city and marched with them to the Guildhall which had been converted into a dormitory. Students cooked and served food to the marchers and washed and bandaged blistered feet. Brian Simon contrasted such help with the strikebreaking of 1926, remarking that by the 1930s students "were beginning to perceive an identity of interest" with workers. However, the motivations were perhaps not so different. Like volunteering to drive a train during the General Strike, aiding the Hunger Marchers was an exciting break from the ordinary university routine, according to the later reminiscences of students such as Barbara Pym, Kit Meredith and Kenneth Sinclair Loutit.[52] Provision of practical support was not necessarily an indication of political agreement with all the Hunger Marchers' demands. Sinclair Loutit recalled that helping the marchers was "a 'popular front' effort," the subject of general consensus among students who represented a broad range of university opinion including the SCM and the University Socialist Society.[53] Pym remembers it was "ludicrous" for her to march behind the October Club banner chanting "students join the workers struggle," but she did so with enthusiasm.[54] As for hundreds of other students across the country, the encounter with the Hunger Marchers had lasting impact. Sinclair Loutit later wrote "though I did not then realise it, this was my baptism into socio-political activity."[55]

Pick and Shovel Peacemaking: Students and the International Workcamp Movement

It was in South Wales in summer 1931 that students pioneered what was to become the major student response to the Depression: camps with and for the unemployed. These camps had been almost entirely neglected by historians until the recently published work of John Field. As Field points out, an extraordinary variety of camp movements flourished during the interwar years.[56] Students had long been involved as volunteers at camps run by missions and settlements, but in the 1930s they became closely associated with two new movements: international workcamping and camps for the unemployed. International volunteer workcamps were developed by Pierre Ceresole (1879–1954), the pacifist son of a former President of Switzerland, on former First World War battlefields in 1920. Strongly influenced by ideas of pacifism and internationalism, workcamps brought together young volunteers from different countries on manual labor projects. The organization Ceresole founded, Service Civil International (SCI), became extremely influential. Early SCI workcamps, held across Europe in the 1920s, focused on repairing and rebuilding houses, bridges and roads after floods and landslides and involved hundreds of volunteers of different ages, occupations and nationalities.[57]

From the start university students were an important source of volunteers, as workcamping was ideally suited to fit in with long summer vacations. Influenced by SCI experiments, from 1925 the Swiss National Union of Students developed a program of camps which was influential in spreading the movement among students elsewhere.[58] Another influence came from a youth movement called *Deutsche Freischar* that began to organize workcamps for students and young people in late 1920s Weimar Germany. In the 1930s International Student Service ran a campaign to promote workcamps which it felt combined social service and self-help, organizing two training conferences in Switzerland in 1930 and in 1937.[59] Scores, perhaps hundreds, of British students gained experience on such workcamps in Europe.[60] As the 1930s went on, however, the model was adapted by less progressive forces including the Bulgarian government and the Nazi youth labor service.[61] Proponents of workcamps continued to emphasize the differences between these compulsory schemes and manual work voluntarily undertaken as part of an international movement. In 1938 the Second World Youth Congress, held at Vassar College in the United States, endorsed the voluntary workcamp model as an ideal method of peace education and education for international understanding.[62] For British students Quaker influence remained strong and there were also strong continuities between the workcamp movement and the older Ruskinian belief in the dignity of labor.[63]

That the first workcamp in Britain should be held in South Wales and organized in part by student groups is not surprising. After two

Welsh students attended the 1930 ISS workcamp training course, the Self-help Council made contact with Peter Scott, a Quaker who was leading an experimental reconstruction project at Brynmawr in South Wales. Other organizations showed interest and the first Brynmawr workcamp in summer 1931 was a joint affair organized by SCI, SCM, the Young Friends' Committee and the Fellowship of Reconciliation with the secretary of the Welsh Student Self-help Council, Kitty Lewis, making all the local arrangements.[64] Despite late advertising, there were twice as many applications as there were places on the camp; in the end 72 British volunteers and five international students based in Britain were accepted with around 30 coming from overseas. Many of the volunteers were students from Leeds University, with others from the colleges of the University of Wales, Woodbrooke College and a smattering from Oxford, Cambridge, London, Manchester, Birmingham, Bristol, Exeter and Loughborough College.[65] The campers worked alongside local people—mainly unemployed or short-time miners—to renovate dilapidated houses and turn a rubbish dump into a swimming pool, a project that had in fact already been started by local men.[66] In the evenings the volunteers held meetings and sing-songs with local people and were taken on excursions at weekends. Reflecting the interest of the student volunteers in peace and internationalism, two "remarkable" League of Nations Union evening meetings were held.[67] A second camp was arranged the following year and the swimming pool was formally opened in July 1932.

After the first Brynmawr camp, a British branch of SCI known as International Voluntary Service (IVS; later International Voluntary Service for Peace or IVSP) was formed to organize camps in England and Wales including at Blaenavon (1934), Birkenhead (1936) and Gateshead (1936). Information about the volunteer workcamp model spread rapidly through the university world by touring speakers, through articles in college magazines and by publicity pamphlets sent to student groups. One keen proponent was Jean Inebnit (1890–1982), a Swiss-born lecturer in French at Leeds University, who apparently concentrated the whole of his university work into two days of the week, and spent the rest of the time touring Britain organizing workcamps and recruiting volunteers. According to Donald Bentley, first paid secretary of IVS, the first nucleus of volunteers were students from Leeds University who would "cram themselves into Jean Inebnit's Morris and later his Ford Sedan."[68] Jack Hoyland (1887–1957), a Quaker educationist who had served as a missionary in India, was another keen organizer of workcamps for students and schoolboys. He became an ardent publicist, publishing two books and numerous articles on the topic in the 1930s. In 1936, he spoke at the Depressed Areas conference at Birmingham University, where he urged students to get involved with the burgeoning—and related—movement for allotments for the unemployed.[69] Hoyland even took part in a BBC radio broadcast on workcamping in 1937, in which Howard Marshall interviewed supporters of the model including a miner from Rhondda alongside an unnamed but outspoken opponent of such workcamps.[70]

Students from universities all over the country became involved a range of camps inspired if not organized by IVS, working alongside local people on various community recreational schemes such as creating cycle paths, bowling greens, community centers, youth hostels, communal allotments and graveyard restoration projects.[71] IVS helped the newly formed Youth Hostel Association arrange workcamps to convert and decorate buildings into hostels. Over the Christmas holidays 1932–1933 students from several northern colleges including Leeds and Newcastle converted the old stables of Abbey House at Whitby into a Youth Hostel.[72] In 1933, Birmingham Settlement organized a small workcamp involving 16 students and 13 unemployed men to lay tennis courts on the large new council estates of Kingstanding in north Birmingham, where the settlement had recently set up an outpost as part of a trend to move social welfare agencies onto newly built estates.[73] The IVS camps were also the inspiration for the SCM's own foray into workcamping. The SCM had for many years been organizing annual summer conferences at Hayes in Derbyshire, and wanted to make an attempt "to bridge the gap between the student-life of its summer conference and the life of the working-class communities around."[74] Such an endeavor, it was felt, should have an explicit spiritual message as well as a material expression. Hence after taking much advice from other camp-organizers, in the summer of 1935 a group of 60 students set up camp, with half the group working as laborers on a dig to convert a slag heap into a children's playground and park and the other half running an evangelistic campaign in the villages around the camp. The students also organized political discussions, tea parties and cricket matches with local people as well as sending theological students to preach in local churches on Sundays. The camp was repeated over subsequent summers until the outbreak of war.

Inspired both by IVSP workcamps and the German youth labor camps of the *Deutsche Freischar*, some students and other volunteers associated with Rolf Gardiner's Springhead ring took part in series of workcamps organized at a land colonization project for unemployed miners in Cleveland, Yorkshire. The project was organized by Major James and Ruth Pennyman in a region of extremely high unemployment. The Pennymans leased uncultivated moorland and recruited unemployed men as volunteers to clear the land and turn it into a communal market garden. The workers received payment in produce and a surplus was sold to pay for tools and seeds. Although Rolf Gardiner (1902–1971), an early adopter of organic farming and a proponent of folk dancing, was a controversial figure with Nazi sympathies, he was invited to speak at the 1937 ISS conference on workcamps. His talk there regretted that the Cleveland camps had failed to gain the support of northern universities which he felt should have taken responsibility for the camps.[75] Perhaps the close involvement of Germans in the camps or Gardiner's controversial view that much British voluntary service was "far too slack and easy" were the deciding factors here.

A key goal of all these volunteer workcamps was the free mixing of people from different social, cultural and class backgrounds. Despite the name, few volunteers stayed under canvas but were put up in village halls or billeted with local people, with the board they paid providing a much-needed income.[76] An Oxford student, Nicholas Gillett, who was a member of Jack Hoyland's workcamp committee, recalled in his autobiography his motivations for taking part in workcamps:

> We wanted to be regarded not as "townies" but as people who knew one end of a spade from the other; not as soft-headed academics but as practical people able to take the rough with the smooth; not as callow youth but as people with a range of experiences; not as the privileged elite ignorant of human suffering but as friends who cared about people. These were high hopes and we were often disappointed. Mixing with other people of many different backgrounds was in itself a first step towards wisdom.[77]

As is often the case when using voluntary organizations' sources it is often necessary to read between the lines, or "across the grain," when interpreting accounts of volunteer workcamps. Many reports adopt a similar narrative form: after initial mutual suspicion, the camp settles down and volunteers and local people begin to understand one another. Writing of his visit to the 1933 IVS Oakengates camp, where workcampers were seeking to convert a slag pile into a new public square, American ISS Secretary Kenneth Holland reported the scepticism of the villages who wondered why these "outsiders" had come.

He concluded that over the course of the camp "to the students, the unemployment problem became understandable in terms of human suffering. To the miners, the students became friendly young fellows, with more than an academic interest in social justice."[78] Each work-camp required months of careful negotiation with local authorities, trade unions and local residents, who often needed much convincing about the wisdom of bringing a volunteer labor force into an area of high unemployment. Before the 1935 camp a circular was sent out promising "IVSP will leave Oakengates as soon as there is any likeli-hood of the work being done by paid labor at Trade Union rates," but pointed to the extensive borrowing of the Urban District Council to prove this scenario was extremely unlikely.[79] The report of the first Brynmawr camp hints that the overseas students were preferred by local people to the British ones.[80] Nonetheless, it was felt that all the students had gained a new understanding of the problems sur-rounding unemployment and had gained admiration for the "courage and tenacity" of local people. Interviewed by Malcolm Chase in 1998 Wilf Franks, a Bauhaus-trained artist and designer who was a volun-teer on the Cleveland project, recalled tensions between the students and miners who apparently "worked three times as fast as them."[81]

Often the most successful aspect of the international workcamps was the strong social life which developed among the volunteers of different nationalities, a further example of the way in which social service often worked to reinforce student identity. This was illus-trated in Brynmawr in 1931 "by the almost exclusive use of Christian names" according to Leeds student volunteer George Beach, a tradi-tion deployed "even when addressing the women helpers."[82] Fahmy Gadalla, an Egyptian student studying at Leeds, recalled "jolly eve-nings" at the Gateshead workcamps discussing international affairs, playing games and singing.[83] Workcamps were one of the few places where men and women students could mix relatively easily in the 1930s, although the camps did sometimes reinforce traditional gen-der roles. On IVS camps the women were known as "sisters" and their official role was to cook, wash, mend and generally look after the male volunteers—"pick and shovel" work was not encouraged—and similar roles were created for women on SCM camps. Women stu-dents were occasionally able to carve out broader roles for themselves. At Brynmawr, for example, a Norwegian volunteer called Inge led a program of color-washing local houses and gardening, while women students on SCM camps led work with children and young people in the vicinity.[84] Strong friendships and several marriages resulted from the camps. Arthur Gillett met his wife through workcamping and

Kitty Lewis married academic Professor Idwal Jones in 1933, after meeting him on a workcamp.

COMPLETION OF A STUDENT'S EDUCATION: UNIVERSITIES' CAMPS FOR THE UNEMPLOYED

A second form of student camps that emerged in the 1930s were camps for the unemployed which placed greater emphasis on taking men—and some women—out of their home environments. Like international volunteer workcamps, these camps drew on a range of influences, but were notably influenced by Ministry of Labour vocational training schemes and instructional camps which had been operating since 1925 to give unemployed young men practical skills and experience of manual labor.[85] As unemployment worsened in the 1930s the Ministry of Labour set up scores of such camps to keep unemployed men occupied and improve their physical fitness. Although student-led camps were organized by different groups across England, Wales and Scotland there was extensive exchange of ideas between camp organizers, and a number were organized through a coordinating body known as the Universities' Council for Unemployed Camps (UCUC). Michael Sims Williams of Westcott House, Cambridge formed the Universities' Council in after 1933 after a trial six-week camp on Lord Somer's estate at Eastnor Park, Herefordshire. To publicize his idea Sims Williams published a handbook, in which he described camping as "a great work for the unemployed to be done by small groups of men who are only able to devote a holiday to the task."[86] Oxford, Cambridge, King's College London and University College Southampton joined the Universities' Council, which was able to draw on uniquely high-level Establishment support.[87] For example, an appeal by the Vice-Chancellors of Oxford and Cambridge elicited a letter of support from the Prince of Wales which was circulated to potential donors.

The members of the Universities' Council organized dozens of camps each summer between 1934 and the outbreak of war in 1939, with camps for boys put on in 1940. Holiday camps for women were arranged by students from Girton, Newnham and Edinburgh.[88] The camps operated with about 15–20 student volunteers and one paid cook for every 80–100 unemployed men. Camps provided unemployed men with three or four hours a day physical labor as well as the chance to develop new hobbies.[89] It was important that the men were not asked to do any job which could be done by paid labor and that that camps should not be in any way billed as "charity."[90] Most camps operated on the pattern of a morning's work followed by afternoon recreational activities including hiking, swimming and sunbathing as well as football, cricket, darts and dominos matches against local teams.[91] The evenings were devoted to discussions, campfires and visits to the local village. Because many camps were run by the same colleges or universities year after year throughout the 1930s, they developed individual traditions such as the Bredon Hill camp's annual magazine and the male-voice choirs formed at Welsh camps. In his analysis of these camps, Field argues that while the camps were "characterized by visible forms of service in which the students participated fully" such as chores and physical work there was a clear hierarchy in which students were seen as leaders. Nonetheless students welcomed camps as one of very few opportunities for lowering class barriers and fostering trust and understanding. One camp leader reported "The spirit of the camp was so informal, that at times I was apprehensive that I had let the thing go too far. The whole tone of the marquee at meal times was one of joking and leg pulling."[92]

The university camps for the unemployed were a novel response by student groups to the Depression and despite much sharing of practice, they evolved in different ways. A number of northern and Scottish universities including Sheffield, Glasgow, Edinburgh, Leeds and Liverpool organized camps independently of the UCUC. These camps were organized on local university initiative, drew on local support networks and were publicized through the local and regional press. Sheffield students, for example, helped the Yorkshire Unemployed Advisory Council run a camp for two hundred men near Hornsea by making a collection at the university and sending volunteers to camp each year between 1937 and 1939.[93] The first camp in Scotland was organized by Glasgow SRC President Harold H. Munro in conjunction with the Community Council for Social Service.[94] In 1935 Liverpool University Settlement started a series of camps with unemployed men and students alike taking part in a "working holiday" on an archaeological excavation at Maiden Castle, Bickerton.[95] For this camp men were recruited from local service clubs and money raised by public subscription in Liverpool, with the largest donations coming from local business people and philanthropists like Harold Cohen, Lord Derby, the Rathbones, the Holts and the Pilkingtons. At Liverpool in 1934, Leta Jones helped organize a summer holiday camp for women in a borrowed house in Wales. Organized on a very tight budget, students enterprisingly secured donations of goods from local and national firms.[96] In an account written just after the camp Jones suggested that it seemed unfair that she and her fellow students "should be given so much by the state, and by their parents, by Providence and should make no return."[97]

Welsh students were behind another shift to the provision of purely holiday camps for the unemployed. These camps started with an experimental scheme by Cardiff University Social Service Group in 1934 in which 50 students held a holiday camp on the Gower for 430 men in smaller groups spread over an eight week period.[98] By 1935, 200 students from all the colleges in Wales were organizing a series of summer camps on the coast for 750 men and 500 women.[99] The camps were democratically run by elected committees of men and students, no work could be demanded from the men and everyone had to share in usual camp duties.[100] Thus these camps were also a form of student self-help because they benefited impoverished students as much as unemployed men and women.[101] Aberystwyth student Alun Davies dubbed the camps a "student utopia" where students from all the colleges in Wales mixed together with unemployed men without any administrative hierarchy and enjoyed "the proletarian pleasures of eating, drinking (*sic*) and sleeping."[102] These Welsh holiday camps were the only student camps to receive active support from trade unions and perhaps enjoyed a greater level of success because students and unemployed campers were drawn from more similar backgrounds.[103] Alive to the criticism of trade unions, Moelwyn Merchant defended holiday camps, arguing that students' sympathetic attitudes had earned them the respect of the unemployed, and that there was value in social service projects before any wholesale economic and political change could occur.[104]

All camps for the unemployed encountered a number of unforeseen problems. One concern was the feeling that some of the men who attended the camps were not the ones that most needed help, although such judgements based on campers' physical appearance were rather unreliable. At the 1936 Bredon Hill Camp run by Cambridge University Rover Scouts, for example, students were disappointed that "when the men arrived, many of them were not the 'down-and-out' sort which we had hoped for."[105] Organizing a camp was a steep learning curve for many students who found that team games were easier to arrange with the younger campers whereas older men preferred sunbathing or that while discussion was enjoyed, formal debating was difficult to organize.[106] Hobbies had only mixed success, often because the men preferred sports and relaxing, but also because the students had few skills as instructors. Hobbies thrived best when one of the men could pass on his own practical skills, such as boot-repairing, which was very popular at a number of camps.[107]

Moreover, camps were beset by many of the same problems of volunteer recruitment and ensuring continuity of interest from university students year after year that regularly faced other student social service movements.[108] Volunteers for the Liverpool women's camp organized by Leta Jones dried up and the camp had to be carried on for the final few weeks with low numbers of students, "which left us exhausted."[109]

The issue of follow-up work by students with the campers when they had returned to their homes was also raised repeatedly by camp organizers. This was more successful where the unemployed campers and students lived in the same city, such as the Liverpool women's camp, where students held small get-togethers and were pleased to find most of the unemployed women had found jobs.[110] However, despite these problems, students' time was valued. The Secretary of a local Council of Social Service felt that the camps were more successful because they were run by students who were "men of varied interests" and not "people vocationally dedicated to good works."[111] Organizing committees recognized that while the primary objective of the scheme was to serve the unemployed, undergraduates benefited considerably from the experience. In their letters to camp chiefs, reports and later memoirs students described how much they had benefited by participating. The benefits of fresh air, exercise and comradeship with fellow volunteers and working men were not only physical but mental.[112] As one student related "When I arrived this year I was feeling rather out of tune and uncertain of myself; but before I left I was feeling very fit, enjoying myself thoroughly, and wishing that I could have another week or more there."[113] Like other forms of student social service, many workcamp volunteers interpreted their experience as an education in its own right. Harry Rée (1914–1991) took part in Cambridge camps in Helmsley, and particularly relished the responsibility that came with running a camp, recalling "I think it probably did us more good than the unemployed."[114] One report judged there was no better way for students to "experience first-hand contact with fellow citizens drawn from an entirely different environment and thereby to learn the depth and extent of the tragedy of unemployment."[115] Student camp leader J. R. Maxwell Lefroy echoed earlier claims about residence at a university settlement when he recorded that volunteering at a camp "is completion of one's education at the University."[116]

There is less evidence of the impact of camps on the unemployed men and women who attended them. Reports generally noted that camps were successful from the unemployed men's perspective, citing men's delight in being under canvas, describing the level of friendly banter and rivalry which developed between tents, and relating their reluctance to go home.[117] However, a set of thank-you letters from Liverpool women sent to Leta Jones reveal the strong impression made on unemployed girls and women by their two-week stay and the passionate attachment to the student volunteers that some of them developed. The women requested Leta to send photographs of herself, implored her to write back and requested that she passed on personal messages to her fellow student volunteers. Taking part in camps appeared to have sparked dissatisfaction with their ordinary lives for several correspondents—whether they were living back at home or, as one woman was, staying in a convalescent home. Eileen Waring wrote poignantly:

> I arrived home quite safe but not so happy, Birkenhead seems such a vile place after spending a quite [sic] and peaceful fortnight at Bulchgwn with such pleasant people...I shall never forget you, you made me feel as if I had known you all my life...I suppose when the new set of girls arrive you will forget all about little Eileen...I find I cannot write another word of this letter because it makes me so unhappy to think I may never see you again.[118]

By the late 1930s camps had become a well-known and widespread form of student social service in Britain. Camps were a "popular front" effort, which drew a wide range of students—socialists, Scottish nationalists, Christians, conservatives—into practical activity. Jenny Harrow sees the rise of camps as part of a wider decline of the university settlement ideal, sending the message that the universities' obligations to the poor could be discharged "in more congenial surroundings than the 'East End' and for only four weeks of the year!"[119] However, camps were part of a wider student social service movement that developed in the 1930s. A "social service supplement" which appeared in the February 1939 issue of *New University* put forward camps as just one of many ways in which students might engage with social problems. Although arguably following, rather than leading, the interests of the wider student movement, NUS congresses in the later 1930s began to discuss social topics and in turn the journal *New University* began to include articles on social problems.[120] A "Commission on Social Service" which reported to the NUS Congress of 1939 reiterated the need for student social study, concluding that "practical experience must be accompanied by factual study of the problems."[121] Through such activities the NUS was taking on a new, activist role promoting and supporting student social service, which it had previously left to groups such as the SCM.

CONCLUSIONS

The Depression brought renewed student interest in social study and experiments in social service after something of a lull in the 1920s. "This is an age of conferences, campaigns and unemployment camps" judged the SCM in 1934.[122] At the universities, students and staff members worked closely with a very wide range of local and national social service agencies to develop innovative schemes such as the camps for the unemployed. Despite some national coordination, these camps reflected the big differences in the British university landscape. Smaller numbers of students were also drawn into service on workcamps that reflected more progressive ideals of pacifism or internationalism and were particularly associated with the Quakers. All types of camps, however, appear to have had the unconscious effect of strengthening student group identity. Camps provided a new way in which undergraduate high spirits, sense of adventure and delight in practical jokes and larks could be turned to a worthy cause in the 1930s. While it must be noted that sympathetic treatment of unemployed men by students was not necessarily an expression of political solidarity and many student activities remained ameliorative, for the first time students were engaged in serious discussion of the causes of unemployment and trade depression through conferences and study schools. Moreover, for some students the negative effects of unemployment had come closer than is usually recognized.

Students played an important part in the wider social service movement in the 1930s as it moved away from provision of direct material relief to embrace a range of "occupational" schemes that aimed to provide unemployed men and women with constructive leisure time activities.[123] Moreover, the practical involvement of large numbers of volunteers marked this movement off from less hands-on activities such as fundraising or social study. Later commentators, such as Mary Morris writing in 1955, felt that the interwar period was significant in the development of a volunteering movement, noting "from small beginnings the social service movement swept over the country."[124] Calls for personal service in the 1930s were undoubtedly made to a broader section of society than previously and students from a wider range of colleges and universities became involved than had been the case with the prewar settlement movement. Of course, student support was never universal. In his contribution to the History of the University of Oxford, Brian Harrison notes that causes such as unemployment often "evoked a deflating humour or even indignation from those who viewed high-minded crusading as bad form" within the Junior Common Rooms which were largely dominated by public school men and sporting men.[125] Yet, it is clear that camps drew on a wide base of support outside Oxbridge. The model of camps for the unemployed was embraced but significantly modified by student groups at the civic universities.

A key factor underlying the growth of a student social consciousness in the 1930s was the increased cooperation between national student bodies including the NUS, the SCM, ISS and the British Universities League of Nations Societies on a range of educational, social and political questions. These organizations shared offices, sent observers to each other's meetings, contributed articles to each other's publications and collaborated on fundraising campaigns and in joint publications. After fluctuating support through much of the 1920s and 1930s, by the late 1930s the NUS began to receive greater support from member universities and university colleges that was in part a result of its social service turn, its new concern for the student experience and its cooperation with other organizations. Although students might mobilize around either domestic or international concerns (addressed in the next chapter) in the 1930s, what they had in common was the desire that relief, volunteering or campaigning activities should stem from their position in society as university and college students, a view which had the unlooked for effect of strengthening student solidarity and building a student movement.

CHAPTER 7

Students in Action: Students and Antifascist Relief Efforts, 1933–1939

In summer 1938, over five hundred student and youth delegates from 45 nations meeting at Vassar College for the second World Youth Congress signed the "Vassar Peace Pact" condemning "any war of aggression" as well as specific tactics such as bombing of civilian populations.[1] Delegates judged that although the primary aim of the world youth peace movement was to prevent war, practical aid to victims of war and oppression was an essential part of the movement. This chapter argues that in the 1930s students sought to collaborate on relief efforts as a practical contribution to the fight against fascism and a means of building a broad-based national and international student movement. International politics, the threat of war and the rise of fascism increasingly impinged on student life through key events including the election of Hitler as Chancellor of Germany in 1933 and his remilitarization of the Rhineland in 1935, the Italian invasion of Abyssinia in 1935, the outbreak of the Spanish Civil War in 1936 and the start of the Sino-Japanese war in 1937. Communist-supporting students took a lead in developing a strong antiwar movement across British universities that by the mid-1930s had succeeded in drawing a wider range of students into a broad coalition. Traditional "support" type activities such as fundraising and collecting gifts-in-kind continued alongside new forms of student social and political action such as boycott and protest. If a student popular front was to become a reality, then cooperation in practical relief efforts was the best way to make it happen.

YOUTH DEMANDS A PEACEFUL WORLD: THE EMERGENCE OF THE STUDENT ANTIWAR MOVEMENT

The late 1920s and early 1930s saw shifts in public attitudes to the legacy of the Great War, which were reflected on university campuses.

As Adrian Gregory points out in his history of Armistice Day, 1929 was the peak of the "war books" publishing phenomenon, with books such as *All Quiet on the Western Front, Goodbye to All That,* and *A Farewell to Arms* setting a new standard for discussion of the war.[2] Such changing attitudes were particularly evident at the universities and colleges. A local peace ballot organized by the Student Christian Movement (SCM) at Manchester University in the academic year 1932–1933, for example, found 69 percent of votes cast by students (464 of whom took part) to be in favor of total unconditional disarmament, a figure far higher than other local ballots.[3] Growing student interest in questions of war, peace and internationalism was channelled through existing university societies including International Student Service (ISS), SCM and the British Universities League of Nations Societies (BULNS) as well as a range of new, more radical student organizations.[4] In the early 1930s BULNS was a significant force with a membership of 7,197 students that amounted to over 10 percent of all university, college and training college students.[5] Supported by two paid secretaries for the universities and colleges, branches organized lectures for nonmembers, ran study groups, supplied speakers for local branches and mobilized volunteers to administer a national Peace Ballot in 1934–1935.[6] In 1933 the most popular study circle topic by far was "Disarmament," followed by the USSR, India and the Far East.[7]

Armistice Day emerged as a focus of student antiwar protest in the early 1930s. Since the 1920s leading antiwar commentators such as Dick Sheppard (1880–1937) had protested about inappropriate commemorations of Armistice Day. From time-to-time there had also been comment and letters about the most appropriate forms of remembrance published in student magazines. In the early 1930s, however, students began to mount protests over increasingly militaristic elements that they felt were being introduced into university Armistice Day commemorations. These were coordinated for the first time in November 1932 when left-wing students at a number of universities organized protests which met with opposition from university authorities.[8] University College held a special debate and passed the motion "In the event of a declaration of war, this house would not support the Government." In Bristol the Socialist Society laid a wreath at the University War Memorial bearing the controversial inscription, "To the dead of all nations, victims of a war they did not make, from those who are pledged to fight against all such crimes of Imperialism." The offensive wreath was removed on the Vice Chancellor's orders, prompting Bristol students to write to every college magazine to raise awareness of this censorship. In Cambridge, unlike other universities, Armistice Day had become the annual student rag, when collections were made for the Earl Haig Fund. However, during 1933 a growing number of students associated with both the Socialist Society and the SCM felt that the rag parade, pranks and stunts were incompatible with the symbolism of November 11. November 1933 therefore saw coordinated effort including the display of a "No More War" exhibition, a demonstration outside a cinema showing pro-war film "Our Fighting Navy"—which developed into a brawl—and a large-scale peace march. Hundreds of students turned out to march and were pelted with eggs and tomatoes by onlookers, including other students.[9] This Cambridge peace march has become a notorious symbol of student pacifism, notably for the involvement of later famous figures such as the poet Julian Bell (1908–1937) and the spy Guy Burgess (1911–1963) who drove the route together in a car prepared for "battle" by being padded with mattresses.[10]

Growing student pacifism was epitomized by the infamous King and Country debate at the Oxford Union in February 1933, when a majority of students passed the motion, "This House would under no circumstances fight for King and Country." Although other unions had been debating similar motions for several years without comment, the Oxford vote generated a press furore which lasted several weeks, and prompted a second vote at the Union seeking to expunge the debate from the Union minute books. Martin Ceadal has argued that the success of the motion can be ascribed to the oratory of the main speaker in favor of the motion, C. E. M. Joad, and that the following controversy was largely generated by the outrage of a previous generation of Oxford men, who interpreted it as a symptom of "a new student radicalism."[11] Mike Day further argues that the real significance of the debate lies in what happened next and the "role NUS [National Union of Students] played in encouraging student organizations to discuss the issue."[12] The then NUS President, Denis Follows, wrote to every students' union or SRC urging them to hold a similar debate. Similar motions were passed at University College, Birkbeck, Cardiff and Manchester, although Reading and King's College London refused to hold a debate and at Armstrong College, Birmingham University and Queen's University Belfast students rejected the motion. However, support for such debates was mixed even at the time. BULNS secretary Norman Poole concluded such debates were only likely to arouse antagonism and reinforce prejudices among the general public toward both pacifism and students.[13] Moreover, he felt, such spectacles did little to advance serious discussion of war and peace in the colleges.

The attention paid to developments at Oxford and Cambridge should not allow us to ignore growing levels of antiwar feeling at a wider range of universities and colleges, which can be traced through student publications and reminiscences. In December 1932, a group from Leeds University wrote an open letter to their student magazine seeking to associate themselves with students elsewhere who deplored the militarization of Armistice Day.[14] From the early 1930s students formed antiwar societies, antifascist committees and peace councils, which were often under left-wing control.[15] Marxist-influenced students "recognised no contradiction in the opposition to both fascism and war" because they were both seen as the products of capitalism.[16] Moreover, a key issue for students as for others in a broader peace movement was the feeling that the British government's jingoism and half heartedness over disarmament represented a greater threat to peace than European fascism.[17] The birth of the Students' Anti-War Council in 1932 was part of the increased pattern of activity of the Communist Party of Great Britain (CPGB) on university campuses, discussed in the preceding chapter. An offshoot of the British Anti-War Council, it was controlled by the Student Bureau of the CPGB as one of its most important mass organizational activities.[18] By the beginning of 1934 the Council could count affiliated committees in 20 universities, although not all antifascist students were initially keen to work with the Communists. At Liverpool, the Anti-War Committee voted not to affiliate to the Students' Anti-War Council.[19] The LNU at Queen's University Belfast (QUB) did affiliate but when it changed its name to "QUB League of Nations and Anti-War Society," the BULNS Committee ruled it could not remain affiliated to BULNS because antiwar action was incompatible with impartial study and the "freest possible discussion of international affairs."[20]

While the leadership of the student antiwar movement owed much to the involvement of Communist students, by the mid-1930s they had succeeded in drawing a wider range of students into a broad coalition. At University College Nottingham, for example, war and peace were topics which brought students together: joint meetings were organized between the SCM, the League of Nations Union and the Anti-War Society.[21] A SCM officers' conference in 1933 passed a motion in favor of complete pacifism (120 in favor, 17 against, 50 abstentions).[22] At Sheffield the movement had grown from 6 students in 1930 to over 100 by 1935 who were interested in the Peace Society either "actively or vaguely."[23] In October 1933, a Peace Council was formed at Bristol University consisting of seven student societies including the LNU, antiwar society, the International Society, the branch of the SCM and representatives of student physicists and chemists.[24] Leta Jones recalled that students "were genuinely concerned in Liverpool and all other universities that war was looming...We discussed pacifism as we thought of ourselves as cannon fodder."[25] The 1934 *Panto Spinx*—the special edition of the Liverpool college magazine sold annually on rag day—featured an antiwar woodcut of schoolboys facing enemy guns.

With few actual fascists to fight in the universities, the broad peace coalition that had developed from the early 1930s became arrayed against a common enemy in the form of the University Officers' Training Corps (OTC).[26] On his return to college after a summer touring Germany in 1934, Kenneth Sinclair Loutit resigned from the Cambridge OTC feeling that it had become overly militaristic and was too supportive of the "New Germany."[27] Somewhat ironically, when serving as a medical volunteer during the Spanish Civil War Sinclair Loutit was grateful for what he had learned in the OTC at school and Cambridge. At a number of universities students organized petitions against the large university grants allocated to maintain the OTCs. Tensions ran high and spilled over into the pages of student magazines and more public conflicts. At Bristol, for example, about 30 OTC members allegedly vandalized a peace exhibition. Several students' unions including Bangor and Manchester voted to abolish their college OTC although university authorities rarely took such votes seriously. At Exeter, the Guild of Undergraduates twice voted down proposals to form a new OTC in 1935–1936 before the Senate overruled the students and allowed its formation to go ahead, although the final vote of 80 against to 71 in favor reveals that the student body was split on the proposal.[28] This incident was sufficiently notorious to prompt Labour MP John Parker to raise a question in the House of Commons.[29] Referring to the "disastrous anti-war debate" at Armstrong College, the editor of *The Northerner* felt that "until this absurd, hysterical, dog-and-cat attitude between pacifists and OTC at college is destroyed, we cannot expect to make any headway amongst ourselves on the question of war."[30] In the later 1930s as the government prepared for possible war, antiwar students sought to disrupt civil defence planning.[31] Students, particularly some medical students, objected to government proposals for gas drills put forward as part of civil defence planning, a need heightened by Italian use of poison gas in the Abyssinian war.[32]

From the mid-1930s the student antiwar movement grew in strength and began to push for greater cooperation with other student groups in a way that had not earlier been possible.[33] Following the model of forming popular fronts against fascism adopted by Moscow in 1934, antiwar students argued that the basis of the movement should be as wide as possible and unite Communist, Socialist, Liberal and Christian students. As Lieve Gevers and Louis Vos reflect "Communist infiltration did not alter the fact that this protest movement against Fascism and war was a genuine social movement, led by students who believed in their cause but who in their actions were drawn by the radical appeal of Communism."[34] In 1934, observers from the more moderate student groups—the NUS, SCM and ISS—began to attend the meetings of the Students' Anti-War Council, which started a new publication known as *Student Front*. A student subcommittee of the British Youth Peace Assembly (BYPA) was formed in 1936.[35] The new group was increasingly representative of the British student movement and may be said to constitute a "student popular front."[36] This committee took over the management of *Student Front*, turning it into *Student Forum*, a supposedly "all party discussion centre" for students with a circulation of 36,000 by 1938.[37] *Student Forum* gradually expanded its editorial board to include BULNS, university Labour, Liberal and Conservative associations, ISS, NUS and SCM by the end of 1938. Despite this all-party editorial board, the offices of *Student Forum* on High Holborn continued to be watched by Special Branch seeking confirmation of Communist Party involvement in the running of the paper.[38] The student antiwar movement was particularly keen to engage with students at teacher training colleges who were important because "their contact with the outside world is greater than that of the students at the universities."[39] Indeed, this recognition was becoming more widespread within the broader student movement. For example NUS changed its constitution in 1937 to allow affiliation of students' unions in training colleges.[40]

THE MOST FRUITFUL WORK TO-DAY: STUDENTS AND THE NAZI REFUGEE CRISIS

In 1935, Albert Einstein noted that help for students "who have not yet made their names in the world is the most difficult but, at the same time, the most fruitful work to-day" as he put his name to an ISS appeal for German refugee students.[41] In 1933, the newly created League of Nations High Commission for Refugees coming from Germany asked ISS to accept responsibility for student refugees. Academics, professionals and students—the so-called intellectual refugees—were early identified by the High Commission as a presenting a "special problem."[42] By 1934 around 1,700 students were counted in the total of 10,000–11,000 intellectual refugees and family members who had already left Germany. The work of the Academic Assistance Council (AAC)—later known as the Society for the Protection of Science and Learning (SPSL)—in assisting well-known scholars to find positions in British universities has been justly celebrated as has the *kinder-transport* to Britain of ten thousand unaccompanied children, but the work of ISS in supporting student refugees is less well known. Norman Bentwich's 1953 book does call attention to the contribution of ISS and it features in a new biography of James Parkes but the organization is neglected in other, more recent work.[43]

The AAC was set up to aid Jewish academics and launched in May 1933 with the support of eminent university men on the initiative of Sir William Beveridge and his fellow London School of Economics professor Lionel Robbins (1898–1984), following a visit to Vienna in April 1933. Another high-profile body was the Jewish Academic Committee (later known as the Professionals Committee) formed by leading members of the Jewish community in the United Kingdom to find places for refugee researchers, doctors, lawyers, teacher and social workers. Recent work by Susan Cohen assesses the help given to women academic and professional refugees—including some students—by the British Federation of University Women (BFUW)[44] Of these related associations, the story of AAC/SPSL is the best known because of the "extraordinary eminence" of some of its early beneficiaries. Of the 2,600 academics helped, many became Fellows of the Royal Society or the British Academy, dozens received knighthoods and 18 won a Nobel Prize.[45] Although the scale of the ISS's work for students greatly exceeds the BFUW's refugee work in terms of money raised and numbers assisted, there have been no academic studies of its work.[46]

During the 1920s the German student movement had become gradually more right-wing as democratic, Jewish, liberal and socialist student groups were increasingly isolated.[47] As the *Deutsche Studentenschaft* gradually came under Nazi control it began to advocate the introduction of a *numerus clausus* (restriction on Jewish students in the universities) and in spring 1933 organized ritual book burning at all German universities. Jewish students were barred from membership of *Deutsche Studentenschaft*, were prevented from taking examinations and became unable to find work in the professions for which they had been trained. Between 1933 and 1936 around seven thousand students were expelled from the German universities. Although many students remained living in Germany, of those who emigrated 90 percent (2,500) sought help from ISS.[48] In Austria too, Nazi-controlled student groups gained support through the 1920s and 1930s, taking over completely with *Anschluss* in March 1938 when they started a campaign to "purify" the student population.[49] With the German occupation of the Sudetenland in March 1939, Czech students also became refugees; student resistance was put down by the Nazis and eventually all universities and colleges were closed. Between 1933 and 1939 ISS helped student exiles to find refuge mainly in the United Kingdom, France, Switzerland and Holland.[50] While the majority were Jewish, ISS recorded requests for help from "Liberals, Socialists, Pacifists and Roman Catholics."[51]

According to a 1933 article ISS took on the task of aiding refugees because "ISS since its inception has fought against any kind of discrimination based on race, nationality or creed" and its staff could draw on the experience of allocating relief to students after the First World War.[52] The story is rather more complicated. Like other relief agencies in the early 1930s, ISS publications and appeals downplayed the Jewishness of those helped; successive appeals were made for "German," "Austrian" and "Czech" students. However, since the late 1920s James Parkes—one of the small number of core staff based at the ISS Geneva headquarters—had taken a serious and scholarly interest in growing anti-Semitism among student groups in central Europe. In January 1929, Parkes arranged a semi-secret conference in France to bring Jewish student groups into contact with nationalist organizations from Germany and Eastern Europe. In 1930 he published *The Jew and His Neighbour*, an account of anti-Semitism, and returned to Oxford to study for a doctorate on the origins of anti-Semitism in 1931.[53] Thus as soon as the ISS committed itself to relief of Jewish students Parkes was the obvious candidate to send on an international fundraising tour, during which he was successful in securing large sums from leading Jews including Israel Sieff, Vice-Chair of Marks and Spencer, and the banker Felix Warburg in New York.[54]

The ISS committee for England and Wales took on a large share of the overall work for refugee student relief. Realizing the likely scale of the work, the committee set up an Advice and Relief Department in London, run by Christine Ogilvy and Gareth Maufe. Its work consisted of rehabilitation and resettlement support for students who found themselves in a foreign country as much as financial aid. By 1936 the London office had assisted over one thousand refugee students from Germany and was to aid smaller numbers of Austrian and Czech students over the coming years.[55] Always a major donor to central ISS funds, the committee agreed to find around a third of the first £10,000 needed, both via college fundraising and by taking part in a number of public appeals with organizations including the AAC and the Refugee Professionals Committee.[56] Following *Anschluss,* ISS joined the new Coordinating Committee for Refugees and in 1938 ISS received £7,300 of the half a million pounds raised by the Lord Mayor's Czech Refugee Fund for work among Czech student refugees.[57]

Only a small proportion of the refugees—with very high academic qualifications or close to the end of their courses—could be assisted to complete their degrees. Ogilvy and Maufe lobbied universities to secure additional student places and fee remissions, secured scholarships for "the most brilliant" and indentified au pair positions to keep living costs as low as possible. In the first two years 152 scholarships were allocated. At Liverpool in 1939, for example, six places for refugees were set aside with tuition fees remitted by the University Senate, while the Guild of Students waived its subscriptions.[58] At Bedford College, students and staff combined in a scheme to "adopt" a Czech student so she could study at the college for three years.[59] ISS worked closely with other organizations like the British Federation of University Women who paid for the postgraduate training of a small number of women students and with NUS to arrange hundreds of invitations for refugee students to spend holidays across the United Kingdom.[60] The SCM gave its support, reflecting that refugee relief was a "field in which to refuse to enter politics is to quit religion."[61]

A major aspect of ISS work was in helping students retrain for work in agriculture, horticulture and in technical and commercial occupations such as chemistry, and in finding work for them, mainly in South America, Palestine or South Africa. For instance, half of the refugees living at an ISS-run hostel and retraining center in Welwyn Garden City in 1934 were working on a local farm and learning carpentry so that they could seek employment as agriculturalists. Such "reorientation" to new activities was necessary amongst refugee organizations of the 1930s. For example, nursing and domestic work were the main occupations found for refugee academic and professional women by the BFUW.[62] The problem was only partly financial. The British government had placed strict restrictions on the entry of refugees to Britain, who needed to demonstrate that they would not become a financial burden on the state. Moreover the mid-1930s was a period of high graduate unemployment and underemployment in Britain and ISS had to tread very carefully to show that an influx of refugee undergraduates and research students would not exacerbate this very real problem. The refugees were retrained only for overseas work and any paid employment they found in Britain was supposed to be of a "strictly non-competitive nature," such as teaching German, translation and interpreting work.[63] For ISS one solution to anti-Jewish feeling was greater international education through encouragement of talks and discussions on refugee problems.[64] ISS also followed a policy of dispersal across as many universities in Britain as possible.[65] In 1936 Jewish students made up around 2 percent of students in Great Britain and Ireland, a figure that increased only slightly in the years before 1939.[66]

Students raised money for ISS in rather more traditional ways than they did for causes such as the Spanish Civil War, for example, through donating proceeds of dances.[67] In 1934–1935, for example, the British committee raised £4,778—sending half to Paris and Geneva and spending half on relief on students in Britain. Although the exact sum is unknown, funds raised in the 1935–1936 academic year were apparently higher than in previous years, perhaps as a result of better information about the treatment of Jews remaining in Germany. It is difficult to calculate the overall response from British students because in addition to contributing to central funds, local ISS committees raised money, organized vacation accommodation and provided varying types of support to the refugee students at their universities. In the 1930s and 1940s Birmingham University received 83 refugee students from 16 different nations, who met in a special club.[68] Aberystwyth students donated £100 to ISS during the summer term 1939, a sum that exceeded all expectations, and was apparently "conclusive proof that students are serious about this serious problem."[69] However, *The Gong* judged Nottingham students' low level of contributions in 1937 to be a "dismal reflection on student apathy" and expressed a hope that English students never needed to join the exodus of refugees.[70] ISS judged that student efforts for refugees were only "satisfactory" in view of the numerous other collections held for causes such as China and Spain.

Relief efforts were hampered by the fact that there were plenty of German sympathizers in the universities, as in society more broadly in the 1930s. In the early to mid-1930s several college magazines published articles in support of the Nazi "miracle" in Germany.[71] There were small, short-lived Fascist groups at Oxford, Cambridge, Armstrong College, Birmingham, Liverpool, Reading and other universities although in general far right groups had only very limited support in universities and colleges.[72] Writing in 1934 Edwin Barker warned that the fascist movement, while still very small, was definitely growing in strength in a few university centers.[73] Sir Oswald Mosley provocatively arranged a series of public meetings of his British Union of Fascists (formed in 1932) in university towns, including Oxford and Cambridge. These often ended in violence, as Elizabeth Longford later recalled of one 1936 Oxford meeting.[74] Interestingly the authorities of Hull University College allowed the local leader of the Hull British Union of Fascists to speak at the college in December 1934, but banned a Communist speaker the following term.[75] By the late 1930s growing awareness of the Nazi policy toward the Jews translated into greater support for refugee relief, as well as increased anti-Nazi protest on campus. Following *Kristallnacht* in November 1938, for example, Oxford students representing a range of university clubs and societies wrote to Foreign Secretary and University Chancellor Lord Halifax expressing dissatisfaction with the British government's failure to condemn the Germany's "monstrous policy" toward the Jews.[76] When German Ambassador Von Ribbentrop gave a talk at London University LSE students organized a protest in which students carried posters bearing the slogan "Fascism destroys Culture."[77]

Although the roll call of those students helped by ISS to study in Britain is impressive, we have little information on those helped and even fewer first-person accounts. The anonymous case histories preserved in ISS reports give little clue as to how students felt about having to abandon their future plans.[78] For example, "AL," a German woman medical student who had been working as a domestic servant in London was advised to give up her plans to become a doctor and supported to retrain as a radiologist. "GS," a male law student, facing the "hopeless prospects for refugee students in the legal profession" was helped to retrain as an optician and found work in South Africa. Paul Mandl (1917–2010), an Austrian refugee student at Aberystwyth who later went on to become a professor of mathematics in Canada, recorded in a letter to the student magazine that he had been made to feel very welcome at the college where he took part in student activities "both serious and gay" and was pleased that "certain characteristics of Wales, both social and geographical remind me of my native Austria."[79] The scientist Ernst Walter Kellermann (1915–2013) later wrote in his autobiography of ISS's "ceaseless work" to overcome barriers and prejudices affecting refugee students.[80] His first contact with ISS however in 1937 was a friendly but disappointing response to letter to asking for help to leave Vienna before the impending *Anshluss*. In the end Kellermann was given an ISS grant of £50 to study with Professor Born at Edinburgh University, provided he could get additional grants to make up what he needed.

The overall relief effort for refugee students was admirable if ulti-
mately limited in its reach by lack of funds and immigration controls.
The cause did not touch the hearts and minds of British students in
the same way as the relief campaign for victims of the Spanish Civil
War did in the mid-1930s. In addition, ISS ambivalence over how
best to deal with the Nazi regime may have undermined relief efforts
and alienated some supporters. The ISS leadership was divided over
the topic of relations with Germany, with some like James Parkes
wanting to suspend all contact with the Nazi-controlled student
movement and others feeling that it was better to maintain links in
order to be able to exert an influence over German students. In 1933
the Geneva headquarters and the committee in England and Wales
were divided over whether to honor the arrangement to hold the ISS
summer conference in Germany.[81] In the end the conference was held
in two parts; most of the delegates travelled to join a second group
of students in Luzeinsteig in Switzerland after the first meeting in
Germany where students had been subjected to an "intense programme of Nazi propaganda."[82] Although relations were suspended
in June 1934 after the murder of German ISS leader Fritz Beck, in
1936 the central ISS controversially reestablished contact with the
Deutscher Kreis für internationale studentische Zusammenarbeit ISS
branch in Germany which lasted until the *Deutscher Kreis* broke off
relations with Geneva in 1939.[83] German students attended the 1937
ISS conference in Nice, where they were a curiosity to others. Leeds
student Alban Hull reported that they "seemed to think and act as
one man."[84] In 1939 an ISS Bulletin sought to justify this conciliatory stance by arguing that maintaining semi-official relations had
allowed ISS to keep abreast of developments in Germany, to bring
German students into contact with wider student opinion through a
series of international conferences, including an Anglo-German conference at Oxford in 1937, and had brought a financial contribution to
the ISS budget for 1937–1938.[85] This account did not acknowledge
the irony of receiving money from one group of German students to
spend on another group of (refugee) German students.

BROAD ALLIANCES: THE UNIVERSITIES AND THE SPANISH CIVIL WAR

No international cause mobilized British students more strongly in
the interwar period than that of the Spanish Civil War, 1936–1939.
As Tom Buchanan has argued, the outbreak of the Spanish Civil
War "intersected powerfully with the growing alarm and political

mobilization of British intellectuals in response to the rise of fascism and the disintegration of the international order."[86] Aid for Spain offered an umbrella movement in which there was something for nearly every student, from protest against British noninterference to fundraising and collecting milk for the victims of war. Indeed many student pacifists somewhat incongruously combined opposition to rearmament in Britain with support for military intervention to help the Republican government in Spain. Jim Fryth has described how the aid for Spain movement was remarkable in its political and social breadth, in the extent of working-class involvement and the role of women in the campaign.[87] The main historical accounts of relief in Spain—by both Fryth and Buchanan—mention university students only in passing, but university and college groups formed a significant part of the overall movement. Students and staff were mobilized to raise funds as well as to become involved in campaigning and other more political acts of solidarity, including organizing student delegations and volunteering in Spain.[88]

Relief for Spain attracted a broad-base of support across British universities. Kit Meredith, for instance, suggested that it was around the issue of Spain that some of the "broadest alliances" within the universities were forged.[89] It was on the issue of Spain that the NUS broke with its nonpolitical traditions by sending student delegates.[90] Talks on Spain could command large audiences. At Nottingham, for example, the aid campaign was launched in November 1938 at a meeting attended by 120 students, while 100 came to hear a returned International Brigadier speak the following year.[91] Spain was also one of the few causes through which students successfully collaborated closely with youth movements outside the universities. Student contributions for Spain were coordinated through the British Youth Peace Assembly rather than through ISS, because aid was not specifically directed at student groups in Spain but aimed to meet broader humanitarian objectives. Moreover, the majority of students supported the Republican side, inline with British sympathies more broadly, and therefore relief work was an extension of political beliefs. Buchanan argues that relief funds which attempted to be genuinely impartial, aiding both sides equally, tended not to flourish.[92] This presented a challenge to the much-vaunted neutrality of ISS, which preferred to concentrate on educational reconstruction rather than broader humanitarian purposes.[93] It is noticeable that of the dozens of conferences on international affairs, peace and collective security which ISS organized in many countries in the second half of the 1930s, Spain did not feature at all. However, from late 1936 the ISS committee in Geneva was on standby in case the war should lead to an exodus of student refugees from Spain, in which case aid would be allocated on the basis of need "whatever may be the political colour of the students."[94]

A major part of BYPA's work was the setting up of a Youth Foodship Committee to collect and send food and tinned milk to Spain. The first ship sailed in December 1936, although from 1937 most of the food and other gifts travelled overland via Paris. Over £50,000 worth of goods and cash was collected by the BYPA for Spain between 1936 and 1939.[95] Students at many colleges sold food vouchers issued by the BYPA in small books. A "BYPA Bread Voucher," for example, cost 3d and would buy 1 lb of flour for Spanish children.[96] At Manchester, one enterprising student managed to collect £5 during his lunch break by leaping on a table and announcing to diners in the refectory that while they were eating, people in Spain were starving.[97] Most universities and colleges formed independent Spanish aid committees to channel money and gift-in-kind contributions to the central BYPA fund or local Foodship Committee, although in some cases the campaign was coordinated by the college ISS branch, the university peace council or directly by the students' union. As might be expected Socialist Societies as well as SCM branches were among the most active groups involved, but so too were university peace councils and Jewish Societies.[98] Indian students formed Spain-India aid committees at some universities, and members in Cambridge took a prominent part in aid Spain demonstrations.[99] At Cambridge the University Peace Council distributed three thousand jam jars to undergraduates to use as collecting jars for loose copper and operated a Spain stall in the market place.[100] In 1939, the rather belatedly formed Spanish Relief Committee at Hull University College organized house-to-house collections.[101] Student fundraising efforts received a boost when, meeting at the second World Youth Congress at Vassar College in August 1938, students from six nations made a pact to outdo each other in the collection of food and funds.[102] British students responded by raising £2,400 in the autumn term of 1938.[103] Individual colleges were matched "in friendly rivalry" with colleges in United States, Mexico, Holland, Belgium and France as well as asked to challenge their local rivals.[104]

A further popular student cause was the support of refugee children through schemes such as "adopting" eight hundred babies in a home near Madrid—a project strongly supported by Manchester Women's Union—or supplying aid to child refugees in France.[105] Students from Southampton University were involved in one of the most high profile relief efforts of the whole Aid Spain movement in Britain—the reception of four thousand Basque child refugees in May 1937 following the bombing of Guernica. Along with volunteers from the trade unions, the Labour Party and the local Guides and Scouts, students helped assemble tents, set up a field kitchen and clean a donated local mansion for use as a sanatorium.[106] Local students were involved in the day-to-day running the refugee camp while a party from Cambridge turned up to help during their long vacation. The broad umbrella of the Spanish aid movement—the National Joint Committee for Spanish Relief numbered 850 individual groups, local, regional and national by 1939—allowed students to become involved with the cause in ways related to their courses such as through the the Artists International Association, the Spanish Medical Aid Committee or the Spanish Teachers' Relief Committee. Undoubtedly students also channelled support in cash and in-kind through religious and political organizations with which they were involved on an individual level or in their home communities, such as the churches, Quaker meetings or the Labour Party.

In addition to these more traditional "support" type activities, the Spanish Civil War pushed students into new forms of social and political action. The British Government, along with France, was seeking to uphold a policy of nonintervention in Spain, despite violations of this agreement by Germany and Italy. The significant strain of left-wing antifascism in the universities meant that students were more likely than the public as a whole to oppose the noninterventionist policy, although in fact there was growing protest about nonintervention as the war continued into 1937 and 1938. Some students therefore became involved with a broad protest movement against the policy preventing the Republican Government from buying arms. In January 1938, for instance, some five hundred students together with a few lecturers of the University of London walked out of lectures to take part in one such "Arms for Spain" demonstration. Student associations sent delegates to an Emergency Conference on Spain in April 1938 and in July students took part in a two-year anniversary "National week of aid for Spain" coordinated by the National Joint Committee.[107] In Cambridge Ram Nahum, President of the Socialist Club, organized a student poster parade to call attention to nonintervention. Such action was not entirely confined to radical Cambridge or London. When the foreign secretary Lord Halifax paid a surprise visit to University College Hull in February 1939 he was met by a hastily organized student poster demonstration and presented with a petition condemning government policy that was signed by

Figure 7.1 Cambridge student Ram Nahum at a poster parade organized in protest against nonintervention in the Spanish Civil War, 1938.

Source: Image from the Brian Simon Archive (Ref: SIM/4/5/1/22) held at the Institute of Education Archive.

90 students.[108] However, not all students agreed with Arms for Spain demands, but as one Student Forum editorial noted "on the question of food, there can be no difference of opinion."[109]

A further expression of solidarity and support for the Republican cause was the organization of student delegations. Although later historians have tended to confuse and conflate these delegations, there were three separate delegations to Spain that included British students.[110] The first such visit took place during the 1936–1937 Christmas vacation, shortly after a cross-party group of British MPs had visited the Republic and returned to set up the National Joint

Committee for Spanish Relief. Six students from Britain joined French and Czech students for a ten-day visit to Madrid, Valencia and Barcelona organized by the World Student Association.[111] This Paris-based body was controlled by Communists and employed James Klugman as secretary between 1935 and 1939. The British group was a relatively mixed one, including Gerald Croasdell of the BULNS and BYPA, John Gardiner of the BYPA, Frances Drew from Edinburgh University, Hugh Gosschalk of London University and the Union of University Liberal Societies, Philip Toynbee of the University Labour Federation and Rajni Patel, an Indian student studying at Cambridge, who represented the Indian Student Organisations of Great Britain. However, Toynbee later revealed that there were eight Communist Party members in the supposedly "all party" delegation of 11.[112] Toynbee was heavily involved in organizing support for the Republican cause in Oxford and later published a series of extracts from his diary of the visit, recording his wild excitement at being in Spain. On arrival in the anarchist city of Barcelona, he reported feeling "wretched" at being "just a student delegate," and noted "I think it will be an act of heroism if I *do* decide to obey Party instructions and go home."[113]

On the students' return to Britain, five thousand copies of a pamphlet reporting the delegation were printed and distributed as part of a "special and urgent appeal to all students" for food, clothing and medical aid. John Gardiner, a Conservative student, was the only one of the delegation not to sign the *Spain Assailed* manifesto because he was "politically unsympathetic to both parties" but did endorse the collection of food and clothing.[114] Rajni Patel was involved in collecting for Spain through a Spain-India aid committee run by the Indian League.[115] After the thrills of his trip to the front, Philip Toynbee found the practical task of collecting dried milk for Spanish children back in Oxford rather an anti-climax though he admitted in his diary it was "a decent enough activity." [116] In *Spain Assailed* Toynbee appealed directly to students to respond as members of British universities in terms reflecting ISS appeals of similar date:

> This is not simply a Spanish issue. If the academic life of yet another great country is destroyed, it will not only mean irreparable loss for the universities of Europe, but a direct threat to the students and professors of the few remaining democracies. Time and again the Spanish students have appealed to us for our help. If we unite in a great student movement to save the universities of Spain, we *can* save them. If they are lost, we shall very soon be lost, too.[117]

This first delegation was not endorsed by the NUS or the *Confédération Internationale des Étudiants* (CIE) and although an account of the tour was published in *New University*, it was criticized in the same issue by the editor of its "University Intelligence" section, Grahame Browne, as "serving little useful purpose apart from to call attention to the situation which was already adequately described in some of our more left-wing newspapers."[118] However, by 1938–1939, according to Brian Simon, the NUS was officially cooperating with the World Student Association because the CIE had become "almost totally inactive."[119] Therefore NUS did send an official representative, George Bean of Liverpool University, on the second student delegation which visited for twelve days in July 1938 and which also included Ted Heath (1916–2005), then President of the Oxford University Conservative Association (OUCA).[120] The third delegation, organized by the BYPA's Student Committee, visited at Christmas 1938 and included London student Rachel Chance and two Cambridge students: Arnold Kettle and Mohan Kumaramangalam.[121] On returning home from these trips delegates were greeted at large receptions where students shared their experiences and impressions with audiences of representatives of student organizations, trade unions and the press. Such visits to a real warzone were hugely exciting for student participants and this enthusiasm carried over into talks given by delegates on their return to raise awareness and appeal for funds.[122] For example, Gerald Croasdell gave "one of the best speeches" at the annual BULNS conference in 1937, where he introduced a resolution against the war.[123]

In addition to these student delegations, small numbers of students went to Spain as volunteers to fight for the Republic, both before and after volunteering was made illegal in January 1937. Although students or recent graduates comprised only a very small number of the approximately 2,500 British men (and a few women) who fought in Spain, their influence on students back in Britain was significant. When the brilliant Cambridge student John Cornford died in Spain the day after his twenty-first birthday in December 1936 it was widely reported in student magazines and his memory regularly invoked as inspiration for all students fighting fascism.[124] Eric Hobsbawm recalled that Cornford's photograph was displayed on all "progressive Cambridge mantelpieces."[125] A fund opened in Cambridge in memory of Cornford and fellow student G. C. McLaurin rapidly raised £2,000.[126] As Brian Simon later wrote "his death symbolized for many, then and since, the close involvement of students in the ominous and threatening political developments of the late 1930s. It also served as a catalyst. In those circumstances it was increasingly difficult to stand aside."[127]

Small numbers of British students also visited Spain to serve with relief agencies such as the British Medical Aid Unit and International Voluntary Service for Peace. A London medical student, 23-year-old Kenneth Sinclair Loutit, was one of the founding members of the Spanish Medical Aid Committee (SMAC) which was set up July 1936. In mid-August a hastily composed unit of 20 volunteers left for Spain with Sinclair Loutit appointed Administrator by the London-based committee. Over the course of next few years the SMAC sent out 150 medical personnel. The original unit led by Sinclair Loutit was eventually absorbed into the medical service of the International Brigade. A number of historians have explored the activities and legacy of the SMAC. For instance, Buchanan devotes a chapter in his 2007 book to the Medical Aid Committee in which he describes its "remarkable achievement" but adds that the story is one of "intrigue and intense personal and political infighting."[128] As Sinclair Loutit noted in his unpublished autobiography, the Committee "with singular optimism, persuaded themselves that I, a student of twenty three, had what it takes to command a field unit in a civil war."[129]

Student involvement with relief and campaign work for Spain was later depicted as a watershed moment in the 1930s student movement by many of those involved, despite the ultimate failure of the Republican cause. Amid the triumphs of poster parades and Spain Weeks throughout 1938 and 1939, students could not ignore the fact that the Spanish Republic was "visibly on its last legs and virtually beyond hope" as Hobsbawm afterwards put it.[130] Brian Simon later noted the long-lasting impact of the campaign, reflecting there were "many in my generation, to take just one example, who would never set foot in Franco's Spain."[131] By 1939 Spain had become a unifying cause among students of different political backgrounds. Reflecting on the situation in prewar Cambridge, John Simmonds concluded that the campaign "brought into political activity hundreds of students who, a year before, would have turned up their noses at a poster parade or a door-to-door collection."[132] It is also perhaps indicative of how far the student movement had moved by the late 1930s that it was Ted Heath, leader of a revitalized and anti-appeasement student Conservative movement in Oxford, who was the one selected to write up the July 1938 delegation's experiences for *Student Forum*.[133]

A FORGOTTEN CAMPAIGN? STUDENTS AND
THE SINO-JAPANESE WAR

A third major cause which mobilized British students' fundraising and campaigning abilities in the 1930s was the second Sino-Japanese War that broke out in 1937. Because aid for China was organized through a large number of different groups, it is harder to assess students' contributions to this relief effort than it is for the Spanish Civil War or Nazi refugee crisis. However, student efforts were directed both through a special ISS appeal and a new independent group known as the China Campaign Committee. When 14 universities were bombed by the Japanese over the summer of 1937, university leaders in China appealed directly to ISS, which agreed to an intentional appeal after an emergency conference with Professor Chang Pengh-Chun of Nankai University.[134] The ISS Committee for England and Wales launched its campaign for Chinese students with a meeting at University College attended by Chang Pengh-Chun (now in London) and such figures as R. H. Tawney and the Chinese Ambassador.[135] Responsibility for aiding Chinese universities and students was delegated to ISS by the Mansion House Appeal, which had already been launched on behalf of the China Association, the British Red Cross and the Conference of British Missionary Societies. Formed to protest about the war and to organize boycott of Japanese goods as well as raise funds, the new China Campaign Committee had strong Communist connections and drew support from trade unions, the Women's International League, left-wing student groups and the BYPA.[136] LSE student Pat Koo (b. 1918), daughter of the Chinese diplomat and politician Wellington Koo, was one of a number of Chinese students in Britain mobilized as speakers at local meetings of Peace Councils, church groups, trade unions and Left Book Club branches.[137]

The ISS appeal for Chinese Universities Relief was supported by a range of national groups including SCM, BULNS, BYPA, the British Federation of University Women and the NUS, which offered to channel funds to ISS through *New University*.[138] Reflecting student desires to offer relief from students to students, an early decision was taken to concentrate aid on a limited number of students rather than allow funds to be "swallowed up in a great civilian relief action."[139] Funds remitted to China by ISS were therefore spent exclusively on student relief, allocated in the usual manner through student-staff committees as well as through the student Young Men's Christian Association (YMCA). Around 85 percent of the funds raised in Britain were sent to China though some money was retained to assist

Chinese students who found themselves stranded in Britain. Drawing on expertise in dealing with refugee students, ISS assisted small numbers of students to complete their studies or to retrain.[140] The committee in England and Wales met its self-imposed £4,000 target, a significant contribution to the global ISS target of £10,000 for 1937–1938.[141] Interestingly, perhaps because of the city's large Chinese and "Eurasian" populations, as well as Liverpool's strong Labour movement, Liverpool University was one of the earliest and largest contributors, sending £440 in a few months.[142] Manchester managed £268 over the academic year 1937–1938.[143] In Birmingham, however, the ISS appeal for China had a less than encouraging response, with a hop raising £10 and staff and student subscriptions a further £40 in total.[144] A so-called mass meeting on China attracted just 60 students who were all either members of the Socialist Club or the SCM.[145] Such sums compare poorly with the money raised for Spain and the even larger amounts raised by rag collections in the late 1930s. Manchester, for example, raised over £4,800 for medical charities at the 1939 rag, and Leeds around half this sum.[146]

As was by now becoming a common way of showing solidarity as well as investigating need, an international student delegation visited China between May and July 1938, ending its tour at the World Youth Congress at Vassar.[147] The group included British Communists Bernard Floud (1915–1967), President of the BULNS, and James Klugman. On his return Floud spoke at ISS-organized meetings at various colleges including Manchester and Birmingham and appealed not just for students to raise funds but also for them to boycott Japanese goods and to lobby the government to send aid.[148] Like, Spain, the aid China campaign offered opportunities for student involvement in more politicized social action through the boycott of Japanese manufactured goods. In December 1937, protest centered on Japanese goods arriving for the Christmas market but by spring 1938 the message was one of "no silk." In February 1938, the China Campaign Committee declared the first "China Week" and 280 poster parades were organized across the country.[149] Several universities collaborated with local Aid China Committees to raise awareness and money as well as to call for boycott. Student groups were involved with poster parades in cities including London, Edinburgh, Cambridge and at Cardiff, where the University Peace Council also opened a propaganda shop.[150] In Southampton and Bristol students became involved with special Aid China conferences.[151] In Cambridge, the University Peace Council organized boycotts in which students leafleted potential customers of shops selling Japanese products.[152] In 1937, the

BULNS also encouraged student athletes to call for a boycott of the Tokyo Olympics then being planned for summer 1940.[153]

Yet despite some successes, the campaign for China was the poor relation of the Aid for Spain movement in the universities as well as in British society more widely. In a memoir published in 1989 former China Campaign Committee national organizer Arthur Clegg (1914–1994) described it as a "forgotten campaign." Analysis of student magazines from the period reveals many more mentions of activities in aid of Spain than China. In 1938–1939 fundraising efforts for the ISS appeal fell short of expectations, despite hopes being raised by a tour of British universities by Dr T. Z. Koo of the Chinese SCM.[154] However, Chinese relief was a subject much discussed at the World Student Conference which met in Paris in summer 1939.[155] Compared to Spain, China was simply too distant and alien for many students to feel strong sympathies with the victims of Japanese aggression. Distance was not the only factor. In her history of the Australian SCM Renate Howe points out that most Australian students were, ironically, also more concerned with the Spanish Civil War than with the Sino-Japanese conflict.[156] In Britain, as in the United States and Australia, students were faced with many competing claims for their time and money both domestically and internationally.

Conclusions

In the 1930s student voluntarism was tested as never before. The universities and colleges were a source of funds, gifts-in-kind and volunteers for a wide range of competing international causes. Reflecting on the steady succession of appeals for each fresh disaster of the modern world, student organizations expressed both pride that the British student movement rallied to each new cause and confidence that British students would give a lead in relief.[157] Relief efforts took place against a broader backdrop of antiwar activity on university campuses, where Communist-supporting students took a lead in developing a strong antiwar movement that by the mid-1930s had drawn a wider range of students into a broad coalition. Brian Simon later referred to these national and international events as part of the "radicalisation of a whole generation of students."[158] The threat of war impacted particularly on students because they were likely to be among the first to be called up, meaning that "maintenance of peace," but not appeasement of Hitler or other fascist powers, emerged as a priority for many students.[159] Cooperation between different student organizations at college and at national level was crucial to maximizing the success of appeals for Spain, China and Nazi refugees. Moreover, the seemingly desperate international situation gave rise to new student responses in the form of boycott, demonstration and campaigning. Although the boycott of Japanese goods or the demonstrations against nonintervention in Spain were not the preserve of students alone, they were certainly some of the more active participants. That undergraduate students should be at the leading edge of protest does not seem strange today, but in the 1930s it did mark a significant change. Writing in 1942 to commemorate the life of Cambridge student Ram Nahum who had been killed by a German bomb, John Simmonds argued that 15 years previously it would have been considered abnormal for a student to carry a protest poster, suggesting sardonically that "if a student had carried a poster, it would probably have advertised for strike-breakers."[160]

Although not all students agreed on the use of such methods, support for protest and boycott was not confined to a small group of Communist students but cut across political and religious divisions.[161] Repeated failures on the part of the British Government to help Ethiopia in 1935, Spain in 1936 or China in 1937 resulted in distrust of the government and a sense of political frustration, which was to create what the SCM called a "time-lag" in swinging student support behind the war in 1939–1940.[162] Moreover students were beginning to perceive a common identity with a broader youth movement at home and overseas.[163] That such cooperation was indeed taking place was shown in the series of conferences held during the spring and summer of 1939, including student participation in the BYPA's Youth Hearing in February, the Youth Peace Campaign's peace pilgrimage to London in February and the National Parliament of Youth in March.[164] By the end of the 1930s the British student movement was more broadly based than Ashby and Anderson or even Brian Simon allowed. Contrary to what later commentators like A. H. Halsey and Stephen Marks have claimed, students framed their relief contributions as a specific student response. A student movement was forged through the development of student social and political action on domestic and international issues and explicitly adopted a "popular front" approach to coordinate its activities. However, the outbreak of war in September 1939 was to put the student movement under unforeseen pressure.

CHAPTER 8

The Students' Contribution to Victory: Voluntary Work in the Second World War and After

Over the Christmas vacation of 1940 hundreds of students from all over the country played their part in a massive relief effort for the Blitzed cities of London and Manchester. Manchester student C. E. Jones, who organized a party of students to help with the grim task of uncovering bodies from the rubble, described it as "a Christmas of destruction, death and misery."[1] In London, 120 students spent part of their Christmas holidays living in the East End and learning new respect for its people. A pamphlet produced by students involved in "this great and terrible experience" contained an urgent "call to the universities of Britain. The society passing through this ordeal is our society; we must make ourselves ready to play our part."[2] By 1941 the rhetoric of a "student tradition of social work" was being employed by the National Union of Students (NUS) and others to promote war work across colleges and universities, but such coordinated student support for the war effort seemed unlikely in the autumn term of 1939.[3] While thousands of students immediately joined the forces, those returning to college faced the multifaceted challenges of evacuation and Air Raid Precautions (ARP) as well as uncertainty over their very future as students. The Communist-dominated NUS leadership launched a robust campaign aimed at defending university education during wartime but its antiwar stance plunged the organization into crisis and shattered the prewar consensus that had been carefully built up across the student world. This chapter examines the impact of the Second World War on students, exploring the ambivalence of many to the outbreak of war in 1939 and the challenges faced by a student movement that had been built on antiwar foundations in the late 1930s. Once again, a new consensus was forged through student involvement in practical social service and war work. The chapter then examines the claim that students' voluntary war work was "markedly different" from prewar efforts "carried on in a spirit of condescension."[4] The chapter ends with a look at the student contribution to rehabilitation and educational reconstruction in Germany and elsewhere in Europe after the end of hostilities.

Empty Notebooks in London: Evacuation and Student Life in the Second World War

Universities and colleges reopening in the autumn term of 1939 were greatly affected by the outbreak of the Second World War. Rolls fell somewhat as male students left to join the forces. At Manchester University, for example, term started with 160 fewer men students than in autumn 1938, although this was only a small percentage of the total of 2,496 students.[5] In Oxford, where most students studied arts, the impact was bigger with a thousand fewer male students enrolling.[6] A greater challenge was that of evacuation of the London colleges, for which plans had been developed throughout 1939.[7] Thousands of students were evacuated to university towns including Cambridge, Oxford, Birmingham, Bristol and Nottingham and to the Welsh colleges.[8] Evacuated colleges began returning to London in 1943 and 1944. In 1939, many other universities found themselves with a new intake of student-soldiers requiring specialist training in engineering faculties.[9] With conscription initially set at 20 years old for men, another challenge was the influx of younger students at 17 seeking to complete their degrees before being called up. Over the course of the war, the lowering of the conscription age to 18 meant that student numbers decreased sharply to about half their prewar figure by 1943. This left around 25,000 students, with more women than men and increased numbers of medical, dental and engineering students whose courses enabled deferment of the call-up. With students expecting to stay only one or two years, after 1943 most universities and colleges introduced shortened honors courses, "war degrees," or a "fourth term" in the summer vacations to reduce the time taken to get a degree.[10] Students in Northern Ireland were less affected by the outbreak of war as conscription was not introduced, but students at Queen's University Belfast, for example, were urged to volunteer for military service and for summer vacation war work.[11]

The evacuation of the universities in 1939 required a massive logistical effort, especially for nonresidential colleges, and caused a number of problems for students and student organizations.[12] Students from one college were often dispersed to more than one center. University College (UC) students, for instance, were scattered across Aberystwyth, Bangor, Swansea, Sheffield and Cardiff.[13] Day students relocating with their colleges had to be found accommodation in lodgings or with host families.[14] Some poorer students, who were only able to survive on their patchwork of loans and grants by living with parents or other relatives, could not afford to move with their college. Others found the higher costs of living at Oxford or Cambridge put a strain on their finances. For example, although 450 London School of Economics (LSE) students moved with their college to Cambridge, in the autumn of 1939, 2,000 others sat "enviously with empty notebooks, unable to live and study away from their London homes through lack of money, unable to study in London."[15] Delays with payments of grants and scholarships were also common. Medical education was especially disrupted as students encountered shortages of laboratory space, inappropriate placements for clinical students and the deployment of doctors unused to teaching.[16] Lecturing staff were called up for the forces and large numbers went into government service. The new Ministry of Information, established by former NUS president Ivison Macadam and based at the heart of the University of London in Senate House, drew many of its first staff from the universities and from student organizations including the NUS. [17]

For host colleges the upheaval of receiving hundreds of additional students was extensive. The evacuation caused overcrowding in lectures and halls of residences and problems with access to libraries and laboratories. [18] There were also a number of examples of clashes of student cultures, such as that experienced at Aberystwyth, where the influx of UC evacuees more than doubled the student population. As the *Dragon* noted, "Aber people, rightly or wrongly, considered London students to have adopted an annoyingly patronizing air."[19] In the halls of residence and colleges scarcity of domestic staff as well as new wartime restrictions led to changes to living arrangements, dining routines and use of facilities. Several Oxford and Cambridge colleges were taken over by other universities and their students "doubled": put two to a room in other colleges. At many halls and colleges students took on domestic work previously left to servants such as carrying coal, waiting at tables, washing up, cleaning their own shoes, making beds and working shifts at the porter's lodge.[20] Students who had never lived away from home before learnt "self reliance" and how to get the "best out of communal life" in hostels, according to one upbeat magazine editorial.[21] Residential colleges supplemented rations through growing vegetables and bee-keeping on college premises.[22] Helpfully for some, "the austerity of war concealed social and financial difficulties" as Nina Bawden (1925–2012), a grammar school girl who entered Somerville College in 1943 later pointed out.[23] However on the surface little had changed at some colleges. "Oh, but they still play croquet. Good!" was the response of one former Lady Margaret Hall student on revisiting her old college in 1940.[24] J. J. Kipling, an Oxford student keeping a wartime diary for Mass Observation, recorded that in the autumn of 1939 few students carried gas masks to lectures and his own greatest concern seemed to be the availability of butter. He reported that undergraduates "still manage to get drunk, even without the influence of third year men. So all must be well with Oxford."[25] Despite wartime changes, many students felt their position of relative privilege was only justified by studying extra hard.[26]

The outbreak of war also immediately affected student leisure time activities. Activities such as dances, society meetings, public lectures and musical recitals were restricted by new, locally imposed rules on the size and time of gatherings.[27] Sports and athletics suffered as colleges found themselves with fewer fixtures and in 1939 the activities of the Universities Athletics Union were "abruptly terminated."[28] At some colleges, including Durham, Swansea and Southampton, building projects for new students' unions and sports facilities were abandoned. Students also encountered problems with university authorities who imposed restrictions on use of union buildings, changed opening hours, introduced new curfews and in some cases took action to curtail political discussions and freedom of speech on campus.[29] Branches of the University Labour Federation (ULF) were particularly active in investigating and protesting against these restrictions on student life. At Sheffield, for example, the Socialist Society led a campaign for better food in the hostels.[30] At Nottingham, the Students' Union committee (of whom five out of six members were socialists) succeeded in overturning a ban on political debate. Student voluntary work was also affected, although commentators continued to look to students to take a lead in social service, particularly with children and youth.[31] Most student rags planned for 1939–1940 were cancelled or scaled back and student energies diverted into collecting money for charities such as the Red Cross or St John's Ambulance. However, Glasgow students were not so easily put off, and together with evacuated London medical students upheld the tradition of rag mags, immunity badges and a "pie eating stunt" to raise more than £8,000 in April 1940.[32] In Birmingham in 1940 the reinstituted Carnival—albeit shorn of its torchlight procession, decorated lorries and free beer—once again raised money for local hospitals, which were recognized to need help even more than before the war.[33] As in the First World War, many women students immediately took up traditional activities such as knitting "comforts for the troops" and taking part in first aid training. The women's colleges also "rallied round" to provide the usual outing for groups from the Women's University Settlement in 1939 and sent money in lieu of Christmas parties in 1940.[34]

Despite its challenges, evacuation brought a welcome boost to the membership and range of activities of clubs and societies at host colleges. Joint student debates, sporting fixtures, dances and society meetings were organized, while evacuated staff formed discussion groups and enjoyed sherry parties with new colleagues.[35] A number of special rugby and soccer fixtures were arranged between composite university teams to raise money for war charities.[36] At Nottingham, the evacuated SCM branches of Goldsmiths and the Institute of Education combined with Nottingham's to plan a joint program of activities and socials, of which study circles were especially popular.[37] By February 1940 King's College students at Bristol University boasted of being "established residents" and cited the engagement of Bristol Lady President Joan Kay to King's Hon Secretary Hugh Bungay as evidence of teatime fraternization.[38] At Oxford, a Mass Observation report on the university in wartime revealed that international clubs were the most flourishing undergraduate societies.[39] Moreover, students found that evacuated children billeted locally often had it much worse than they did, and were "in need of help and company" which students were well-placed to provide.[40] Many colleges helped arrange sports and social activities for evacuees.[41] In Aberystwyth, for example, students formed a joint Aber-London committee to investigate and report on the situation of children evacuated from Liverpool schools to the Welsh coast and to organize entertainment for the children.[42] In Oxford, students associated with the university Jewish Club held a youth group for Jewish evacuees from London. Women students often took a lead in such activities, and in general the war gave women greater opportunities for leadership and influence in the universities. Women formed a greater proportion of students, tended to stay in residence for longer, and were on average a couple of years older than their male contemporaries. Mass Observation found Oxford "clubs which never numbered women among their highest officers are now dominated by them."[43] University College's Women's Union president urged students to seize unprecedented wartime opportunities and regretted that women had let men take the lead in student life prewar. [44] Unfortunately the first female president of the NUS, Mary Corsellis, was elected in 1940 but never became president owing to the constitutional crisis that engulfed the NUS that year. [45]

The outbreak of war led to much confusion among student political organizations. In 1939, the ULF—which included Communist Party members—broke with the Labour Party in coming out strongly against the war. The ULF towed the Comintern line, which following the Nazi-Soviet pact, held that the war was an imperialist war, "waged for profits and world domination." [46] Moscow's position had split the leadership of the Communist Party of Great Britain (CPGB) and it was not until Hitler invaded the Soviet Union in June 1941 that the CPGB—and the ULF—announced full support for the war, when, as Francis Beckett notes, many Communists were relieved to abandon a line "which they had never in their hearts really believed in." [47] Throughout 1940 and into 1941 the ULF remained outspoken in its criticism of the war, and its members devoted much time to indentifying and documenting cases of poor ARP planning at the universities, student hardship and infringements of students' rights. [48] Its stance against the war was deeply controversial among students and caused ULF founder, Arthur Greenwood MP, to resign the organization's Presidency. [49] In contrast, student Conservatives backed the war from the outset while the Liberals saw the war as a chance to improve people's standards of living and place "Imperial relations on a new footing." [50]

It is harder to judge the feelings of the wider student population, but during the academic year 1939–1940 there does seem to have been ambivalence toward the war linked to a high degree of uncertainty over the very continuation of the universities in wartime. [51] A key cause was the government decision in October 1939 to pay its annual grant to the universities (of around £2 million) for six months only. Kipling reported to Mass Observation that Oxford was full of rumors about the university closing down and all the dons being given government jobs. [52] Many universities organized discussions and conferences on the topic of higher education in wartime, and motions condemning the war were passed by some unions and debating societies, although not always with large victories. [53] At Birmingham, for example, R. H. Lambourne reported that while most students were not actively opposed to the war there was "very little feeling of enthusiasm for the war cause." [54] At Aberystwyth, apparently, few students were "wholly convinced that the Allied cause is just." [55] Brian Simon, who served as NUS President 1939–1940, later argued that the intentions and character of the Chamberlain Government "were viewed with extreme scepticism by, I would say, the vast majority of students; and this was reflected in the outlook of the NUS."[56] This may have been overstating the case. Support for the NUS campaign in "defence of the universities" during 1939–1940 was widespread though not universal. Early in 1940 the NUS distributed 3,500 copies of a pamphlet written by Simon called *Defend the Universities!*[57] Key planks of the campaign were securing the continuance of the Treasury grant in wartime, negotiating postponement of military service and pushing for more financial aid for poor students. The campaign was also pushed by a new Coordinating Committee set up in the autumn term of 1939 and formed of representatives of SCM, International Student Service (ISS), British Universities League of Nations Society and the three university political associations. However, some members of this group, notably the SCM, expressed concern that the Coordinating Committee was seeking to foster "a mass student movement which shall be a political weapon," rather than respecting the independence of its members.[58] Student attitudes to conscription varied widely.[59] Writing of Oxford, Kipling further noted that students were not agreed on support for the NUS proposal to postpone the call-up, with some feeling they had no right to be granted postponement when people their own age "were being led off to the battlefield."[60] The University Conservatives opposed postponement, while student Liberals also gave temporary conscription their support.[61]

There is plenty of evidence that many students were happy to put up with some level of disruption of everyday life as the inevitable consequence of war, and there were reports of students disrupting meetings of antiwar or left-wing groups. At Aberystwyth women students evacuated from London organized a petition seeking a later curfew, an action that was not supported by their Welsh peers.[62] At King's College, Newcastle, (formerly known as Armstrong College) a *Northerner* editorial claimed that students accepted the restrictions of wartime such as early closing of the union and couldn't understand the attitude of students elsewhere who were opposed to such measures.[63] Throughout 1940 King's continued to oppose the NUS line on the war as "unnecessarily paranoid" and unrepresentative of the views of British students and to object to the editorial policy of *Student News,* a view shared by a number of other colleges. Despite support for the save the universities campaign in 1939–1940, UC union society, for example, considered that by mid-1940 NUS was "antagonising a section of the educational community and spending money on biased political work."[64] Kipling recorded a good deal of acceptance of the war among students at Oxford, combined with a desire to think and study about the problems to come after the war.[65] At other universities opinion was similarly divided. The pages of Birmingham's *Guild News*, for instance, suggest students had come to terms with the war but believed strongly in the importance of maintaining the Universities as centers of thought. *Guild News* published a wide range of opinion on topics such as compulsory physical training and Russia's invasion of Finland.

Students' ambivalence toward the war came to a head at the British Student Congress, which was held in the new Leeds University Union over Easter 1940 and attended by six hundred delegates. The congress was organized by the NUS in association with the Coordinating Committee.[66] A series of study groups, meetings and local conferences took place in the run up to the Congress.[67] The aim was that the Congress should broadly reflect the British student movement, with members of all student political parties and organizations taking part. A survey of 332 delegates found that 60 percent belonged to no student society other than the NUS and three quarters (73%) had attended maintained secondary schools. Around 50 members of the SCM attended.[68] This mixture of delegates led one Manchester student to reflect "one learned that Conservatives could be intelligent, and Liberals could be active as well as broad minded; that Communists, at close quarters, were not altogether outrageous."[69] However, a Mass Observation reporter who attended the Congress and interviewed delegates concluded it was not representative of student opinion as a whole but only of the "active and articulate" university opinion, which tended to be left-wing.[70] Delegates felt that the majority of British students were "apathetic and only interested in going to lectures," while students with more right-wing views hadn't attended the Congress.

The Congress framed a "Charter of Students Rights and Responsibilities" that called for full freedom of speech and association, as well as a share in the governance of universities.[71] Preparatory work included a "Commission on the Universities and the People," which concluded that "students had responsibilities to the community as a whole, and that only by fulfilling these could there be gained a general appreciation among the people of values of universities."[72] Despite much reasoned discussion, the Leeds Congress became notorious for its poll on the war, in which 281 students voted in favor of a statement that "the continuance of the present War is not in the interest of the people in any country." Writing in 1991 former NUS Secretary Margot Kettle, née Gale (1916–1995) reflected that student Communists at that time felt "it was their duty to move resolutions of the kind at every opportunity."[73] In fact 150 students voted for an alternative motion expressing deep hatred of war, but supporting "the continuation of the War for the defeat of Nazi Germany," although this was rarely mentioned in the succeeding press furore.[74] Commenting from the 1980s Simon argued we should remember that "this was still the period of the so-called 'phoney war'" and that Chamberlain was still the prime minister, with Halifax as Foreign Secretary.[75]

The controversial vote lost the NUS leadership the support of former allies, including the usually supportive Association of University Teachers, members of the SCM, several students' unions and Eleanor Rathbone (MP for the Combined Universities) as well as inviting condemnation from the NUS's own Council.[76] Indeed the fallout over the poll contributed to a power struggle between the NUS student leaders and its trustees that came to a head with what Simon described as an attempted "coup d'etat," in which the trustees sought to close down NUS for the duration of the war.[77] Simon and his supporters fiercely resisted these moves and by Easter 1941 new President Peter Rivett, of Leeds University, was able to announce that NUS had emerged from the crisis with renewed vigour and strength.[78] The strength of the 1930s student antiwar movement meant that the transition to work in support of the war effort was never going to be an easy one, while the leading role played in student politics by Communists affected NUS policies for the duration of the Nazi-Soviet pact. While never the unanimous standpoint, it seems opposition to the war was not the preserve of an extremist minority either. A 1940 SCM report argued that student attitudes to the war were transformed during the last few weeks of the summer term 1940 with the change of government and the evacuation of Dunkirk.[79]

SHOULDERS TO THE WHEEL: STUDENTS AND WAR WORK

A 1941 article in NUS paper *Student News* judged that "the student tradition of social work was never more necessary than now," and pointed to a long list of organizations requiring student voluntary help.[80] Perhaps the biggest change to university life during the war was the introduction of war work, but ambivalence toward the war and uncertainty over the future meant the student movement was slow to take up the opportunities. However, despite its poll on the war, the 1940 Congress did endorse student participation in such activities as educational work in the forces, Workers Educational

Association and voluntary service among evacuees. Students coming up to university in 1940 were more prepared than their predecessors to put their "shoulders to the wheel of war work." The distractions of its constitutional crisis over and its work under "full student control," the NUS helped coordinate this contribution to the war effort, for example by publishing a series of pamphlets detailing how students could help out and acting as a clearing house for volunteers.[81] New activities included sending a group of 40 students to Somerset to volunteer with evacuated children in summer 1940.[82] The Blitzkrieg attacks on major British cities, which began in September 1940, provided new opportunities for student voluntarism. In Manchester, around 180 students organized themselves to help out at canteens, shelters and at rest centers.[83] Jones, the President of the Manchester Technology Union, got together a party of 34 students to help the paid rescue squads in the grim and dangerous work of recovering bodies from bombed houses. Students were put, two or three at time, with the paid rescue squads and helped dig out bodies, guided by "the smell of putrifying [sic] flesh." Many of the party ate their Christmas dinner from mobile canteens.[84] Another group arranged baths for bombed out children at the Students' Union. Despite such acts of service, some students reported difficulties with persuading the authorities to take their volunteer help seriously, with medical students, for example, failing to persuade Manchester Corporation to allow them to staff first aid posts in shelters.

Students led by NUS President-elect Mary Corsellis had begun volunteering with homeless people at clubs and settlements in the East End of London on a small scale at the end of the long vacation 1940. Over the Christmas vacation, the University of London Union worked in partnership with London County Council to provide student helpers for rest centers and air raid shelters, accommodating students in two flats in Shadwell. Around 120 students from all over the country took part in this scheme.[85] In addition to performing simple tasks that relieved full-time shelter staff, many students wanted to make a contribution which only they as students could offer such as arranging talks on current events, science and health. More controversially, anxious to avoid "the Lady Bountiful activity of dealing out a pity-prompted charity," students also conducted a survey of conditions in air raid shelters. In a report of the experience written by Corsellis, students in other cities were advised to begin preparations for providing relief work "before the bombs fall" by conducting surveys of shelters, organizing meetings of student volunteers and making contact with relief agencies and authorities.[86] As a "privileged section of society" Corsellis argued, students should be ready to help the community but "unless we know what to expect we may be a handicap instead of a help...learn now and prepare."[87] During 1941 students at colleges including King's College, Newcastle, Leeds and Edinburgh followed this advice and drew up detailed plans of how students would help out their respective cities during a Blitz.[88] Such plans were implemented by Liverpool students after the city was bombed in May 1941. Further support for victims of the Blitz was given by Oxford students to groups of people from heavily bombed districts sent to stay at colleges holidays paid for by the Lord Mayor's War Fund Appeal in summer 1941.[89]

Students' voluntary work in the London Blitz may have been uniquely well organized, but it is a useful case study to examine in more detail in light of claims made in a chapter—actually written by then NUS president Jack Allanson—in Brian Simon's book on the universities that wartime volunteering marked a shift from earlier models. The Blitz project evidently drew inspiration from some of these other models. Students in collective residence in the East End mirrored a university settlement, but the students slept on mattresses on the floor and shared the domestic chores of cooking and cleaning, recalling the camaraderie of camp life. If the written account of the experiment is to be believed, these students were also a more heterogeneous bunch than prewar student volunteers, including working-class students whose homes were not so different from those in the neighborhood in which they were helping as well as wealthier students for whom the "East End was a world completely new and incomprehensible."[90] In the evenings students set the world to rights through keen discussion on the social, economic and religious conditions "of the world as it was and as it might be."[91] In the best student tradition, social education thus went hand in hand with practical service and local social workers and clergymen were invited to the flats to speak of their experiences in the East End. The SCM's annual report for 1940–1941 noted that the combination of relief and discussion was evidence that "even the Blitz may bring a blessing."[92] Student recognition of the need to help make a better world after the war reflects what was going on more widely in educational and social reform circles during the 1940s and does mark a departure from the written accounts we have of volunteering on camps for the unemployed in the 1930s, for instance. Perhaps more than any previous student voluntary action, the intensity of wartime experiences did begin to break down the sense of separation many university and college students felt from wider society.[93]

The Blitz experience stimulated calls for students to get more closely involved in the war effort and this was facilitated by changing student attitudes toward the war. Speaking at a ULF conference in January 1941, George Matthews praised student work in the Blitzed cities and argued that ULF members should start to play a leading role in the endeavor, in order to "prevent it becoming mere charity work."[94] In a change of emphasis from 1940, NUS congresses from 1941 called for students to take up war service of every kind as part of the wider student contribution to winning the war.[95] The Scottish Union of Students similarly pledged its members to use their spare time for war work and social service, particularly with youth organizations.[96] By the academic year 1941–1942 most universities and colleges had a more or less formal war work scheme in place. The NUS urged students to cooperate with university staff and "cheerfully accept" duties such as fire watching, first aid training and ARP work.[97] For able bodied men students enrolment in senior training corps or air squadrons was usually made compulsory, while those unfit for service and women students were engaged on a wide range of voluntary projects including helping out in canteens, shelters and first aid posts; making camouflage netting; working as hospital cleaners; looking after children whose mothers worked in factories; and putting on talks and activities for locally stationed troops.[98] In 1942, for example, the Liverpool Guild "adopted" a local anti-aircraft regiment, offering soldiers a program of talks, debates and small group tutoring.[99]

Student News began to publicize examples of college war work and in October 1941 NUS secretary Lena Chivers (1915–2007) gave a radio broadcast about the ways in which students were trying to aid the war effort.[100] Notably, students were encouraged to prioritize voluntary work for which their education or training particularly fitted them over unskilled service.[101] Examples included arranging social and educational activities for troops and teaching skills in music, handicrafts or physical training to local youth.[102] From 1942 several women's unions and colleges—such as Manchester, Liverpool, Leeds and Oxford—began to introduce compulsory national service programs that combined domestic work such as serving in the refectory, firewatching, gardening or telephone duty with first aid training and social service at canteens, play centers, guide groups, youth clubs or hospitals.[103] In addition to term-time service, women students gave up part of their vacations to volunteering in play centers, nurseries or summer schemes for evacuated children or paid work in factories

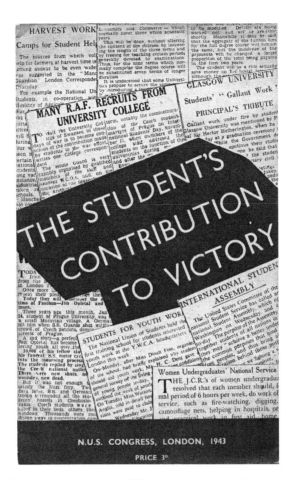

Figure 8.1   Front cover of the NUS Congress report, 1943.

Source: Image from the Brian Simon Archive (Ref: SIM/4/7/8) held at the Institute of Education Archive. Image reproduced by kind permission of the National Union of Students.

that enabled other women to take a holiday.[104] Another major activity coordinated by NUS and the Scottish NUS was the organization of agricultural harvest camps on behalf of the Ministry of Agriculture and the Ministry of Labour—for which students received a set wage—beginning with three hundred students in summer 1940 and peaking at almost two thousand students at the end of the war. Judging from student publications and memoirs, students were proud of involvement in this range of wartime service and derived much

satisfaction from taking part. Although such work could be weary-
ing, tiresome and sometimes distressing, it was also very often fun. At
Somerville College Nina Bawden found her wartime duty of "entertaining American soldiers" by serving as a waitress in the Red Cross
Club to be "no hardship."[105]

The Reconstruction of University Life: World Student Relief in the 1940s

Alongside voluntary war work at home, British students continued
to support the work of International Student Service which in 1940,
together with the World's Student Christian Federation (WSCF)
and the Catholic international student body Pax Romana, launched
an extensive relief program for student victims of the war, known as
European Student Relief and later World Student Relief.[106] The program initially focused on the needs of student refugees and on the
provision of study material to both Allied and Axis student prisoners
of war.[107] Later, activities widened to include sending of food supplies
to students in occupied countries and showing solidarity with students
worldwide on International Students' Day, designated as November
17 in memory of those killed or imprisoned during the Nazi attack
on the Czech universities in 1939.[108] In Britain, one key area of work
was for the hundreds of student refugees who in May 1940 fell under
the government's new internment regulations and were transported to
the Isle of Man, Australia or Canada.[109] This internment prompted a
chorus of protest led by ISS and the Committee of Vice-Chancellors
and Principals. An ISS appeal called on the student body to "feel
ashamed" at the fate of "co-students who sought refuge in this country
from Nazi oppression."[110] ISS staff worked with the Vice Chancellors'
Committee and students' unions to support interned students, and
was successful in securing their release within a year. In addition, ISS
continued to support refugee students throughout the war; around
150 students were helped with grants each year and another 500–600
supported with information and advice in the mid-1940s.[111] However,
it is noticeable that aid for refugee students did not figure highly in
accounts of British students' war work, and Eleanor Rathbone's 1945
claim that not enough was being done for them seems justified.[112]

Through contributions to World Student Relief, British students
played a key part in postwar educational reconstruction in Europe
and the Far East. WSR was recognized by the United Nations Relief
and Rehabilitation Administration (UNRRA) as a relief agency spe-
cializing "in the reconstruction of university life."[113] As after the

First World War, the principle of self-help ran through relief efforts; students couldn't possibly rebuild the destroyed universities, libraries and laboratories but they could offer short-term emergency aid to stimulate student self-help in war-torn countries. In summer 1945, NUS Congress resolved that British students were unaware of the true "extent and urgency" of the need for relief in European universities, partly because of the low profile of ISS committees at some universities.[114] The NUS, SCM and ISS began working together to increase awareness, resulting in a big increase in ISS funds. Along with students in the United States, the British Committee of ISS was one of the major donors to WSR in the 1940s, raising £16,357 in the 1945–1946 academic year of which £10,951 was collected in the universities and the rest through a national appeal.[115] Students showed a "great versatility" in fundraising through large-scale events on the pattern of prewar rag days.[116] In Liverpool, for instance, a Flag Day and Pageant raised over £1,000 and at Cambridge a large-scale Whitsuntide fair attracted thousands of visitors. This fundraising effort was seen as more impressive when set against a background of abnormal university conditions, as the immediate postwar student intakes consisted of a large number of ex-servicemen with "heavy personal responsibilities" such as wives and children.[117] The increased income allowed the British ISS branch to expand operations considerably, renting a large office with storage for relief supplies and residential accommodation for volunteers. In the 1940s ISS employed six secretaries based at key university towns in England and Scotland, whose work was supported by hundreds of student volunteers.[118] In the late 1940s British students raised money and supplied food, clothing and study materials to scores of universities across Europe as well as to Burma and Indonesia.[119] In addition to fundraising in the colleges, the British ISS committee solicited assistance for students overseas in the form of funds and supplies from the Council of British Societies for Relief Abroad and the Aid to Greece campaign. More than one hundred tons of food aid was shipped to European students between autumn 1945 and spring 1947. Compared to what it described as the "cold and impersonal" relief of official bodies, ISS claimed to have passed on a welcome "message of University Solidarity" to students and professors "whose lives were lived during the past few years in the fog of suspicion, fear and hatred attendant on conquest and occupation."[120]

A further form of postwar university reconstruction was the provision of rest centers for students from liberated Europe. The aim of such rest centers, which also operated in France, Italy and China, was to bring together "young people who have lived for years in unnatural conditions of imprisonment, slavery or underground resistance." [121] After a visit of British ISS leader James Henderson to see conditions in Eindhoven in April 1945, ISS opened a rest center for Dutch students in a rented country house called Ashton Hayes near Chester, selected for its proximity to the large student populations of Manchester and Liverpool.[122] Dutch students had been persecuted after the Nazi occupation of Holland, because the Nazis had viewed the universities as a breeding ground for opposition to their regime. Groups of 25–30 students—including survivors from Dachau and Ravensbrück concentration camps as well as those who had been active in the Dutch Resistance—travelled on three-month visas, spending a month at Ashton Hayes and a further two months in private houses all over Britain.[123] Over three hundred Dutch students and smaller numbers of Finnish, French and Italian students stayed at Ashton Hayes.

Students could do as they liked, some were keen to study while others content just to spend time in the house, chatting, listening to the radio and organizing dances with fellow students and local people. The ISS committees in Liverpool and Manchester arranged concerts, lectures and visits for the recuperating students and allowed them access to university facilities and libraries.[124] Unfortunately these civic universities' facilities were not universally admired. After a visit to Oxford "the dream of every student," student Adi Vries remarked "I hope my friends in Liverpool and Manchester will forgive me my strong preference for this old place."[125] Parties of students climbed Mount Snowdon or went hitchhiking without the persistent need to "lie low" and the "worry of false identity cards."[126] The stay in an English country house must have represented a whole new world for students used to life under the Nazis, where as one remembered, as a student "you carried your life in your hands...The Gestapo were waiting for you; you did not go home; you changed your address each night."[127] It was also a valuable form of intercultural education for British student volunteers. In addition to the rest center, a joint NUS-ISS student exchange scheme was also up and running in the first academic year after the war with students from countries including Italy, Denmark and Norway. British students thus played their part in a wider movement offering hospitality for youth groups from the occupied countries, displaced person camps or concentration camps.[128]

As after the First World War, student relief efforts were a central part of renewed attempts at promoting international student solidarity. After the war NUS helped establish a new International Union of Students, which agreed its constitution at a World Student Congress in Prague in 1946.[129] Making contact with German students was to be an important aspect of this work, but the question of sending aid to Germany was one on which the international student movement was divided in 1945. A report of the British ISS Committee was careful to note that aid sent to Germany in 1945–1946 was solely for "displaced persons."[130] Although a conference at Manchester University in August 1945 considered the topic of "Germany in Europe," the first postwar international Assembly of ISS held in March 1946, concluded there could be no question of establishing contact with German student organizations "which were still suspect."[131] At another gathering held in Cambridge in summer 1946 the needs of German students were raised once again and this time conference voted to send a commission to Germany.[132] The delegation that visited German universities in all four zones reported that "help must go to German students" who needed "food for their minds" in order to "recognise and value truth and tolerance."[133] This message was reinforced by a 1947 NUS delegation to the British zone, which urged that students should do all they should to help the aid work.[134] The emphasis of the relief efforts was on sending books and other literature, "adopting" German universities, as well as organizing student correspondence and exchange visits. For example, ULU "adopted" the Technical University of Berlin in 1946–1947.[135] Various voluntary organizations—including German Educational Reconstruction—collaborated in bringing parties of German students to work alongside British students and others on Ministry of Agricultural harvest camps. German students who participated in the 1947 camps valued the opportunities for "practical contact with democratic life" and chances to get to know and understand British young people which the camps afforded. The kindness of lorry drivers and others they had met on their travels at the end of the camp period was a particular feature of letters from students.[136]

The many British student delegations that visited Germany in the 1940s were an important aspect of moves to bring Germany back into contact with the rest of the world. The trip reports that appeared regularly in student magazines helped educate British students about the appalling living conditions of many Germans and emphasized the need for relief efforts that were not "charity" but essential intellectual contacts that would help to reduce Germany's isolation.[137] A further aspect of the denazification work was the involvement of British students in a burgeoning workcamp movement in postwar Germany. In September 1946, ISS Secretary Jim Henderson visited the British zone at the invitation of workcamp organization International Voluntary Service (IVS) and the Education Branch of the Civil Control Government (the interim military government responsible for the British zone), to witness the denazification process at first hand.[138] After some trial workcamps with students from Göttingen University, IVS had convinced the Control Commission to sanction workcamps.[139] International involvement was central to the social mixing judged necessary for a successful workcamp and from the late 1940s IVS sent a steady stream of British volunteers—many of whom were students—to Germany. Topics of discussions, both formal evening discussions and spontaneous conversations, were carefully recorded by each camp leader and in summer 1946 included "German youth," "Work camps, compulsory or voluntary," "Conditions of internment camps under the British," "The refugee problem" and "Esperanto."[140] Workcamps therefore emerged as a key strand in postwar reconstruction, offering British students opportunities for travel and cultural exchange, for developing practical skills and for making friends. Reporting in 1948 on the interest in overseas workcamps and the "thirst for adventure" among British students and young people, IVS envisaged a great future for overseas volunteering.[141]

By the later 1940s Cold War politics were threatening both student relief efforts and the wider movement for international student solidarity. The International Union of Students was dominated by the Eastern bloc and by 1950 NUS had disaffiliated and was involved in setting up a new International Student Conference. Although much postwar aid had been targeted at Eastern Europe, in March 1950 World Student Relief received a message that these students no longer wanted aid from the West. The WSR program was wound up in September 1950.[142] British students continued to raise money for ISS—known as World University Service from 1950—and as the scope of its activities contracted in Europe, the organization turned its attention further afield, as will be discussed in the next chapter.

CONCLUSIONS

By the middle years of the war, students left in the universities were committed to combining study with war work that would form what they termed the "students' contribution to victory." The crisis faced by NUS in 1940 found resolution in the coming together of students for the war effort and NUS embraced its new role in coordinating and publicizing students' leisure time and vacation war work. In addition to a big increase in scale, there was also a substantial change in the nature of voluntary work. Students helping in air raid shelters, rest centers and in rescue parties came face to face with the physical destruction and human cost of modern warfare on civilian populations. Entertaining troops or evacuated children, working in canteens, hosting refugee students and helping at nurseries may not have taken the same emotional toll, but they drew large numbers of students into contact with a wider range of people than they would otherwise have encountered. Wartime volunteering had, according to Jack Allanson, "eradicated entirely the anti-social student of the pre-war years."[143] Analysis of student voluntary activities during the war does suggest a shift in the attitudes of student volunteers. Few students taking part in the camps for unemployed during the 1930s, for instance, appeared to have questioned the economic structure that had produced unemployment. Their concerns were largely ameliorative. Moreover, earlier efforts constantly sought to bridge a perceived gap between students and "the community," without considering that students might belong to the communities discussed.

By 1942 there was also a strong theme of planning cutting through student responses to the war. Students, like others, were looking toward the postwar world. Records of the well-attended student congresses—over one thousand students in 1941, 1942 and 1943—showed that the relations of students to wider society were under much discussion, as well as wholesale reforms to university education.[144] In 1944, the NUS report on the "Future of University and Higher Education" explored the idea of a "Pre-University Year of Social Service," which might help break down the barriers that existed between students and other people and between universities and the outside world.[145] Such a suggestion reflected a long-standing idea that students' contributions to communities should stem from their position in society as university and college students—a reworking of the Platonic "education for leadership" idea. However, the report found students did not universally welcome this early suggestion for a "gap year" and concluded that the problems of integration might be better solved by drawing university students from a wider section of population than previously. From the mid 1940s the NUS and other student organizations consistently argued for increased access to university for students from a broader range of social backgrounds and better financial support. Despite domestic concerns, British students continued to look outward through fundraising for World Student Relief during and after the war and through participation in educational reconstruction efforts including exchanges with students in Germany and former occupied countries. This may be seen as part of a longer-term shift to student involvement in overseas aid that was to develop much more in the 1950s and 1960s.

CHAPTER 9

Experiments in Living: Student Social Service and Social Action, 1950–1965

A meeting held in February 1948 to decide how to allocate the balance of prewar funds of the Cambridge branch of the Universities' Camps for the Unemployed, concluded that "no form of social service in England now appealed to undergraduates in the way unemployed camps appealed to them before the war; and that what undergraduates wanted was to work abroad, in Germany and other European countries."[1] While reconstruction efforts did have strong appeal, such pronouncements on the death of domestic student voluntarism were to prove premature, and in time students' experience of overseas service was to inject new life into voluntary action in universities and colleges in Britain. Contrary to initial fears within the voluntary sector, the increase in state-provided welfare from the 1940s opened up more rather than fewer opportunities for volunteering. Although sometimes seen as a "forgotten decade" between the upheaval of world war and the significant social and cultural changes of the 1960s, this chapter shows that the 1950s marked the beginning of a new wave of student social action on a range of international and domestic issues, including juvenile delinquency, apartheid and antiracism, refugee students, and the antinuclear movement. There were innovations in domestic student volunteering in the 1950s—particularly in the field of youth work—that laid the groundwork for bigger shifts in the later 1960s. Increasingly wary that older models of student social service—such as clubs, camps and settlements—might be seen as patronizing, students developed new projects that aimed to meet changing social needs. In a period when perceived common youth identities began to trump older class consciousness, students had to seek new outlets for the student social consciousness. Exploring student voluntarism is one way to understand the significance of changes to student funding, residence and social life that marked the two decades after the war, and to recognize important shifts in students' position in society. By the mid-1960s, the universities had become a necessary constituency of support for a range of new voluntary organizations and campaigning groups, a theme that is taken up more fully in the succeeding chapter.

A STRONG MORAL ELEMENT? POSTWAR UNIVERSITY EXPANSION, RESIDENCE AND LEISURE

The three decades after the Second World War were marked by sustained growth in student numbers in Britain, with a particularly strong increase in the second half of the 1960s, a "spectacular" increase that was reflected across Western Europe.[2] Underpinning growth in absolute numbers was a range of factors including demographic shifts, changes to the secondary education system and the raising of the school leaving age, government desire to widen access combined with increased financial support for students, as well as the considerable widening of the definition of "higher education" to include both full-time and part-time students in a range of colleges and polytechnics in addition to the traditionally defined universities.[3] Before the war there had been around 50,000 students in universities across Britain, a figure which had more than doubled by 1962–1963 to 118,000—although this still represented just 4 percent of the age group.[4] By 1970, there were 262,000 students in British universities (of whom 30% were women) out of a higher education field of 600,000.[5] By 1980 827,000 or 13 percent of the age group were in full-time higher education.[6] In the 1960s overseas students made up 7 percent of the undergraduate body and a third of postgraduates, with most of these concentrated in London.[7]

Growth was due to considerable expansion of existing institutions, the gaining of university status by some former technical colleges and the foundation of new universities—there were 44 universities in Britain by 1970.[8] The first major postwar higher education institution—opened in 1949 as the University College of North Staffordshire (later Keele University) —influenced a series of new campus universities on greenfield sites, including Sussex (1961), York (1963), Essex (1964), Kent (1965), Warwick (1965) and Stirling (1967).[9] A number of technical colleges, including Bath, Loughborough, Brunel, City and Surrey, were granted College of Advanced Technology status in the late 1950 or early 1960s and also received university charters by the end of the 1960s. At the same time plans for a radically different "University of the Air" or Open University (OU) were under discussion by groups including the Labour Party and the BBC throughout the 1960s, and the OU admitted its first students in 1971. A significant factor behind expansion in the 1960s and 1970s in Britain was the findings of the Committee on Higher Education, which reported in 1963. Chaired by London School of Economics (LSE) professor Lionel Robbins, this was the first commission ever charged with investigating the UK higher education system. A key principle underlying the report's recommendations was that courses of higher education should be available for "all those who are qualified by ability and attainment to pursue them," a goal that envisaged an increase from around 4 percent to 10 or 15 percent of the age group.[10]

The social background of students was also changing, albeit slowly. In the 1950s and early 1960s university students were still overwhelmingly middle class.[11] In 1961–1962 almost three-quarters (71%) of British undergraduates came from the families of nonmanual workers. Reflecting prewar patterns, the proportion of working-class students taking science and technology subjects was higher than for arts or medicine, and it was higher in Wales and at English civic universities than at Oxford, Cambridge or London. Indeed the Robbins Report concluded that between 1928 and 1961 there was almost no change in the number of students coming from working-class homes. By the 1950s three-quarters of university students in England and Wales received some state or local authority assistance (although only half of students in Northern Ireland did so).[12] The number of local education authority (LEA) awards in England and Wales made to new university students doubled to 15,000 a year between 1950–1951 and 1957–1958, and these grants were brought in line with the scales of the more prestigious state scholarships.[13] The Education Act of 1962 phased out state scholarships and introduced means-tested LEA grants to cover the costs of maintenance and fees for all students with a university place and two "A level" passes.[14] In Scotland, these grants were administered centrally by the Scottish Education department. Grants were reduced by parental contributions assessed according to an income scale, although a minimum grant was payable however wealthy the parents. Women students remained a minority, around a quarter of all students in the early 1960s. As Shelia Rowbotham notes "young women in the 1960s were more likely to get to 'teachers' training colleges' than universities."[15] Postwar changes in schooling, however, meant that only a fifth of undergraduates (22%) had attended independent schools, with the rest mainly coming from grammar or direct grant schools. With improvements to grants and a greater range of choice of institution, students' social backgrounds widened further in the later 1960s and 1970s. There were also higher numbers of mature students, part-time students and students living at home. In 1970 part-time students and Open University students together accounted for 16 percent of university students.[16]

In addition to student publications and memoirs, evidence for the postwar student experience comes from the mass of data gathered as part of the Robbins Committee on Higher Education and several independent studies including Peter Marris's 1964 research for the Institute of Community Studies and Ferdynand Zweig's 1962 survey of Oxford and Manchester students undertaken at the request of the *Daily Herald*.[17] Harold Silver and Pamela Silver have argued that much of the research into students in the 1950s and 1960s focussed on issues of success and failure, particularly mental health and "wastage."[18] Marris's research, for example, revealed that despite students coming from more diverse backgrounds than before the war, higher education remained a minority experience which tended to cut students off from the majority of their age group. In Marris's analysis universities were "institutions for the recruitment of a social elite," which led to students suffering "a sense of anomie which impairs their existence." Similarly, Zweig uncovered strained relationships with siblings who were left behind in "educational and social terms" as a result of not going to university.[19]

In contrast to the prewar generations it was much more common for students to undertake paid work during the vacations in the 1950s and 1960s, often in manual roles as barmen, taxi-drivers, kitchen hands, shop assistants, dustmen or hospital orderlies.[20] Such jobs "would enable [students] to mix as equals with men and women from whom, later, their career would set them apart" according to Marris.[21] Vacation jobs had been all but impossible for prewar students—not least because of high unemployment and trade union opposition—but labor shortages in the 1950s led various local authorities to look to students. In March 1956, for example, Nottingham City Transport appealed for three hundred students for vacation and Saturday work as bus conductors because of a "desperate shortage" of regular staff.[22] However, term time work was still relatively uncommon, with 90 percent of students undertaking no paid work or working for less than five hours a week in 1962.[23] A further change was national service. At the end of the war 18-year-olds continued to receive call-up papers but in 1947 a formal scheme of national service was introduced for all men who had to enrol for two years. Although they could defer until after graduation, the majority of men with a university place chose to do national service first, arriving at university with greater maturity and a wider range of experiences to draw upon.[24] While previous generations had often gained independence through living at boarding school, this was less the case in the 1950s and 1960s, when increasing numbers of students came to university without ever having been away from home for longer than a few nights.

Residential patterns had also changed somewhat, with students less likely to live at home in 1962 compared to before the war. However, residence was still determined by long-standing traditions. In the Scottish universities it was very common to live at home with parents and over a fifth of students at the larger civic universities like Manchester (21%), Liverpool (31%) and Newcastle (20%) stayed at home.[25] Students from poorer backgrounds were less likely to live in university accommodation. Halls provided the center of social life for residents with regular programs of dances, talks, concerts, hobbies clubs, sports fixtures and summer plays.[26] However, as the age of majority was only lowered from 21 to 18 in 1969, for most of the period under study students were *in statu pupillari* and many halls were run on old-fashioned lines with all powerful wardens, gate-hours and visitor restrictions that conflicted with students' desire for greater independence. Yet the concept that residence was necessary for the building of corporate culture remained widespread. Despite extensive building programs at many universities, the supply of halls of residence struggled to meet demand, while the first students enrolling at the new universities found that accommodation blocks had often not yet been built. In the 1950s and 1960s living in lodgings was a common experience for many students, and student handbooks contained pages of advice about how to master "the art of lodgership," including tips on how to get on the good side of landladies.[27]

Recalling Nottingham University in the 1950s, Dulcie Groves argued that student life was built around university societies.[28] Perhaps surprisingly, in the 1950s and early 1960s students were more likely to be actively involved in a religious society than a political one. For instance, around a quarter of students belonged to a university based religious group or society at Leeds (23%) and Southampton (24%) and this rose to 31 percent at Cambridge.[29] Zweig found the Catholic Society—with 450 students—to be the most popular and active society at Manchester University, followed by the Film Society and the Rhythm Club.[30] Around a third attended a religious service at least once a week. The national membership of the Student Christian Movement (SCM) had shrunk to around 7,500 in the mid-1950s, its membership depleted by the growth of denominational student societies since the war, but its influence remained out of proportion to its numbers.[31] In Oxford, one student reported that "the SCM is like the...Communists; they're behind everything."[32] At the new universities the first intake of students had to found societies for themselves, often the first such to be created were film clubs, drama groups, debating societies and rag committees.

In the 1950s and 1960s many students' union buildings were rebuilt or extended to cope with greater numbers of students as well as to meet growing demands for licensed bars, coffee bars and other facilities. Of course many students also took advantage of the social and cultural life of the towns in which they were located, particularly cinema and theater-going, as well as classical, jazz and, later, pop music concerts. Another sign of the changing times was the occasional report in student papers of the increased consumption of marijuana and other drugs. Yet Zweig reflected that the students he encountered were serious and prematurely old, describing a typical student as "conscious that he was kept by the tax-payer and had to repay his debt to society."[33] Indeed, as Michael Sanderson remarked of the new University of East Anglia, there was a "strong moral element in student leisure life" from the start.[34] Changes to residential patterns, funding, national service and part-time employment meant that students often had knowledge and experience of a greater range of individuals and communities than before the war. Male students were on average two years older than their female counterparts in the 1950s. However, opinion varied on how much contact students had— or ought to have—with the world outside the university, a debate that intensified with the spread of the greenfield campus model of university.[35] In 1960, Sheffield student E. C. Barrett concluded that "an undergraduate population is one of the most selfish communities in Britain today" in an article criticizing fellow students for living in a university "fortress."[36] Barrett suggested it was perfectly possible for students to combine academic work, university activities as well as be "engaged in some form of service to our adopted home town." [37] Such motivations were behind moves in the 1950s and 1960s to find new outlets for the student social consciousness, which this chapter now explores.

A STUDENT VOLUNTEER BOOM?

In the 1940s and early 1950s consternation about the possible impact of state welfare services on the voluntary sector and volunteers was widespread.[38] Speaking at an International Student Service (ISS) conference in summer 1948, Professor W. Rose raised the concerns of the

British ISS committee about the threatened "extinction" of voluntary organizations under the socialization of the state.[39] While ISS had experienced a rising income in the mid-1940s on the back of student commitment to European relief and reconstruction, by 1950 it had to retrench and reduce its staffing levels, with the Treasurer remarking rather bitterly that while government "leaders stress incessantly the importance to society of voluntary work" this was not matched by financial support.[40] Fears of extinction were of course not to be realized, and while it was expected at the time that the expansion of state welfare would leave some continuing role for voluntary organizations, the actual form this might take was unclear.[41] In particular, this was a debate about the changing nature of voluntary work, especially the place of volunteers in the state-run welfare services. Voluntary sector leaders were loud in proclaiming the continued need for volunteers, particularly in National Health Service management, hospital visiting and domiciliary services for old and sick people. A 1949 House of Lords debate on Lord Beveridge's *Voluntary Action* report recognized that the work of voluntary organizations was sustained by "a small number of paid officers, but mainly by a great multitude of unpaid workers."[42] Several of the contributors to this debate specifically mentioned the role of volunteers. For example, speaking on behalf of the Government, Lord Pakenham noted that "It is quite wrong to assume that nationalisation of any social service excludes the volunteer."[43]

Voluntary organizations which had traditionally relied on student fundraising and volunteering were particularly concerned. The 1940s and 1950s were a tough time for university settlements which faced a slackening of support from their sponsor institutions at the same time as having to deal with the underinvestment and physical damage of six years of war. In 1950, for example, students at women's colleges responded to an emergency appeal on behalf of the Women's University Settlement to help plug its operating deficit.[44] In 1952, the Head of Cambridge House, Mr Deuchars, indentified student indifference as stemming both from a negative "contemporary attitude to the necessity for voluntary service" and the changing social background of undergraduates, who no longer had either the income to financially support settlements or the leisure for voluntary service.[45] Yet settlements and boys' and girls' clubs did continue to receive steady if low level support from students and recent graduates, particularly those also active in the SCM, although the nature of such help was changing.[46] The British Association of Residential Settlements recorded that while fewer people were able to give full-time unpaid service, greater numbers of part-time volunteers were coming forward.[47] In the 1950s most settlements continued to have some long-term residents, often students and trainees who lived cheaply in exchange for help with clubs and activities.[48] Connections were maintained with universities through short residential courses for undergraduates interested in social service and by continued sports fixtures, camps and club visits to colleges. Cambridge House, for example, not only had 25 long-term residents including medical students and postgraduates but also received 79 Cambridge undergraduates on short visits during 1958–1959.[49]

Having survived for almost a century it was not until the later 1960s and 1970s that the residential volunteer model was fundamentally questioned.[50] With all meals provided in the settlements, residents had little occasion to shop locally or visit neighborhood pubs and it was recognized that "it is difficult for residents largely from a middle-class background to feel much of a part of the local community."[51] Although some settlements tried to revitalize their residential programs in the 1970s, by the 1980s few settlements had residents, and links to universities were tenuous at best. The umbrella body— the British Association of Settlements—had already dropped the word "residential" from its title in 1967. Annual reports repeatedly expressed surprise that the settlement model should have survived into the 1960s and 1970s. As Kate Bradley notes, the central idea that a settlement resident should be a leader of the local community "held little weight before the Second World War; it held less afterwards."[52]

By the 1960s there was general agreement that "everyone's basic needs should be met by statutory sources if they are unable to meet them by their own efforts," as voluntary sector commentator Mary Morris summed up.[53] Hence voluntary organizations were no longer needed to provide basic food, shelter or medical care, but were seen to retain a vital role in giving additional help to individuals, communities and causes as well as in pioneering new services. One of the outcomes of fresh thinking about the nature of voluntary service during the later 1950s and early 1960s was a big expansion in organizations that recruited and deployed young volunteers.[54] By the early 1970s this change was so significant that the Director of the newly formed Volunteer Centre, Mike Thomas, felt the general stereotype of volunteers had shifted from "middle-aged do-gooders" to "long haired youngsters alternating between decorating old people's flats and trying to organise a revolution."[55] Indeed, the 1960s were portrayed by commentators as marking a "youth volunteer boom," a phrase coined by Tim Dartington in his 1971 account of youth volunteering agency Task Force, but popularized in several articles by Jos Sheard in the 1980s and 1990s.[56] Sheard argued that after a low ebb in the immediate postwar period, the 1960s saw a major revival of interest in volunteering as it was realized that volunteers could make significant contributions to state run services and that volunteering was a safe and constructive outlet for the otherwise unpredictable energies of young people.[57] This thesis has recently been challenged. Far from being an afterthought introduced in the 1960s and 1970s, the introduction of state welfare services in the 1940s and 1950s depended on the work of volunteers.[58]

The expansion of volunteering by young people in the 1960s built on developments from the mid-1950s which included a number of new university initiatives organized to meet the perceived needs of a new generation, with a strong focus on "unattached" youth and young "delinquents." Concern about juvenile delinquency had been high on the policy agenda from the 1940s and featured as the subject of several government commissions, academic research papers and conferences in the 1950s.[59] Part of the debate centered on inadequate provision of suitable leisure time activities for youth, and the challenges of securing appropriate paid and volunteer youth workers. For instance, the Albermarle Committee on the youth service, which reported in 1960, called for a national campaign for more voluntary helpers in youth clubs.[60] In the late 1950s and 1960s several universities took up the challenge. In 1958, Queens University Belfast founded a new youth club in the vicinity of the university, aiming at bringing so-called teddy boys and "social misfits" into closer contact with the wider community. Staffed by a full-time warden supported by student volunteers, the club was in part funded through rag collections.[61] A similar youth project established by Nottingham Students' Union in 1960 opened its own youth club in 1963, while the University of London Union (ULU) established a "Youth Council" in 1960 to encourage students to become volunteers in London youth clubs.[62] Zweig reported that many Oxford students were interested in youth work in clubs, boys' brigade or borstals.[63] The National Association of Boys' Clubs employed a series of University Liaison Officers in the late 1950s to tap universities as a source of volunteers for youth clubs; officers toured the universities and arranged undergraduate visits to clubs and remand homes.[64] One of these staff, Patrick Coldstream, found it easier to attract interest at Oxford and Cambridge where it was possible to "reawaken a dormant tradition of this kind of service," than at other universities.[65] Moreover, attempts to encourage large-scale volunteering with youth clubs were hampered by students' reluctance to appear patronizing or condescending. Despite recurrent appeals for volunteers, the general trend in youth work was toward trained, paid staff, supported by leaders recruited from the club's own membership.

Another new development that drew on Oxford's long tradition of Christian-inspired social service was the Oxford-Borstal camp scheme that ran between 1957 and the early 1970s.[66] These "adventures in living" brought undergraduates of all Christian denominations to share camp life with boys from borstals (detention centers for young offenders) with the goal of establishing lasting bonds of friendship. Participating colleges were paired with different borstals; while within each camp two Oxford "men" shared a tent with two borstal "boys." Campers took part in activities very similar to those of the interwar camps for unemployed men including manual labor, hiking, sports and visits to places of interest including RAF stations and public schools.[67] The initiative originated in the desire of the Chaplain of Pembroke College Oxford to find some practical vacation volunteering for undergraduates because he felt the traditional college mission model no longer suitable for a mixed denominational student society. Over the period around two thousand students took part, and the model spawned imitators at other universities including Cambridge, Nottingham and Glasgow. Like earlier attempts at cross-class comradeship, relationships between undergraduates and borstal boys were not easy to build because of "difference of accent, vocabulary, interests and present way of life."[68] One borstal trainee reported that "what we thought was fun they thought it was stupid. What they [students] thought was fun, we were just bored."[69] Yet friendly relations were often established and correspondence and visits continued for some time after the camps. The program had an explicit goal of social education for the students, who after the camp were able to spend four or five days living in a borstal. As with much student volunteering, reminiscences of participants dwelled on the enjoyment and the enriching experience, without much reflection on the wider impact of the scheme.[70] However, for those student volunteers who took part, the experiences gained in boys' and girls' clubs or on borstal camps was often inspiration for careers as social workers, probation officers, teachers and almoners.[71]

In the 1950s, then, there were a number of largely unsuccessful attempts to reestablish links between the universities and clubs or settlements, together with a few new initiatives that often drew on older patterns of service. It was clear that new outlets for the student service ethic were needed. One such was the Hull University Social

Service Organisation (HUSSO), set up in 1960–1961 on the initiative of Derek Forster, a mature student from a working-class background, in order to "improve relations with the citizens of Hull."[72] Its first large-scale activity was in planting a scented garden for blind people. Similarly, in 1959 and 1960 groups of Christian students at Sheffield University organized workcamps decorating community centers and flats for blind people.[73] Students formed similar university social service organizations at several universities including London, Bristol, Cambridge, Hull, Manchester, Birmingham and Swansea. Data collected by the National Union of Students (NUS) in 1969 estimated that around 5 to 10 percent of the student population was involved in such community service schemes.[74] Typical activities included decorating and gardening projects, visiting hospitals or children's homes, working with children and older people. Practical gardening and decorating projects drew on the workcamp tradition, which was itself revitalized in the late 1950s with a number of new projects led by the Civic Trust and other organizations.[75] Activities such as visiting older people in their homes, once the preserve of ladies' visiting societies, were colonized by youth and student service groups. Thus students played a leading part in a wider youth social service movement from the late 1950s that resulted in the formation of a number of new schemes including the Duke of Edinburgh's Award (1956), Voluntary Service Overseas (1958), Community Service Volunteers (1962), Task Force (1964), Young Volunteer Force Foundation (1968) and scores more regional and local organizations.[76] Many of these bodies recruited staff that had cut their teeth as student volunteers at boys' and girls' clubs, workcamps or settlements.

OUR HEADLINE MUST BE HUNGARY: INTERNATIONAL CONCERNS AND UNIVERSITIES IN THE 1950S

Although a stereotype of 1960s student radicals tends to dominate our view of postwar student activism, it was the 1950s that marked the beginning of a new wave of student social action on a range of international issues including apartheid and antiracism, refugee students, and the antinuclear movement. Soviet intervention in Hungary in October 1956 together with the British and French invasion of the Suez Canal, were important turning points for the student movement as for the emergence of the New Left.[77] Student publications repeatedly stated that events in Hungary and Suez had moved the universities more deeply than anything since the Spanish Civil War and had shattered "the apathy of the student world."[78] By 1960 a student editorial could assert that "most undergraduates are usually angry about something whether it be the bomb, birth control, refugees, apartheid, [or] anti-Semitism."[79]

The Soviet invasion of Hungary in October 1956 had a big impact on British universities. When the uprising—which began as a student demonstration—was put down by Hungarian state police supported by Soviet troops (who invaded on November 4), there was widespread and immediate "revulsion throughout the student world."[80] Students organized protest marches and rallies in cities including Glasgow, Cardiff, Bristol and Birmingham.[81] University College, for example, organized a petition of 1,256 signatures which it presented to the Soviet Ambassador and a silent "dead march" of 1,500 students past the Soviet Embassy. In Bristol, the Hungarian flag was flown at half mast on the union buildings and students laid a wreath at the city's cenotaph to show sympathy with the suffering of Hungarian students.[82] Around a thousand Manchester students signed a petition supporting the student rising, and hundreds crowded into the union hall to hear about conditions in Hungary from Hungarians already living in the city.[83] Some talked of recruiting an international force of students to go Hungary to fight, a "second International Brigade," that the Sheffield University paper *Darts* considered wholly unrealistic, despite the sincerity of its organizers, and the scheme was quickly abandoned.[84] Others began to raise money for the Red Cross or the Lord Mayor's Fund and recruited volunteer parties to prepare refugee centers.[85] Two Oxford students travelled to Vienna to start relief work among refugees with money from a special fund raised by the university.[86] Shaken out of apathy—as one report put it reflecting New Left rhetoric —college branches of the SCM in most universities instigated or participated in meetings, debates and petitions about Hungary.[87] As in the world more widely, Hungary impacted on student politics— the Glasgow University Communist Club was apparently the only student organization in Britain to stand by Russian action.[88] Attempts by the leaders of the Sheffield University Communist Society to denigrate the Hungarian uprising caused outrage at a meeting, and led to a front page *Darts* protest article by two refugee students.[89] Caroline Hoefferle has recently argued that the Suez crisis elicited more student protest than Hungary, but my analysis of student newspapers reveals that the Hungarian crisis and subsequent relief effort had a bigger impact on the student population as a whole.[90] For every student who felt moved to political action over Suez, such as campaigning, protesting or writing to his or her MP, there were several others who felt that taking practical steps for Hugarian refugees was the better course of action.[91] Indeed one article in ULU paper *Sennet* noted that although it was still the Suez crisis making headlines in the daily press, "our headlines must be Hungary."[92]

The most significant university response was in raising money to enable Hungarian refugees to study in British universities and colleges. Initial fundraising for general relief soon turned to raising money for this specific cause. Help and support for refugee students had been a theme running through student social service from campaigns for exiled Russian students in the 1920s to programs in the early 1950s for Arab students following the termination of the British Mandate in Palestine.[93] Work for Hungary was on a much bigger scale. Following an emergency visit to Austria by several university leaders, in November 1956 the Committee of Vice Chancellors and Principals made available 150 places for selected student refugees in British universities, and further groups were admitted in 1957.[94] Refugee students who arrived through other channels were put into contact with World University Service, which led a coordinating committee to manage the different agencies helping students. Universities waived fees and raised money through local appeals amounting to over £56,000, but the main bulk of the money to support students (around £145,000) came from the Lord Mayor's Fund, which had opened in early November, and from other sources including the Ford Foundation.[95] After initially agreeing to admit just 2,500 Hungarian refugees, Britain ended up admitting over 21,000.[96] Although the numbers are little unclear, perhaps around one thousand Hungarian students sought assistance in Britain and in 1959 there were five hundred studying in British universities and technical colleges.[97] Others were helped with advice, retraining or in finding jobs. About 90 percent of the refugees arriving were men, and most were medical, dental or engineering students who might be "expected to fit easily into the economy of the country."[98]

This effort for Hungarian students was described by Sir John Lockwood (1903–1965), then Vice-Chancellor of the University of London, as "one of the most impressive acts of cooperation in the history of the universities of the UK."[99] Refugee students were spread across Britain with Oxford, Cambridge, Manchester, London, Glasgow and Edinburgh taking the largest numbers. Student reception centers were established at five universities and undergraduates were involved in setting up hostels and welcoming the arrivals. In London, for example, staff and students worked together to equip a hostel, organize Christmas visits to host families, provide meals in the ULU refectory and recruit volunteer staff and students to teach

English.[100] The refugees' arrival caused widespread interest and curiosity on campus. Durham's newspaper *Palatinate* declared it was the duty of everyone "from the Warden down to the youngest and newest student" to support the Hungarian students in Durham.[101] At Cardiff University College, the vice-chancellor deemed it a moral obligation for students to pay a 10 shilling "levy" voted by the students' union, which had aroused some protest.[102] In Edinburgh, it was soon clear that students did not have the clothing to face a Scottish winter, and after new suits and boots were ordered, "morale improved immensely."[103] Participation in the relief effort was widely seen as rewarding and worthwhile by those involved, while the cause was strengthened by reports depicting Hungarian students as "of good material," and appreciative of all that was done for them.[104]

In 1958 two LSE students—Alan Dare and Paul Hollander, himself a refugee—conducted a survey into the experiences of Hungarian students in Britain which found that the refugees had "received extremely favourable treatment" and were on the whole satisfied with their university experience.[105] It revealed that the students had largely adapted to life in Britain, were generally satisfied with financial and material conditions and had formed friendly if not intimate relations with British people, despite unsurprising problems of loneliness and homesickness.[106] Far fewer refugee students had returned to Hungary than refugees from the wider population. Magda Czigány's 2009 study of Hungarian student refugees similarly argued that the refugees had found a warm reception in British universities. However, a number of Hungarians felt that many British students were "badly informed, isolated from and indifferent to what they feel to be the vital issues of our time."[107] Writing of his first year in England, Hollander remarked that he and his fellow students were being looked after still in a way which seems "unprecedented in the long and gloomy history of refugees in this century."[108] Perhaps the universities' effort for Hungary in 1956 was a way of making unspoken amends for what now seemed a wholly inadequate response to the plight of Jewish students in the 1930s, but it also reflected new Cold War considerations.[109] One motivation cited in the papers of the vice-chancellors' committee was that other countries such as West Germany and France had offered to accept students.[110] However, the records of the relief committee do reveal some consternation that the reception should not be overgenerous. Dare and Hollander reported that a number of "fairy stories" were circulating about the levels of grants for refugees.[111] In a period before grants were automatically allocated to all students with a university place, there were concerns that refugee students' claims be handled in an equitable fashion "and in a way that is fair to the poorer students always within our own country."[112]

MARCHES ARE ALL THE FASHION NOW: INTERNATIONAL CAUSES IN THE UNIVERSITIES

Shifts in fundraising methods reflected students' changing position in society in the 1950s. An increasing amount of money was raised for WUS and other causes through students' "personal service" or "bob-a-job" schemes, where students cleaned shoes, ironed shirts, darned socks, polished cars, trimmed hedges, washed hair and made sandwiches in return for small donations.[113] It is hard to imagine pre-war undergraduates taking part in such activities and may have been part of a deliberate attempt on the part of students to show themselves in a new light to the public in the 1950s. This was a time when the NUS, in particular, was keen to challenge a widespread image of students as a "privileged, irresponsible and lazy minority."[114] Women students continued to play an important role in fundraising efforts in the universities; WUS and rag secretaries in the 1950s and 1960s were very often women. After a wartime hiatus the student rag tradition was revived with increasingly outrageous stunts avidly reported by an eager local and national press; rags were raising around £200,000 each year in the 1950s.[115] Rag continued to be a focal point of extra-curricular life in many universities and colleges, involving large numbers of students.[116] News of rag preparations and after-the-event postmortems dominated student newspapers in the 1950s. Colleges and universities founded in the postwar period, such as Keele, found that rags could be useful in fostering a common student identity, as well as being one of the few known ways for students to make contact with the community outside the university. However, students' exuberance could cause problems with local communities if rag pranks crossed over into vandalism or criminal damage. In 1958 the NUS executive issued a statement urging restraint lest the "interests and reputation of students generally" be damaged.[117]

Stunts were a key plank of student rag and increasingly adapted as fundraising methods for other causes in the 1950s, notably World Refugee Year (WRY), a United Nations designated fundraising and awareness-raising campaign that ran from July 1959 to July 1960. In Britain, WRY was coordinated by a committee which counted Queen Elizabeth II as patron and was peopled by establishment figures.[118] One of the originators of WRY, journalist and future politician Timothy Raison (1929–2011), pointed to the universities' "terrific efforts" as one of the most remarkable aspects of the whole campaign.[119] Scores of student events were organized to raise money for Oxfam, Save the Children Fund, Christian Aid and War on Want under the aegis of WRY, as well as for the central WRY committee. Sponsored marches ("all the fashion now" according to Raison) and the technique of starvation or bread and cheese lunches (pioneered by SCM members for War on Want in the mid-1950s) were two of the most popular methods. At Bristol University these bread and cheese lunches, which attracted 250 students each week, became *the* place to be seen.[120] Bristol students also ran a "Refugee Gift Shop" in the city center over Christmas 1959.[121] Many colleges donated the profits of their 1959–1960 rags to the cause, as well as indulging in a range of other stunts such as an "action painting" contest in Oxford, a Manchester refugee village camp, a march on crutches through Edinburgh and a number of "commando raids" on offices in the city of London.[122] London students' 130 mile "Pilgrimage of Youth" from Winchester to Canterbury attracted considerable media attention.[123] Edinburgh raised £4,000 during a special "WRY Week" and ULU organized a Carnival, which raised £3,000 jointly for WUS and World Refugee Year through a fashion show, jazz night, beer drinking contest and street collection.[124] Despite the total being three times the previous year's sum raised for WUS alone, the organizing committee pointed to donor fatigue at the end of a year that had featured so many student fundraising events. Although intended to promote awareness as much as raise money, WRY in the universities turned into a sort of year-long glorified rag. Yet student involvement in WRY contributed considerably to the "blend of innovative campaigning, energetic organisation and theatricality," as Peter Gatrell describes it, which saw the UK campaign raising over £9 million out of a world total of £35 million.[125]

Although ISS/WUS had been a pioneer organization in mobilizing British students for international causes and while it continued to fund development projects in universities across Asia, Latin America and Africa, by the late 1950s and early 1960s WUS was losing ground to a number of other organizations concerned with international affairs as well as to student political groups infused with New Left thinking.[126] Universities were well-placed to contribute time and money to immediate crises and one-off causes like Hungary, WRY or the Universities and Colleges Aid to Congo appeal fund (started to help refugees and victims of the war in Congo 1961). However, there was a widespread feeling that student support for any international cause was hard to sustain.[127] As part of these reflections, students began to question the value of fundraising stunts such as those organized for WRY or the Freedom from Hunger Campaign in the early 1960s. Although students recognized that "students can stunt and get away with anything...we realise that a stunt is no substitute for understanding the problems of hunger."[128] By the end of the 1960s an altogether more earnest approach to fundraising which went hand in hand with development education was being developed by new groups such as Third World First, as the next chapter discusses. In addition to fundraising, other forms of volunteering and social action were developed by students through their participation in a range of causes in the 1950s and 1960s. There is little space here to discuss these different campaigns and organizations in any detail—and they have been extensively studied elsewhere[129]—but it is worth noting that student support for such new causes as the Campaign for Nuclear Disarmament (CND), the Anti-Apartheid Movement and Amnesty International was significant, and to briefly outline students' contributions.

From the mid-1950s the universities and colleges became "saturated" by discussion on the topic of nuclear disarmament; as students emerged as a group more opposed to the testing and manufacture of nuclear weapons than many other sections of society.[130] Several colleges held polls on the H-Bomb in 1958–1959 and a 1960 survey of 2,919 students across seven universities found a high degree of awareness of the problems of nuclear weapons; 60 percent of students had read a book or pamphlet on the topic and 37 percent had attended a meeting or debate on nuclear disarmament.[131] A large majority (87%) were in favor of controlled disarmament by international agreement, but given the existing situation students were divided on what Britain's response should be, with 21 percent in favor of unilateral disarmament but 29 percent prefering continued development of the British nuclear deterrent with American aid.[132] This high level of concern was reflected in the mass character of support for CND on campuses in the early 1960s.[133] At University College, for instance, the CND branch had 400–500 members out of a possible 3,500 students.[134] Students took part in significant numbers in the wave of antinuclear protests called by CND, particularly on the Aldermaston marches from 1958. However, as Jodi Burkett argues, CND's middle-aged leadership was not entirely comfortable with this mass student membership, which it had neither expected nor wanted.[135] In 1960 a "specialised group," the Colleges and Universities CND (CUCaND), was started to coordinate the activities of college branches and to publicize and support the work of both CND and its breakaway direct action arm the Committee of 100.[136] Large numbers of Christian students in the movement also gave rise to a specific Christian section.

CUCaND organized study conferences, distributed material to fresh-
ers and supported the wider CND movement by deploying students
in "flying columns" in advance of big marches. For example, at Easter
1962, a thousand students formed the "flying column," leafleting,
canvassing the public, holding street corner meetings and selling the
CND journal *Sanity* at points along the Aldermaston march route.[137]
Participation gave many students experience of a range of protest,
campaigning and direct action methods. By the mid-1960s, however,
CND was in decline across the universities as in wider society and the
peace baton was passed to other groups, notably university "Peace in
Vietnam" societies.

The question of South Africa also appeared on students' agenda in
the mid-1950s as articles critical of the introduction and extension of
apartheid laws began to appear in student papers. One London student used interest in the Hungarian crisis as a way to raise the profile
of South Africa, where conditions were "even worse than the recent
suffering of the Hungarian people."[138] The attempted reintroduction
of legislation to segregate South African universities in 1959 prompted
a higher level of student protest than previously, and also drew larger
numbers into fundraising to enable non-white South Africans to "beat
the bill" and enrol at universities before segregation became law.[139]
Prevented by its constitution from speaking out about apartheid in
general, in November 1959 NUS Council passed a motion calling on
unions to implement a boycott of South African goods as a protest
to the Separate Universities Bill. The boycott developed widespread
support across universities and colleges, although there were problems drawing up a list of goods and firms to boycott.[140] The Separate
Universities Bill also prompted one of the largest student demonstrations ever seen in London when ten thousand students marched from
Hyde Park to Trafalgar Square.[141] Students also became a reliable
constituency for smaller antiapartheid protests around the country—
for example, students made up just under a third of the 150 strong
march in Newcastle in November 1959.[142] One Cardiff supporter of
the boycott claimed that students had "never been more united than
in their fight against apartheid."[143] However, despite strong support
for the boycott from student Labour, Liberal and religious organizations as well as such new groups as JACARI (Joint Action Committee
Against Racial Intolerance) at Oxford—at this early date boycott of
goods or sporting events was not unanimously accepted throughout
the student world as the most effective way of attacking apartheid.[144]
Although support fluctuated, by 1965 there were antiapartheid groups
at most universities and the newly formed Anti-Apartheid Movement

(AAM) had begun publishing a special student newsletter. In his history of the Anti-Apartheid Movement, Roger Fieldhouse notes that despite varying levels of interest at the universities, student support was crucial in AAM demonstrations and rallies as well as in the long-running boycott of Barclays Bank in the 1970s and 1980s.[145]

Student concern for peace, equality and antiracism worldwide found expression through a wide range of organizations in the 1950s and 1960s. The universities emerged as a key constituency of support for Amnesty International, launched in 1961 by lawyer Peter Beneson (1921–2005) initially as short-term campaign on the model of World Refugee Year.[146] In its first year Beneson spoke at most of the universities and found students quick to form "threes"—groups who undertook to work for the release of three prisoners. Oxford University had 12 active groups by summer 1962, while the LSE, Keele, Sheffield and St Andrews were also among the first to form groups.[147] Amnesty's early campaigns of letter writing to prisoners of conscience generated great enthusiasm among students.[148] In addition to college CND or Amnesty branches, groups including the United Nations Student Association (UNSA), SCM, political societies and various international clubs also discussed and took action on topics including racism in the United Kingdom, nuclear weapons, apartheid South Africa and Rhodesia. Membership of student organizations overlapped considerably and participation in college activities fluctuated according to the charisma, skill and publicity-consciousness of student leaders. However, Ian Hopwood, an UNSA student volunteer in the 1960s, identified a number of challenges with the structure of many student organizations, whereby success was judged on rising or falling branch membership rather than the effectiveness of particular campaigns.[149] Many student groups, he argued, were so concerned with pleasing the parent body that they failed to work with other groups in coordinated action. Dissatisfaction with such organization was a key factor behind the rapid success of the innovative Third World First movement in the universities in the later 1960s.

Conclusions

Students were to be central to the "explosion of social innovation" that marked the 1960s, yet in the two decades after the end of the Second World War, undergraduates and staff were uncertain of the best outlets for the student social conscience.[150] The traditional institutions and models of student social service—clubs, camps and settlements—continued to appeal to some students, especially at the older universities, but they were increasingly irrelevant to the new generation of grant-aided students, conscious of charges that these activities were condescending or patronizing to people outside the universities. A strong moral—and indeed often specifically Christian—strand of thinking ran through student social action in the 1950s and into the 1960s. Moreover, despite continued accusations of "apathy", as in previous generations, students sought to engage with the perceived social needs of the day—such as the concern for vulnerable and sick people living in institutions and older people living alone—through new, student-run conduits like workcamps and university social service groups. There was an increase in term-time volunteering for students who were more likely than in previous generations to live away from home and to undertake paid work in vacations. From the mid-1950s the focus of British student interest and sympathy in overseas affairs shifted from European reconstruction to issues of refugees, racism and educational inequality worldwide. Events in Suez, the Hungarian refugee crisis, the H-bomb tests and growing awareness of apartheid led to greater student discussion of social and political issues that at any time since the 1930s. While activism on any issue—whether Suez, antiapartheid, CND or antiracism—was confined to a small minority of students, activities to aid refugee students or high-profile campaigns such as WRY succeeded in drawing larger numbers of students into voluntary action. Rag weeks, bread-and-cheese lunches, fundraising hops and spectacular stunts were well-supported regular features of student leisure life in the 1950s and early 1960s. The concept of international student cooperation—in support of students in South Africa or Hungary, for instance—remained a strong motivating factor for British students and WUS was an important recipient of student fundraising throughout the 1950s. As student numbers increased to represent a greater proportion of the population during the later 1960s and 1970s, this idea was to be replaced by a broader commitment to those facing poverty or injustice worldwide. From the early 1960s student support was a vital force behind the rapid growth of such new groups as CND, Amnesty International and the Anti-Apartheid Movement, and thus many other nongovernmental organizations came to recognize students could be a key constituency, as the next chapter explores.

From Service to Action? Rethinking Student Voluntarism, 1965–1980

In February 1969, two thousand students at Birmingham University took part in a "Community Action Week" on 30 projects ranging from surveys on hypothermia and attitudes to mental health; parties and entertainments for underprivileged children; and a series of redecoration schemes at social institutions across the city—including two homes for unmarried mothers, Birmingham Settlement youth center, a hostel for vagrants, an old people's home and the Institute for the Deaf.[1] Involving a third of the university's undergraduates—a greater proportion than any of the higher profile university sit-ins or protests of the "long sixties"—the Birmingham Community Action week reflected growing dissatisfaction with a lack of contact with communities outside the university, and was a key episode in the development of a national Student Community Action (SCA) movement in Britain. Just nine months later, National Union of Students (NUS) conference in Margate passed a motion decrying the lack of student activity in the community, urging unions to make community action a "majority activity" of students and mandating NUS to establish a SCA program. In the same month, February 1969, a group of Oxford students began knocking on doors, talking to friends about problems of third world development.[2] Within 20 days they had persuaded one thousand students to donate 1 percent of their grant to overseas aid organizations and the campaign had spread to nearby Warwick and Reading universities, giving rise to a national network called Third World First (3W1) that enjoyed rapid success across universities.

Reflecting wider changes in British student attitudes, 1969 was a key year for student social action and this chapter argues that both SCA and Third World First should be seen as "alternative approaches" to protest that emerged out of the mêlée of student militancy in the late 1960s.[3] Although seen by commentators at the time as a positive outcome of wider student protest, SCA has not received the historical attention paid to university sit-ins or protests over the Vietnam War. Students who had returned from a period of voluntary service overseas were among the first to demand a shift from "service" to more politicized forms of "community action." The chapter therefore starts by exploring how in the United Nations' first "development decade" students around the world were inspired by a new movement for overseas volunteering. Tracing the growing student interest in development assistance overseas and community action at home reveals much about students' changing role in British society, as numbers in the universities swelled and student voices grew louder and more confident. By the late 1960s and 1970s students were widely perceived as a privileged group whose grants enabled, perhaps even necessitated, their involvement in a wide range of social and political campaigns. A new generation of nongovernmental organizations (NGOs) began to recognize the value of mobilizing students for fundraising and campaigning, and invested in staff responsible for work in universities and colleges. In turn, student involvement shaped organizational priorities and students made significant contributions to a range of domestic and international causes. However, as student voluntary action became a more mainstream activity of students' unions, it also came under greater external criticism than at any earlier period.

A CHANCE TO SERVE: VOLUNTARY SERVICE OVERSEAS AND THE UNIVERSITIES

In the 1950s and 1960s an emergent model of long-term volunteer placements overseas received impetus and organized promotion from students and lecturers in higher education institutions around the world. In the later 1950s, groups that arranged volunteer workcamps—including International Voluntary Service and NUS—began to report a significant increase in applications for service at both home and on the European continent.[4] Experiments with workcamping in developing countries in the 1950s formed one strand underlying the emergence of the new volunteering movement, in line with the belief that newly independent former colonies needed technical assistance alongside capital investment.[5] The model also had roots in the international student service movement, which had been encouraging student involvement with overseas aid and development since 1920. A key consideration of the 1950 World University Service (WUS) conference in Bombay (the first to be held in Asia) was how students in richer countries might support those in developing ones on a basis of equality rather than condescension. It was an informal meeting between Australian and Indonesian students at this conference which gave rise to the first long-term overseas volunteer project. The students approached others within the Australian Student Christian Movement (SCM) and the National Union of Australian University Students (NUAUS) to develop their idea of a new model of technical assistance—a graduate volunteer scheme that would eventually win the backing of both the Indonesian and Australian governments.[6] This was the first program specifically aimed at assisting development overseas through long-term volunteer service.[7]

This is not the place for a history of international volunteering, but it is worth briefly outlining its development to show the importance of university students to its emergence and to highlight that British volunteers returning from the developing world to enter higher education were profoundly affected by their experiences in ways that had important impacts for the future of domestic student voluntarism. A key figure in the British movement was Alec Dickson (1914–1994), a colonial youth worker who founded Voluntary Service Overseas (VSO) in 1958. In developing plans for VSO Dickson was said to be inspired by the voluntary work of an international group of students who he had met when they were operating a refugee rescue service along the Austro-Hungarian border during October and November 1956.[8] An important factor influencing developments in Britain was the phasing out of national service between 1957 and 1962. As part of this planning, a number of commentators were concerned that its abolition would "leave a gap in our national life."[9] It created something of a crisis for a cohort of young men who no longer had to enlist but who still had to wait a year or two for their university place. This "year between" was seen as an opportunity for a year of adventurous service overseas by Dickson and supporters, who sent the first group of VSO school-leaver volunteers overseas in 1958.[10] Although the leading British volunteer sending organization today, in fact Dickson's scheme was just one of several British programs that sent small numbers on long-term placements to developing countries in the late 1950s and early 1960s.[11]

Around the world, a new range of graduate-level programs was developing. In 1959 the New Zealand University Students Association began to send volunteers to Indonesia.[12] In Canada, several university groups developed volunteer schemes during 1960–1961, and in 1961 the first 17 volunteers of what was to become Canadian University Service Overseas (CUSO) were sent overseas. This new sending agency had the backing of the Canadian SCM and the Canadian

WUS as well as individual universities. In the United States, the proposal for an international youth service scheme articulated by John F. Kennedy in a speech at the University of Michigan in October 1960 drew instant enthusiasm from thousands of American students and many college-based societies were set up to support and promote the idea.[13] Drawing on a wide range of sources of influence, including American academics, the Peace Corps was established in 1961 and immediately became the largest volunteer sending organization in the world. In the early 1960s similar schemes were set up either on voluntary initiative or increasingly with government backing in many other countries including France, Germany, Denmark, Sweden and Japan. Most schemes shared goals of promoting social and economic development in host countries; encouraging friendship and mutual understanding between the youth of different countries; and fostering an international outlook among volunteers.[14]

Back in Britain, students at several universities—including Cambridge and Birmingham—began to develop their own overseas volunteer programs in 1961 and 1962 response to a perceived lack of opportunities for graduate-level volunteers, since VSO remained committed to sending school-leavers.[15] Zweig found strong support for voluntary service overseas among students he interviewed in Oxford and Manchester.[16] The NUS launched its own volunteer initiative in 1962 on the grounds that students' unions were well placed to recruit volunteers and identify appropriate placements through contacts with student leaders overseas, and the Scottish Union of Students also began to recruit small numbers. According to David Wainwright in his account of the British Volunteer Programme (BVP), the NUS plan proved that "the impulse for volunteering is a genuine and spontaneous feeling among young people, and not the fulfilment of any government-inspired policy."[17] All these ideas contributed to mounting pressure for the creation of an official UK scheme, and in May 1962 the Macmillan government announced that the Department of Technical Co-operation was to part-finance a graduate volunteer program.[18] A unique feature of the British scheme was the cooperation of autonomous volunteer-sending agencies coordinated by a committee chaired by Sir John Lockwood, Master of Birkbeck College.[19] The National Council of Social Service provided a secretariat and government contributed half the operating costs, although host countries were expected to cover volunteers' board, lodging and pocket money.

The Lockwood Committee's ambitious targets required the successful recruitment of around 3 percent of all British students graduating each year.[20] Despite the high level of student interest in the idea, the BVP faced a number of challenges in recruiting volunteers to serve for a year or more overseas. By the spring of 1963 the Committee had begun making grants to student groups who could promote the idea of overseas service in colleges and universities.[21] These Voluntary Overseas Service Association (VOSA) groups not only raised awareness of the work of volunteers overseas but also started other activities including offering support to international students in Britain, carrying out social service locally and helping volunteers to access supplies from the United Kingdom. Student newspapers carried positive articles on the work of overseas volunteers.[22] The NUS in particular was struggling to recruit volunteers and to raise sufficient funds to support them.[23] These financial problems meant that by the end of 1966 NUS had withdrawn from the BVP, leaving ten of its volunteers overseas in 1967.[24] Writing in 1968 NUS historian Frank Rhodes described the failure of Graduate Service Overseas as "a deplorable indication either of an increasing lack of communication or of increasing student indifference."[25] However, NUS was arguably not the best-placed agency to train and support volunteers overseas, and its withdrawal did not damage the overall BVP, which was recruiting around two thousand graduates a year by the early 1970s. Although agencies like VSO today recruit experts with an average age of 38, university students in the 1960s helped establish the concept of volunteering as a legitimate contribution to international development. In the 1960s many students believed in volunteer technical assistance in helping to develop education systems, healthcare and welfare services across newly independent nations and as a positive engagement with the process of decolonization. In the 1970s, however, students would reject the "1950s spirit" allegedly behind groups like VSO, and would start asking new questions about how far international volunteering was a form of neo-colonial exploitation that did nothing to decrease the dependency of host countries on the West.[26]

FROM RAGS TO RADICALISM: STUDENT COMMUNITY ACTION AND THIRD WORLD FIRST

In the late 1960s, changing student attitudes to the outside community and the wider world led to a more politicized understanding of voluntary service at home and international development work overseas. There were a number of factors underlying these changes. First, the "rediscovery" that poverty remained a persistent problem in Britain resulted in the formation of new campaigning organizations to tackle the causes of poverty, including Shelter and the Child Poverty Action Group. The issue of housing and homelessness was one of the first to mobilize large numbers of students. The Notting Hill Housing Trust, formed in 1964 by Reverend Bruce Kenrick (1920–2007), who would go on to found Shelter in 1966, began to draw public attention to the poor state of inner-city housing. Students from the United Kingdom and overseas became involved in practical restoration and renovation work channelled through a series of International Voluntary Service workcamps in Notting Hill.[27] In 1966, Ken Loach's BBC documentary "Cathy Come Home" caused widespread public concern about the issues; it was screened at many universities, schools, churches and other groups. Second, the idea that university students should play a role in voluntary organizations that was wider than simply helping deliver existing services was gaining ground. For example, an SCM leaflet from the 1960s advised students to "remember that service is not just doing things but agitating for things to be done."[28] Such attitudes were often problematic for professionals trying to work with particular communities. For example, Shelter's Youth Director Eileen Ware recalled that she hated talking to student groups because of an apparently widespread attitude that it was better to let homeless people "sink so low that they would be rioting and therefore the Government would be forced to do something."[29] Recognizing the fundraising potential of students, in 1967 Christian Aid appointed a special staff member with responsibility for universities and colleges, as other charities had done.[30] However, there was a sense that students should not simply support existing organizations but create new ones. Caroline Jackson felt her voluntary work for Oxfam as a student in Manchester was "just wallpapering over the cracks...and the theme in the late sixties was very much that you needed to get out and make your own models, you needed to start again."[31]

A third factor underlying the shift from service to action was the impetus from students who entered university after a period of service with VSO and who were unimpressed with what they saw as the childishness of rag and the ineffectiveness of much student community service. At the recently founded University of York, for example, it was a returned VSO volunteer, Tim Berry, who set up a project for students to visit a local mental hospital in 1965.[32] Berry's year of service in Malawi made him "more self-confident and grown up" than many of his peers and led to his involvement in several social schemes in York.[33] At Birmingham another returned VSO student, Alan Barr, led the moves away from rag toward the new community action model. Barr later reflected "I'd changed fundamentally in a year...lots of other people who did VSO as cadet volunteers—as we were called—came back I think with a different perspective."[34] Barr summed up the case against rag in his 1972 book *Student Community Action*.[35] Student rags raised comparatively small sums, failed to promote better understanding between students and local communities and were dangerous because they gave students a delusional sense of having made a contribution to society when in fact they reinforced the elitism of higher education. Although students at the universities that opened during the 1960s had the chance to invent their own traditions of voluntary action, many institutions decided to import the tried-and-tested rag model.[36] One of the first activities of students at the University of Essex, opened in October 1964 with 120 students, was to set up a Charities Committee to organize a rag for March 1965, with half the proceeds to go to War on Want and the rest to local charities.[37] A *Wyvern* editorial noted its origins stemmed from the "initial over-enthusiasm" of students in the autumn term, but in the end the event was deemed successful.[38] At Lancaster, opened the same term, early hopes for a 1965 rag had to be abandoned, but students held their first Charities Week in 1966 with a fashion show, rag ball and street procession.[39]

As the new universities were holding their first rag weeks, students at older institutions, including Birmingham and Liverpool, were appointing union committees to question the value and purpose of rag.[40] In 1968 and 1969 universities including Birmingham, Aston and Southampton put on alterative "action weeks" in which students largely took part in practical decorating and gardening tasks.[41] Understandably, there was some resistance to such attempts to replace rag, while others felt that a week of community projects just once a year would in fact do more harm than good.[42] Justifying the change, Derek Palmer of the Birmingham Carnival Committee argued that although students may claim to be radicals "most of the time they are following the established patterns that stretch back over 50 years...The majority of rag committees in this country are unimaginative, traditional and aggressive."[43] Although rags did continue in some form at most colleges, emerging from these early activities was a SCA movement that spread rapidly across the university world, helped initially by a Barrow Cadbury Trust-funded development project run by Alan Barr at Birmingham.[44] It was the older universities such as Manchester, Bristol and Cardiff that were among the first to set up new action projects. In London, a new intercollegiate group—Organisation for Student Community Action (OSCA)—was started to stimulate student participation in community service, which was judged to be lower than at provincial universities.[45] These local initiatives led to national action that demanded a wholesale change in student voluntary work to place it on a "higher and more political level."[46] Barr traces this influence to the first National Conference on Student Social Service held at Liverpool University at Easter 1968 when students came together to discuss new ways to get involved in local communities.[47]

A fourth factor in the politicization of student voluntary service was the influence of the growing agitation for university reform on campuses at home and overseas. With the expansion in higher education during the 1960s students' unions in Britain began to take on more campaigning roles, focussing on such issues as grants, access to records and files, the rights of students to have a say in the content and structure of their education as well as the need for greater links with trade unions and community organizations.[48] British developments were influenced in part by student protest in other countries, particularly in France and the United States. In the United States, students were at the forefront of the civil rights movement and anti-Vietnam protests, and American methods of awareness raising and protest such as "teach-ins" and "sit-ins" were being adapted in British colleges from the mid-1960s.[49] However, British student activists also drew on direct action methods learned through participation in CND and the Anti-Apartheid Movement at home.[50] Left-wing influence was important in shaping both SCA and the wider student movement. Socialist societies at many universities became increasingly influential in students' unions, and at national level groups like the Radical Students Alliance (1966–1968) and Revolutionary Socialist Students' Federation (1968–1970) sought to discredit NUS as a conservative body out of touch with the wider student world, and to push it to adopt more political positions on a range of topics.[51] In the five years after the famous sit-in at the London School of Economics in March 1967, sit-ins and occupations were held at about half of all British universities.

Recent work on student radicalism has begun to challenge some of the myths created by the media during the 1960s, which tended to dismiss student protest as the work of an extreme minority on campus, foreign-led and imitative of student unrest overseas. Nick Thomas, for instance, argues that while only a minority of students took part in protest, they could often rely on the support and sympathy of an "apathetic majority," while student protests made an important contribution to wider social change.[52] Caroline Hoefferle's new book traces the British student movement from the late 1950s to the early 1970s, concluding it was a "widespread, nation-wide movement" consisting of students who framed their protests around "issues of student rights, racism and the Vietnam war."[53] In many cases it was protest over moral issues that raised concerns over students' lack of power to enforce their resolutions coupled with resentment over the discipline meted out to student radicals, that drew a larger number into support for protest and sit-ins. It is surprising that neither Thomas nor Hoefferle looked at SCA as an integral part of the wider student movement, because SCA did make an impact on national student politics from the academic year 1969–1970. From 1969, the newly politicized NUS under President Jack Straw began to show interest in the burgeoning SCA movement.[54] For instance, one of the first motions passed under the revised NUS constitution enabling discussion of social and political questions was on "Students and the Community" in November 1969.

A central question was how the emergent SCA movement should relate to student protests. Initially, some students sought to use their involvement in social service to generate publicity that would counter negative perceptions of radicalism. In July 1968, an open letter to the *Times* signed by then NUS President Elect Trevor Fisk and London OSCA's secretary Pamela Cherry among others, noted that student service was a beneficial student activity that had not received much attention in the press furore over sit-ins.[55] At Birmingham, the organizers of the 1968 community action week were at first wary of identifying their venture with the occupation of the university's administrative building that began in the autumn. However, as plans emerged for the 1969 week, students began to feel more connected to this wider questioning of the values of higher education and to realize that an "apolitical approach" was inadequate.[56] However, the change of emphasis came too late to affect the image of the 1969 action week, in which the students were portrayed by the local press and the university authorities as a responsible majority to be contrasted with the radical, trouble-making minority.

Indeed, SCA was regularly welcomed as a positive outcome of wider student unrest by a wide range of commentators who held negative attitudes to other forms of student radicalism. The *Observer* hailed SCA as indicative of a "new mood" among students who were becoming "bored" with campus questions of discipline and representation.[57] The *Times'* Education Correspondent welcomed SCA because "students in Britain are the most privileged in the world, and yet the least active, in spite of their rhetoric, in fighting to combat the evils they see around them ... Student community action would show the students' mettle and test the genuineness of their consciences."[58] Similarly, SCA was praised in a 1969 House of Lords debate on student participation in higher education as "a most successful attempt by students to make a positive contribution to the society from which they are getting so much."[59] Although generally dismissive of activism as the concern of a small minority in the universities, Michael Beloff's book on the "Plateglass" universities suggested that much British student idealism was channelled into voluntary service.[60] For the most part, however, students involved in SCA came to regret that it might be seen as a "do-gooding" public relations exercise designed to improve the "tarnished images of students at the expense of the underprivileged in our society."[61] By the academic year 1969–1970, its leaders were framing SCA as an alternative form of radicalism, different to but aligned with student occupations or sit-ins. One article in *Sennet* described SCA as a "second front" of student revolution that had emerged out of the "failures of confrontation politics," but also formed a rejection of Old Left politics.[62] There was a high degree of overlap between student involvement in community action, protest over Rhodesia, South Africa or the Vietnam War and actions to gain greater student representation and rights on campus. The motion passed at NUS conference in November 1969 recognized that SCA needed to be placed in "political context as there can be no solution to these problems by social service alone."[63] It also linked SCA to a host of other concerns including squatters' rights, solidarity with travellers and support for militant tenants' associations.[64] Following conference, NUS secured grant funding for the new SCANUS program based in its Education and Welfare Department that aimed to transform SCA "from a minority activity confined to religious societies, or small action groups, to a majority activity of students."[65]

Third World First should also be seen as an alternative approach to protest. Starting in 1969, the campaign to get students to donate 1 percent of their grants to Oxfam and other overseas aid charities enjoyed an immediate and impressive success rate. By 1971, 16,000 students had signed banker's drafts.[66] It spread rapidly through universities thanks to the dedication of its founding members: Philip Maxwell, Peter and Lesley Adamson and Trevor Chalkey and a team of keen student volunteers. Third World First saw the pledge of money only as a first step in engaging students with the broader issues of development, aiming to "involve people in the subject politically rather than just charitably."[67] The organization was innovative in a number of ways. Although student giving through banker's orders was not new—WUS had been encouraging students to sign banker's

orders since at least the early 1960s—the idea of pledging a proportion of one's grant was. One percent of the average grant in the early
1970s was around £25 a year, although students often subscribed less
than this. Third World First's founders quickly realized the advantage of a form of giving which many would not bother to cancel once
they had graduated. Its leaders argued 3W1 was necessary because
mainstream development organizations—such as Oxfam or Save the
Children—could never attract mass student interest, but that existing student organizations with an interest in overseas development
including SCM, WUS and the United Nations Student Association
(UNSA) were losing their constituencies of support.[68] Financial backing from Oxfam was important in setting up the central organization
and by the start of the 1970–1971 academic year there was a team
of paid field workers in place, who shared a house in the Oxfordshire
village of Britwell, believing that co-residence would maintain cohesion and drive. The house drew on the long tradition of residence in
student voluntarism, and provided a central base for volunteer visits,
conferences and seminars. Students who had signed a banker's order
received a magazine known as *The Internationalist* each term—this
had a circulation of nearly 40,000 by January 1973. So successful was
this publication that in 1973 it evolved into the *New Internationalist*,
an independent magazine aimed at a more general audience.

Such a bold, well-resourced organization could not help but cause
some resentment among existing student groups. Socialist students
involved in SCA at Birmingham dismissed 3W1 as "posing as ever-
so-radical" while in fact were only "mixed up liberals with inadequate analyses of the world."[69] However, many college 3W1 branches
worked closely with other student societies on joint campaigns and
fundraising efforts.[70] At Aberystwyth, for example, student members
of UNSA, WUS and 3W1 formed a joint Development Group. At
Leeds, 3W1 supported the Barclays' boycott and at University College
students worked with the Afro-Asian society and UNSA. The rise of
3W1 was also helped by high-profile external events such as the 1970
cyclone disaster in East Pakistan and the famine in Biafra, which
resulted in big fundraising drives in the universities.[71] Such high levels of interest were hard to sustain. In the mid-1970s a typical 3W1
college meeting was a film showing, talk or discussion attended by
around 30 students and engagement with the wider body of students
was limited to specific campaigns or fundraising appeals. An independent evaluation noted a reduction of interest among students that
was held to reflect declining support for overseas development aid in
the population more widely.[72] Without such disasters to keep them in

the headlines, major issues such as hunger and starvation had receded from public consciousness by the late 1970s while domestic problems such as inflation and price rises dominated.[73] Relatively, of course, students were more still engaged with and better informed about issues of development assistance than the wider public.[74] Moreover, the devastating famines in Africa in the mid 1980s would bring questions of emergency aid and international development back onto the student agenda.

MORE SOCIALLY COMMITTED THAN EVER BEFORE: STUDENTS IN THE SEVENTIES

The 1970 Cambridge House annual report suggested that undergraduates were more socially committed "than perhaps ever before" and reflected that visits to the settlement could fill out and give body to students' desire to become involved in the community.[75] It seems likely that a higher proportion of students in the 1970s took part in some form of volunteering, fundraising or social action than in any previous generation. SCA was one of the most important new areas of activity for students' unions, and evidence of this high level of social commitment is demonstrated by the integration of most college SCA groups with their respective students' unions. By 1978 there were around one hundred SCA groups across universities and colleges, many of which employed paid workers.[76] SCA projects involved up to 500 students at the bigger universities, and in 1978 it was estimated that around 50,000 students volunteered each year across the whole field of universities, polytechnics and colleges.[77] At Glasgow University, for example, around 250 students took part in activities ranging from hospital visiting, decorating projects for older people, youth club work or running an allotment to student support service Nightline.[78] College-level activity was supported by visits of NUS project staff, conferences and training events and the SCANUS newsletter.[79]

Central to the SCANUS program in the 1970s was a deliberate strategy to move college-based activities away from social "service" and toward community "action." The national SCA leadership was determined to mark a break with past models of student involvement in communities. Students were enjoined to "ask deep questions" about the problems of housing, social services, education and industry.[80] Because even "reformist" activities such as decorating and organizing soup kitchens were "emotional experiences" they might give students the motivation and strength to get stuck into political or community work, such as supporting council tenants with a rent strike.[81]

Thus SCA was part of a wider rejection of the very terminology of "volunteering" in the 1970s. When Labour MP Richard Crossman (1907–1974) was asked to deliver the Sidney Ball lecture at Oxford in 1973 he was warned that the use of the word "volunteer" would deter students because it was felt to be "dated, square, positively embarrassing," reeking of "middle-class do-gooding."[82] Similarly, students involved in community action projects or short-life housing schemes in the 1970s recalled that they did not classify themselves as "volunteers" at the time.[83]

Responding to changing social needs, student voluntarism expanded to cover a very wide range of activities in the 1970s, which

Figure 10.1 Newsletter of the NUS Student Community Action project, 1973. Reproduced by kind permission of the National Council for Voluntary Organisations.

can only be mentioned in passing here. Work included teaching English to immigrants; innovative paper recycling schemes; community oral history and reminiscence projects; support for single parents; help at women's refuges, unemployed centers and with welfare rights advice.[84] As in earlier generations, students in the SCA movement targeted much of their voluntary work at children and young people, often those with disabilities, living in institutions or from deprived backgrounds. According to a 1974 report on the SCANUS pilot program, children were often targeted by students because they were the "most resilient and least cynical."[85] Much of this work was informed by theories about the necessity and value of "play" for children, which formed a regular topic of SCA conferences and training workshops. A "play supplement" to the May–June 1974 SCA newsletter contained articles ranging from practical tips for involving volunteers to advice on how to help counter "propaganda" on gender difference or the so-called naturalness of competition.[86] Students criticized local-authority run playschemes and noted that children were at a serious disadvantage when they were deprived of the opportunities for stimulating and expressive play either through lack of materials or lack of attention. A common SCA intervention was setting up and helping to run an adventure playground, while other activities included afterschool clubs, tutoring programs and summer holiday schemes. However, many activities suffered from a high turnover of volunteers with a consequent loss of knowledge and experience year after year. Lack of confidence in students' abilities was another concern. One report on an Oxford tutoring scheme for immigrant children noted that "some teachers feel that students are left-wing, neurotic and too inexperienced to be much good with kids."[87] On Sinclair Goodlad's "Pimlico Connection" initiative, however, through which students from Imperial College tutored pupils at local comprehensive schools, students received formal training and met regularly to discuss progress, while the whole scheme was subject to ongoing evaluation.[88]

Mental health and mental disability emerged as important new fields for student voluntarism. In a 1969 overview of the work of 28 student social service groups just four specified mental health as an area of work but this grew significantly over the following decade as public attention was focused on the treatment and care of people with mental health problems and disabilities.[89] Such concern arose following a number of abuse scandals at hospitals and homes for the mentally ill and what were called the "mentally subnormal." Visiting patients had become a common activity among students at universities located near large psychiatric hospitals.[90] For example, Nottingham students began visiting Rampton Hospital in October 1971, and reported pioneering "a few social improvements" such as being the first visitors to take part in evening socials and dances with patients.[91] The SCANUS pilot report noted sardonically that the attraction of mental hospitals to students lay in their "similarity, both in appearance and routine" to colleges of higher education.[92] Bristol medical students suggested that mental hospitals were "becoming a trendy place for voluntary work" and were concerned that their involvement should not merely prop up the status quo, but encourage students to question, innovate and improve.[93] Relationships with some psychiatric institutions were difficult to maintain, with students experiencing poor relations with staff and a lack of support for ideas and initiatives.[94] Relations may not have been helped by the involvement of students in campaigns for patients' rights, such as PROPAR (Protection of the Rights of the Patients at Rampton), which followed a May 1979 television documentary detailing allegations of brutality.[95]

Developing from early support for Shelter, housing and homelessness also became major issues for students in the 1970s. [96] In part this was because the growth of student numbers and the shift to national recruitment to universities had contributed to a chronic student housing crisis that generated headlines at the start of each new academic year. The problem was exacerbated by the rapid inflation and subsequent rent rises of the early 1970s. In many towns and cities students' greater purchasing power in the private rented sector enabled them to displace poorer groups, and thus students *were* the "housing problem," much as many did not care to admit it. Nick Plant, a student at Southampton in the mid 1970s, recalled that his involvement in a short-life housing cooperatives stemmed from a self-help, mutual aid motivation but led to wider campaigning including conducting a survey of housing conditions that managed to embarrass Southampton City Council.[97] Groups at many universities conducted similar housing surveys which also helped raise student participants' consciousness of poverty and inequality. Students from the SCA network did much to make the issue of housing an area of concern for NUS. However, repeated surveys could also cause resentment among local people. A former SCA worker at Manchester University recalled one local resident threatening, "If anybody else comes round here with a clipboard again, they're over that balcony!"[98]

In the long tradition of supporting academic refugees, the coup by General Pinochet in September 1973 overthrowing the Allende government led to a new WUS campaign for student refugees from Chile. Groups were established in 60 universities and polytechnics and WUS was able to award around one hundred scholarships to postgraduates and undergraduates. In 1974, WUS secured funding for the scholarship program from the new Labour government, with the result that over a ten-year period around nine hundred Chileans were enabled to study in Britain.[99] At the end of 1970s several SCA groups were also involved in anti-cuts campaigning. Against those who tried to maintain that SCA should not get involved in politics, others pointed out that student groups involved in seemingly innocuous activities such as painting council houses were in fact taking political action: "by painting it you are supporting the cuts in painters and decorators employed by the council."[100]

Since the Edwardian period, students had seen social study as an essential aspect of the practical service they could offer to communities. Merely visiting older people or helping create adventure playgrounds for children could not give students an understanding of the wider structural issues of poverty. Students needed to be able to locate volunteering in broader social context through studying social problems. Yet despite appeals such as Brian Simon's 1943 call for social study to be integrated into all university courses, it remained an extracurricular activity for keen students. In the 1970s SCA became connected to a wider movement for higher education curriculum reform. Students considered that many of the failures of student voluntary action in the past had arisen from a perceived conflict between academic work and extracurricular volunteering. The leaders of SCA argued that students could achieve "social change for the benefit of the deprived" only by combining practical community action with demands for changes in the curriculum.[101] Barr's 1972 book outlined a range of ways in which courses could be adapted to take more notice of the real world. However, despite a series of conferences, workshops and a number of experimental projects in the early 1970s, the topic of curriculum reform remained largely a minority concern within a wider movement keen on projects in local communities. Writing in 1975 Alec Dickson regretted that SCA had "left the curriculum more or less intact" and suggested that the establishment of social action groups in many universities had actually deflected attention away from the need for such change.[102] Yet as higher education institutions expanded in the 1970s, student awareness of the lack of contact between universities and the communities in which they were located deepened. Universities wielded considerable economic power as well as putting pressure on housing and transport systems, but students recognized that universities rarely consulted local communities about expansion plans.[103] One response was the campaign for "community access" that aimed to make students' unions and their resources (typewriters, meeting rooms, films, books, copy and print services) more accessible to local people, although this movement had made only poor progress by the early 1980s.[104]

By the mid-1970s some disillusionment about the progress of SCA was setting in across the wider student movement. In his 1975 book on student politics former NUS President Digby Jacks warned that the SCA movement had not achieved as much as it set out to do—describing its members as "a motley collection of social engineers, do-gooders and ultra-leftists."[105] It was too easy for activists "to slip into the old 'do-gooding' mould, and assuage middle-class guilt through paternalistic, non-contentious activities such as decorating old people's homes."[106] Criticized on the left for being too reformist, SCA was held up by the right as too radical. Indeed, during the Conservative backlash of the early 1970s, public attitudes to students had never been so negative. External critics began to question the legitimacy of students' involvement in community action projects on the grounds that they did not experience the continual poverty or disadvantage of the residents in the areas where they operated. Such a charge could have been levelled against student voluntarism at any period in the preceding hundred years, but it rarely had been. In a 1973 article Robert Holman, a Birmingham University lecturer, argued that "lack of continuity, inconsistency and a high drop-out rate" characterized student community involvement.[107] However, the 1973 report of the Community Work Group pointed out that students were no more illegitimate than many other "pressure groups drawn from professional organizations."[108] Moreover, students' "outsider" status, while it could cause gulfs of misunderstanding, sometimes served to relieve tensions, as earlier generations had found. In 1970s Belfast, it was noted that student volunteers of different nationalities, religion and class were accepted by Catholic families whose children attended a summer playscheme held just a few months after Bloody Sunday in a way which other strangers were not.[109] As American student volunteer Lisa Huber suggested "outsiders do have a useful and worthwhile role to play in such short-term projects...at its crudest, some of us were Protestants that weren't shooting at them, and who didn't fit the stereotype."[110] In 1978, a financial crisis at NUS brought on by the collapse of the travel department meant that funding for the SCANUS program was withdrawn. At this date, and despite the push toward community action by the movement's national leadership during the 1970s, most SCA groups were still pursuing a more traditional community-service-and-social-education model.[111]

As part of the wider movement for women's liberation that was taking hold in the universities, in many cases led by women radicalized in the student movement, some students started to challenge the division of labor in voluntary action that previous generations had taken for granted. This book has shown that women had long taken on leadership roles in social service and fundraising efforts in the universities. Ironically, the politicization of voluntary action in the late 1960s actually pushed women students out. A traditional voluntary service group dominated by women was easy to dismiss, as one male student writing of Strathclyde University did, as an "exclusively female clique."[112] Although women students remained closely involved in SCA at college level, men came to dominate the SCA movement's leadership as they did the student movement more broadly. Out of 19 members of the SCANUS advisory group in the mid 1970s, for example, just six were women. Men were the major contributors to a "Student Community Action Kit" produced by the SCANUS pilot program. Moreover, fundraising efforts until the 1970s often relied on sexist publications, beauty pageants and competitions to select a "Rag Queen."[113] This was in tune with the wider representations of women in the student press which into the early 1970s continued to decorate college newspapers with photographs of attractive women students. Despite evident interest in women's liberation, it does not seem to have been until the late 1970s that women in the SCA movement began to testify to their outrage at the sexist behavior of male colleagues and to seek to combat sexual stereotyping in volunteer work by holding separate women's groups and meetings.[114]

Gay, lesbian and bisexual students had also long been silenced within the wider student movement, but the gay liberation movement—the British Gay Liberation Front was launched at LSE in 1970—was another outcome of student radicalism in the 1960s.[115] For most of the period under study, homosexual acts by men had been criminalized, and even in the 1970s gay students faced additional discrimination because under the 1967 Sexual Offences Act homosexual sex below the age of 21 remained illegal. Activist students like Peter Tatchell, Jamie Gardner and others worked to make the NUS and the wider student movement recognize sexuality as a political issue.[116] NUS Conference first passed a motion on gay rights in 1971 and in 1973 launched a more extensive campaign aimed at repealing the 1967 Act.[117] The SCANUS newsletter—like student newspapers in general—included several articles on gay rights in the 1970s although these were not always uncontroversial. At college level, gay students organized self-help groups to combat prejudice, campaign for gay rights and provide peer support. However, in many places continued fear of exposure and discrimination meant college groups struggled to recruit members.[118]

An important moment for student voluntarism came in 1978, when the independent Student Community Action Resource Project (set up after the SCANUS program was closed down) succeeded in securing funding from the Voluntary Services Unit (VSU) within the Home Office.[119] The Student Community Action Resource Project moved into offices in the Oxford House settlement in 1979. Government funding was a significant step in the development of a national student volunteering infrastructure that would survive under a range of different names until 2007.[120] Established during the Heath government of 1970–1974, the VSU administered grants to set up a national Volunteer Centre in 1973 and develop a network of local volunteer bureaux.[121] Such moves were part of the wider professionalization of the voluntary sector. Students who had been active in SCA contributed to the rapid expansion of this voluntary sector workforce in the 1970s and 1980s, as they moved into jobs in community work, housing, women's aid, supporting refugees and other fields after graduation.

CONCLUSION

Student social action on a range of issues formed part of a changing consciousness on questions of community relations, academic freedom and the purpose of higher education that characterized the student movement of the 1960s and 1970s.[122] International concern was not new for the student movement, but the overseas volunteer schemes that emerged in the 1960s gave thousands of students and new graduates opportunities for travel, adventure and service that their predecessors had found in other ways. Worldwide, students in the 1960s helped turn what was an untested concept of long-term international volunteering into a viable contribution to development assistance. Through their support for overseas volunteering initiatives, emergency aid and development NGOs British students built a reputation for humanitarian action of which they were rather proud. Student newspapers praised the large contributions raised for overseas aid charities and NGOs fell over themselves to court the student donor with special publications, dedicated staff members and even, in Oxfam's case, financing a new student network, Third World First. Moreover, students pushed existing aid organizations to greater radicalism, and in the 1970s began to question the aims of overseas volunteering programs and offer a critique of international development goals.[123] Often experiences overseas had changed returned volunteers' ideas about poverty, social need, international development and voluntary work, with the effect that many became dissatisfied with existing forms of student voluntarism and helped shape a new SCA movement.

Infused with a strong moral element, British student radicalism was always about more than student representation and SCA and Third World First were perhaps two of the more sustainable movements to emerge from the mix of radicalism in the 1960s and 1970s. Underpinning the birth of SCA was the continued expansion of higher education and deep-seated changes in student attitudes to education, politics and their place in the community that were more important than extreme outbursts of militancy and use of specific protest techniques such as the sit-in.[124] Study of student voluntarism is also a means to look at how wider cultural shifts such as the changing position of women, liberalizing attitudes to homosexuality and concerns about racism and immigration were reflected on campus. As in earlier periods, social education remained central to student voluntarism, whether led by students themselves or mediated through the materials produced by the increasingly professionalized domestic voluntary and overseas aid sectors. However, student voluntarism came under greater and more sustained criticism than it had earlier faced. Despite the rhetoric about the shift from service to action, during the 1970s most SCA groups operated on a continuum between traditional social service activities and more radical campaigning and community action.

CHAPTER 11

Conclusion: Students and Social Change, 1880–1980

This book has taken a long view of the student experience in Britain and the ways in which students have engaged with local communities, social causes and international affairs. The prevalence of voluntarism in every student generation makes it an ideal lens through which to examine what it was like to be a university student in Britain over a hundred-year period. The book has sought to address the neglect of a range of activities including volunteering, fundraising and social action, which have rarely received the same academic or popular attention as political protest on campus, despite involving greater numbers of students. Such neglect is perhaps not surprising given a media preference for sensationalist or negative stories about higher education, but academic neglect may be related to the strong association between voluntary social service and women students, themselves marginal in higher education history. Although often excluded from the leadership of student organizations, from the late nineteenth century women's strong influence in student social service may have contributed to its lower status compared to political action. Women's colleges and unions developed strong traditions of social study, fundraising and volunteering—although women were largely accepting of their subordinate positions within universities until the 1970s.

Seeking out the stories of those women and men involved in social service broadens our understanding of students across the period 1880–1980. For example, recognizing the important role of the pre–First World War Student Christian Movement (SCM) as the first national student association, and its active promotion of service and social study as a way to engage a larger body of students, provides a useful corrective to earlier emphases on representative student politics as the only unifying force in the student world. Examining the work of European Student Relief and its successors makes it clear that student involvement with overseas aid and development was not invented in the 1960s but dates back to 1920 at least. The case of the 1930s student self-help movement shows the innovative ways students in previous generations coped with financial hardship, provides a longer history to students' unions services, and reveals how students in northern England and Wales, in particular, saw themselves as part of a wider European student movement. Likewise, framing Student Community Action (SCA) as an aspect of wider student radicalism in the late 1960s and early 1970s helps us to recognize the broader social and educational concerns of this most active of student generations.

Student voluntarism in one form or another has proved to have greater longevity than political protest in the universities. Having survived the criticisms of the student community action movement, student rag enjoyed something of a rebirth in the 1990s and groups today continue to raise around £2 million for charity, though the carnivals and processions, sexist and racist "rag mags," and beauty contests that characterized rags in mid-century have largely disappeared. In addition, university students—now a much larger proportion of the population than ever before—continue to take part in regular volunteering for a range of charities; local, national and international. People and Planet (formerly Third World First) still engages thousands of students in campaigns on global poverty, claiming to punch above its weight in terms of impact and profile. With large injections of central government funding in the 2000s, student volunteering became more commodified, less interested in wider goals of social education and less student-led than in earlier years. The recent rise of the Student Hubs network—with its ambitious aim of encouraging every student to make a difference during their time at university and inspiring "a new generation of socially-active citizens"—may yet reverse this trend. Today's higher education sector places a premium on the "student experience" and on the value of student volunteering for enhancing employability and in shaping long-term career choices.

The book has shown that student social service was core to the emergence of a distinct "student estate" in twentieth-century Britain. Much rhetoric on student voluntarism emphasized service as a way of "bridging" perceived gaps between students and "the community," although the results rarely lived up to the promise. Social action did however succeed in strengthening student identity, particularly at nonresidential universities, where student rag or college social service committees were some of the earliest societies bringing students from different backgrounds together. Before the formation of the National Union of Students (NUS) in 1922, the SCM's social service committee and the Universities' Committee of the Imperial War Relief Fund provided valued meeting places for student leaders from Oxbridge, the London colleges and the civic universities. In the 1930s a "student popular front" was forged through increased social and political action on domestic and international issues, and although consensus was shattered in 1939/1940, students eventually came together again in support of the war effort. Efforts for Hungarian refugee students in 1956–1957 marked the beginning of a new wave of social action in the universities. In the 1970s community service projects became mainstream activities of many students' unions, allowing the SCA movement to exert strong influence in national student politics.

A driving force behind student voluntarism 1880–1980 was the leadership that came from students themselves. In each generation there has been a small group of active, committed women and men on top of a larger base of the vaguely interested that has been mobilized to greater practical involvement in fundraising, service and social action at particular moments. Coordination at national level through bodies like the SCM, Universities' Committee, International Student Service, NUS or Third World First supported the activities of students at universities and colleges, encouraged greater levels of participation and sought to demonstrate the impact of students' involvement in communities to outside audiences. From SCM travelling secretaries to the SCA project staff at NUS, the movement has relied on professional organizers to promote and support student action. However, by the 1970s, the movement was more student-led than in previous generations with far less deference paid to senior experts.

Students have made significant contributions to social change in Britain through their commitment to a wide range of causes and campaigns. Through fundraising, social service, social education and community action students have attempted to engage with the social issues of the day at local, national and international levels, in ways that deserve wider recognition. Although numbers of students and higher education institutions grew over the period, students remained a small minority of the age group even in the 1970s, and this elite status fostered a sense of social responsibility. Despite regular criticisms of student apathy, students over the period 1880–1980 have shared a strong moral impulse, although this has manifest itself in ways that may not have seemed particularly progressive to later generations, such as General Strike volunteering. Indeed, students have routinely sought to disassociate current activities from those of their predecessors, making it harder to assess the student contribution to social change. Yet domestic and international causes including postwar educational reconstruction, youth clubs, unemployment, refugee relief, Aid for Spain, the antiapartheid movement, nuclear disarmament, housing, overseas volunteering and international development owe much to the input of students. Settlements are anomalous in that they enjoyed support (albeit fluctuating) from students over many decades, and their model of university-educated resident volunteers supported by ad hoc help in fundraising and service from current undergraduates did not substantially change over time. Indeed, Samuel Barnett's central idea of the "mutual benefits flowing from cross-class friendships"—as Jenny Harrow termed it—had a long life in the universities, inspiring settlements, camps for the unemployed, and models of work with young people into the 1970s and beyond.[1] Similarly, a strong strain of student Christian social concern remained a powerful lever for service and social action until almost the end of the period. At the same time there have been constant new initiatives but this hundred-year survey has revealed that the continuities in student social action have often been as important as the shifts in theory and practice over time.

Like the voluntary sector in British society more widely, student voluntary action showed remarkable resilience, continually being reinvented by new generations of students and reflecting changed social conditions. A central idea that resurfaces across the period was that university students had special responsibilities to the community and the nation, and it was only through fulfilment of these obligations that students could demonstrate the wider social value of higher education. A key feature and strength over time was the ability of student-led groups to respond rapidly to changing need, both domestically and internationally. An important aspect of this was the role of charitable trusts and foundations in funding innovations in student social service, from interwar camp movements to SCA development projects in the 1970s. Furthermore, many voluntary organizations—from the Imperial War Relief Committee to Shelter, university settlements to Third World First—saw the potential to enlist students' time and money in support of their cause. Students were a reliable constituency of support for many new social initiatives. However, despite the best attempts of various groups and individuals, student social service and social action remained extracurricular activities throughout the period. British universities were reluctant to make formal links with any social service institutions—they even eschewed legal connections with the settlements that bore their names—and until very recently were unreceptive to attempts to make teaching and research more responsive to social or community needs. Nevertheless, volunteering arguably had a greater impact on communities and organizations when it was most closely linked to students' skills and academic interests. Students have made contributions to social research and social reform through their participation in surveys of social problems and local need. The most effective activities included social education that helped students locate voluntary work in broader social contexts and maintain a critical perspective on the consequences, intended and unintended, of their activities on communities.

Across the generations, however, the educative function of voluntary action for students has often been seen as more important than its impacts on communities or causes. Participation gave higher education students social education, schooling in citizenship and training in leadership. Practical experience combined with widened horizons provided routes into paid and unpaid careers in a range of established and emergent professions, including public administration, social work, education and community development. In recent decades former student volunteers and SCA officers have provided a key recruiting ground for organizations in the voluntary sector, which by 2013 counted 2.6 percent of the UK workforce.[2] Social service and social action were also sources of fulfilment and fun for generations of students, resulting in many long-lasting friendships, relationships and marriages. A strong strain of humor, larks and high-spirited enthusiasm ran though many student fundraising and social service projects. Perhaps most importantly, student voluntarism strengthened group solidarity and in so doing contributed to the emergence and growth of a student movement in Britain and the wider world.

Notes

1 Introduction

1. Talk by Harold Silver at Open University, Milton Keynes, November 2011.
2. Ruth Rouse, "Pioneer Days among Women Students," *Student World* 27, no. 1 (1934): 54–60, at 54.
3. Brian Harrison, *Seeking a Role: The United Kingdom, 1951–1970* (Oxford: Oxford University Press, 2009), xx.
4. Harold Silver and Pamela Silver, *Students: Changing Roles, Changing Lives* (Buckingham: Open University Press, 1997), 10.
5. See, for example, Carol Dyhouse, *Students: A Gendered History* (Abingdon: Routledge, 2006); Nick Thomas, "Challenging Myths of the 1960s: The Case of Student Protest in Britain," *Twentieth Century British History* 13, no. 3 (2002): 277–297.
6. Reba N. Soffer, *Discipline and Power: The University, History and the Making of an English Elite 1870–1930* (Stanford: Stanford University Press, 1994), 67–77.
7. Keith Vernon, *Universities and the State in England, 1850–1939* (Abingdon: Routledge, 2004), 3.
8. Callum G. Brown, Arthur J. McIvor and Neil Rafeek, *The University Experience, 1945–1975: An Oral History of the University of Strathclyde* (Edinburgh: Edinburgh University Press, 2004); Andrea Jacobs, Camilla Leach and Stephanie Spencer, "Learning Lives and Alumni Voices," *Oxford Review of Education* 36, no. 2 (April 2010): 219–232.
9. Mike Day, *National Union of Students, 1922–2012* (London: Regal Press, 2012); see also Mike Day, "'Respected not Respectable: A New History of the NUS," Unpublished manuscript. I am grateful to Mike Day for letting me read this in draft.
10. Catriona M. Macdonald, "'To Form Citizens': Scottish Students, Governance and Politics, 1884–1948," *History of Education* 38, no. 3 (2009): 383–402.
11. John Field, "Service Learning in Britain between the Wars: University Students and Unemployed Camps," *History of Education* 41, no. 1 (March 2012): 195–212.
12. Jodi Burkett, *Constructing Post-Imperial Britain: Britishness, Race and the Radical Left in the 1960s* (Basingstoke: Palgrave Macmillan, 2013).

13. See, for example, Tissington Tatlow, *The Story of the Student Christian Movement* (London: SCM Press, 1933); Ruth Rouse, *The World's Student Christian Federation: A History of the First Thirty Years* (London: SCM Press, 1948); Ruth Rouse, *Rebuilding Europe: The Student Chapter in Post-War Reconstruction* (London: SCM Press, 1925).

14. Renate Howe, "The Australian Student Christian Movement and Women's Activism in the Asia-Pacific Region, 1890s–1920s," *Australian Feminist Studies* 16, no. 36 (2001): 311–323; Meredith Lake, "Faith in Crisis; Christian University Students in Peace and War," *Australian Journal of Politics and History* 56, no. 3 (2010): 441–454; Johanna M. Selles, *A History of the World Student Christian Federation, 1895–1920* (Pickwick, 2011); Paul Axelrod, *Making a Middle Class: Student Life in English Canada During the Thirties* (Montreal: McGill-Queen's University Press, 1990).

15. Arthur Marwick, "Youth in Britain, 1920–1960: Detachment and Commitment," *Journal of Contemporary History* 5, no. 1 (1970): 37–51.

16. Eric Ashby and Mary Anderson, *The Rise of the Student Estate in Britain* (London: Macmillan and Co., 1970), 59.

17. Brian Simon, "The Student Movement in England and Wales During the 1930s," *History of Education* 16, no. 3 (1987): 189–203; David Fowler, *Youth Culture in Modern Britain c. 1920–1970* (Basingstoke: Palgrave Macmillan, 2008).

18. Most recently see Caroline M. Hoefferle, *British Student Activism in the Long Sixties* (Abingdon: Routledge, 2013).

19. Lieve Gevers and Louis Vos, "Student Movements," in *A History of the University in Europe: Universities in the Nineteenth and Early Twentieth Centuries (1800–1945)*, Vol. 3, edited by Walter Rüegg, 269–363 (Cambridge: Cambridge University Press, 2004).

20. Nigel Scotland, *Squires in the Slums: Settlements and Missions in Late-Victorian London* (London: I. B. Tauris, 2007); Katharine Bentley Beauman, *Women and the Settlement Movement* (London: Radcliffe Press, 1996), 189; Martha Vicinus, *Independent Women: Work and Community for Single Women, 1850–1920* (London: Virago, 1985).

21. Katharine Bradley, *Poverty, Philanthropy and the State: Charities and the Working Classes in London, 1918–1979* (Manchester: Manchester University Press, 2009).

22. Ruth Gilchrist, Tony Jeffs and Jean Spence eds., *Essays in the History of Community and Youth Work* (Leicester: Youth Work Press, 2001).

23. Brian Simon, *A Student's View of the Universities* (London: Longmans, 1943), 124.

24. In 2010–2011, the author collaborated with Student Hubs on a project entitled "Students, Volunteering and Social Action: Histories and Policies."

25. Frank Prochaska, *Christianity and Social Service in Modern Britain: The Disinherited Spirit* (Oxford: OUP, 2006), 21.

26. On neglect of beneficiaries see Anne Borsay and Peter Shapely, *Medicine, Charity and Mutual Aid: The Consumption of Health and Welfare in Britain, c.1550–1950* (Aldershot: Ashgate, 2007).

27. Simon, "Student Movement," 202.

28. Leta Jones, *Coward's Custard* (London: Minerva Press, 1998), 5.

29. Arthur Clegg, *Aid China 1937–1949: A Memoir of a Forgotten Campaign* (Beijing: New World Press, 1989).

30. Simon, "Student Movement," 203.

31. Silver and Silver, *Students*, 11.

32. The Student Community Action papers now form part of the "Volunteering England Collection" at the London School of Economics.

33. The organization latterly known as World University Service went into administration in 2010, some papers are held at the Modern Records Centre, Warwick University.

34. "Editorial," *Student Vanguard* 2, no. 1 (October 1933): 3.

35. Stephanie Spencer, "Advice and Ambition in a Girls' Public Day School: The Case of Sutton High School, 1884–1924," *Women's History Review* 9, no. 1 (2000): 75–94.

36. Mass Observation, established in 1937, deployed a panel of volunteer writers to study the everyday lives of ordinary people in Britain.

2 A New Era in Social Service? Student Associational Culture and the Settlement Movement

1. Alon Kadish, *Apostle Arnold: The Life and Death of Arnold Toynbee 1852–1883* (Durham, NC: Duke University Press, 1986), 156.

2. Francesca Wilson, "Dame Kathleen Courtney," KDG/K12/13, Women's Library (WL), 9.

3. C. R. Attlee, *The Social Worker* (London: G. Bell and Sons, 1920), 187.

4. Matthew Grimley, *Citizenship, Community, and the Church of England: Liberal Anglican Theories of the State between the Wars* (Oxford: OUP, 2008), 43.

5. Keith McClelland and Sonya Rose, "Citizenship and Empire, 1867–1928," in *At Home with the Empire: Metropolitan Culture and the Imperial World*, edited by Catherine Hall and Sonya Rose (Cambridge: CUP, 2006), 285.

6. Derek Heater, *Citizenship in Britain: A History* (Edinburgh: Edinburgh University Press, 2006), 166; Julia Stapleton, "Citizenship versus Patriotism in Twentieth Century England," *Historical Journal* 48, no. 1 (2005): 151–178.

7. Jose Harris, "Political Thought and the Welfare State 1870–1940: An Intellectual Framework for British Social Policy," *Past and Present* 135 (1992): 116–141; See also Melvin Richter, *The Politics of Conscience: T. H. Green and His Age* (London: Weidenfield and Nicholson, 1964).

8. Jose Harris, *Private Lives, Public Spirit: A Social History of Britain 1870–1914* (Oxford: OUP, 1993), 250.

9. H. Scott Holland, "Introduction," in *Lombard Street in Lent,* rev. ed. (London: Robert Scott, 1911), x.

10. Edward Caird, "The Nation as an Ethical Ideal," in *Lay Sermons and Addresses* (Glasgow: James Maclehose and Sons, 1907), 118–119.

11. Ibid.

12. Nathan Roberts, "Character in the Mind: Citizenship Education and Psychology in Britain 1880–1914," *History of Education* 33, no. 2 (2004), 180; Reba N. Soffer, *Discipline and Power: The University, History and the Making of an English Elite 1870–1930* (Stanford: Stanford University Press, 1994), 14–15.

13. Stefan Collini, *Public Moralists: Political Thought and Intellectual Life in Britain* (Oxford: OUP, 1991), 113.

14. Gary McCulloch, *Philosophers and Kings: Education for Leadership in Modern England* (Cambridge: CUP, 1991).

15. John Springhall, *Youth, Empire and Society: British Youth Movements, 1883–1940* (London: Croom Helm, 1977), 16–17; D. L. Ritchie, "Dr John Brown Paton," *Progress* 6, no. 2 (April 1911): 87.

16. Grimley, *Citizenship,* 43.

17. Keith Vernon, *Universities and the State in England, 1850–1939* (Abingdon: Routledge, 2004), 100.

18. Frank A. Rhodes, *The National Union of Students 1922 – 1967* (1968; Published Coventry: SUSOC, 1990), 13. I am grateful to Mike Day for giving me a copy of this thesis. See R. D. Anderson, *Universities and Elites in Britain Since 1800* (Cambridge: CUP, 1995), 14–15 for information on student numbers.

19. James Robb, *The Carnegie Trust for the Universities of Scotland, 1901–1926* (Edinburgh: Oliver and Boyd, 1927), 102.

20. Julie S. Gibert, "Women Students and Student life at England's Civic Universities before the First World War," *History of Education* 23, no. 4 (1994): 405–422.

21. Carol Dyhouse, "The British Federation of University Women and the Status of Women in Universities, 1907–1939," *Women's History Review* 4, no 4 (1995): 465–485, at 469.

22. McCulloch, *Philosophers and Kings,* 18–19.

23. J. A. Mangan, *The Games Ethic and Imperialism: Aspects of the Diffusion of an Ideal* (1986, repr., London: Frank Cass, 1998); Kathleen E. McCrone, *Sport and the Physical Emancipation of English Women* (London: Routledge, 1988); M. C. Curthoys and H. S. Jones, "Oxford Athleticism, 1850–1914: A Reappraisal," *History of Education,* 24, no. 4 (1995): 305–317.

24. Mabel Tylecote, *The Education of Women at the Manchester University 1883–1933* (Manchester: MUP, 1941), 39.

25. M. Pinkerton, *Patrick Geddes Hall: Scotland's First Hall of Residence* (Privately published, 1978), 7.

26. Eric Ashby and Mary Anderson, *The Rise of the Student Estate in Britain* (London: Macmillan and Co., 1970), 59.

27. Tim Macquiban, "Soup and Salvation: Social Service as an Emerging Motif for the British Methodist Response to Poverty in the Late 19th Century," *Methodist History* 39, no. 1 (2000): 28–43.

28. Ashby and Anderson, *Student Estate*, 21–22.

29. Hugh Martin, *The Student Christian Movement: A Survey of Its History and Growth* (London: Student Christian Movement, 1924), 3.

30. Soffer, *Discipline and Power*, 168.

31. Sir William Fletcher Shaw, "Foreword," in Ian G. Gregory, *In Memory of Burlington Street: An Appreciation of the Manchester University Unions 1861–1957* (Manchester: Manchester University Union, 1958), vii.

32. *Mermaid* 1, no. 4 (March 1905): 92.

33. Gilbert, "Women Students," 411–412.

34. "Letter from Kathleen Courtney to Her Mother," February 7, 1897, KDC/A3/8, WL.

35. Wilson, "Dame Kathleen Courtney," 8.

36. *Mermaid* 1, no. 1 (October 1904): 2.

37. Quoted in Helen Bosanquet, *Social Work in London 1869–1912: A History of the Charity Organisation Society* (London: John Murray, 1914), 74.

38. *University of London Students Handbook 1910*, UN/5/7/1, University of London Archive, Senate House Library (SH), 45.

39. Ian M. Randall, "The Social Gospel: A Case Study," in *Evangelical Faith and Public Zeal: Evangelicals and Society in Britain 1780–1980*, edited by John Wolffe, 155–174 (London: SPCK, 1995).

40. T. M. Parker, "The Tractarians' Successors: The Influence of the Contemporary Mood" in *Ideas and Beliefs of the Victorians: An Historic Revaluation of the Victorian Age*, 120–125 (London: Sylvan Press, 1949).

41. B. F. Westcott, *Social Aspects of Christianity* (London: Macmillan, 1887), 140.

42. Judith Harford, *The Opening of University Education to Women in Ireland* (Dublin: Irish Academic Press, 2008), 31–32.

43. D. W. Bebbington, *Evangelicalism in Modern Britain: A History from the 1730s to the 1980s* (London: Routledge, 1988).

44. Kathleen Heasman, *Evangelicals in Action: An Appraisal of their Social Work in the Victorian Era* (London: Geoffrey Bles, 1962), 26–27; D. L. Moody, *An Address to Young Converts* (Dublin: G Herbert, 1883).

45. Eugene Stock, "The Missionary Element," in *The Keswick Convention: Its Message, Its Method and Its Men,* edited by Charles F. Harford, 133 (London: Marshall Brothers, 1907).

46. Randall, "Social Gospel," 171; K. S. Inglis, "English Non-Conformity and Social Reform 1880–1900," *Past and Present* 13, no. 1 (1958): 73–88.

47. Dyhouse, *Students*, 187.

48. Gregory, *Burlington Street*, 42.
49. "Students' Night at the Theatre Royal," *QCB* 6, no. 4 (February 1905): 2–3; "Panto Night," *Mermaid* 2, no. 4 (March 1906): 110–111.
50. Ashby and Anderson, *Student Estate*, 21–22.
51. Ibid., 47.
52. *University of London Students' Handbook 1910*.
53. "The Inter-University Congress," *Mermaid* 1, no. 1 (October 1904): 11–13; "Account of the British University Students Congress," *Mermaid* 5, no. 1 (November 1908): 19–20.
54. "Inter-Universities Students' Congress," *University Review* 2, no. 1 (June 1905): 209–210.
55. "The Congress 1906," *Manchester University Magazine* 3, no. 17 (November 1906): 17.
56. Ashby and Anderson, *Student Estate*, 60.
57. Henrietta Barnett, *Canon Barnett: His Life, Work and Friends* (London: John Murray, 1918), I, 302–303.
58. Sir Baldwyn Leighton ed., *Letters and Other Writings of the Late Edward Denison* (1871; repr., London: Richard Bentley and Son, 1875).
59. J. R. Green, "Edward Denison – In Memoriam," *Macmillan's Magazine* 24 (May–October 1871): 376–383.
60. Leighton, *Edward Denison*.
61. Robert Woods and Albert Kennedy eds., *Handbook of Settlements* (1911; repr., New York: Arnos Press, 1970), ix.
62. *Review of Reviews*, 24 (July–December 1901): 677; F. K. Prochaska, *Women and Philanthropy in Nineteenth-Century England* (Oxford: Clarendon Press, 1980), 75.
63. S. P. Grundy, "Social Service 3: What Public School Men Can Do," *Hibbert Journal* 10, no. 3 (April 1912): 685–692; Nigel Scotland, *Squires in the Slums: Settlements and Missions in Late-Victorian London* (London: I. B. Tauris, 2007), 104.
64. For examples, see Thomas Hinde, *Paths of Progress: A History of Marlborough College* (London: James and James, 1992), 142–143; W. McG Eagar, *Making Men: The History of Boys' Clubs and Related Movements in Great Britain* (London: University of London Press, 1953).
65. Georgina Brewis, "From Working Parties to Social Work: Middle-class Girls' Education and Social Service 1890–1914," *History of Education* 38, no. 6 (November 2009): 761–777.
66. Carol Dyhouse, *Girls Growing Up in Late Victorian and Edwardian England* (London: Routledge and Kegan Paul, 1981), 27–30.
67. Jennifer Stephens, *The Peckham Settlement 1896–2000: A Story of Poverty, Privilege, Pioneering and Partnership* (Fordingbridge: Stephens Press, 2002).
68. Doris Burchell, *Miss Buss' Second School* (London: Frances Mary Buss Foundation, 1971), 49; *Church of England High School Magazine*, April 1901, 2; *Ulula*, December 1909, 208.

69. Barnett, *Canon Barnett*, I, 308.
70. Jenny Harrow, "The Development of University Settlements in England, 1884–1939," PhD Thesis (London: London School of Economics, 1987).
71. Robert Woods, *English Social Movements* (London: Swan Sonnenschein & Co, 1895); N. B. Kent ed., *Cambridge in South London: The Work of the College Missions 1883–1914* (Cambridge: W. Heffer and Sons, 1914).
72. *The History and Function of Cambridge House* (Cambridge: Bowes and Bowes, 1934), 10.
73. Kent, *Cambridge in South London*, 191.
74. Tylecote, *Education of Women*, 41.
75. Vicinus, *Independent Women*, 229.
76. Marian F. Pease, "IV," *Hilda Cashmore 1876–1943* (Gloucester: Privately printed, 1944), 15.
77. Hilda Jennings, *University Settlement Bristol: Sixty Years of Change 1911–1971* (Bristol: University Settlement Bristol Community Association, 1971), 7.
78. Robert Hamilton and Jean Macleay, *Glasgow University Settlement: A Centennial History* (Glasgow: University of Glasgow, 1998), 27–28.
79. Walter Besant, "Art and the People," in *As We Are and As We May Be* (London: Chatto and Windus, 1903), 267.
80. Percy Alden, "American Settlements," in *University and Social Settlements*, edited by Will Reason, 137–151 (London: Methuen and Co, 1898).
81. Alden, "American Settlements," 137; Woods, *English Social Movements*.
82. D. M. Brodie, *Women's University Settlement, 1887–1937* (London: Women's University Settlement, 1937), 6.
83. Sir John Gorst, ""Settlements" in England and America," in *Universities and the Social Problem: An Account of the University Settlements in East London*, edited by John Knapp (London: Rivington, Percival and Co. 1895), 9.
84. Ibid.
85. Eagar, *Making Men*; Beauman, *Women and the Settlement Movement*, 189.
86. Liverpool University Settlement, "First Annual Report," D7/3, Liverpool University Settlement Archive, University of Liverpool Special Collections (UL).
87. Harrow, "University Settlements," 328.
88. Muriel Wragge, *The London I Loved: Reminiscences of Fifty Years Social Work in the District of Hoxton* (London: James Clarke and Co. 1960).
89. Ibid., 12.
90. "The Inter-University Congress," *Mermaid* 1, no. 1 (October 1904): 12; "University Students Congress," *Manchester Guardian*, July 2, 1904, 14.

91. Notably in institutional histories of individual settlements. See also Martha Vicinus, *Independent Women: Work and Community for Single Women, 1850–1920* (London: Virago, 1985), Ch. 6; Scotland, *Squires.*

92. Though see Harrow, "University Settlements."

93. Barbara Stephen, *Girton College, 1869–1932* (Cambridge: CUP, 1933), 158; C. F. Andrews, "Reminiscences II," *Modern Review* 17 (March 1915): 271–278; *Toynbee Hall General Information* (London: Toynbee Hall, 1906), 3.

94. Barnett, *Canon Barnett*, II, 21; *WUS Tenth Annual Report*, June 1897, 20; *Brown Book*, December 1911, 33–34; *Student Movement Oxford*, June 1906, 36.

95. *Women's University Settlement Fifth Annual Report* (London: WUS, 1892).

96. *WUS Fifth Annual Report*, 6; *Women Workers: The Official Report of the Conference Held at Nottingham 1895* (Nottingham: James Bell, 1895), 200; Mrs. Dunn Gardner, "The Training of Volunteers: Paper Read to the Council of the Charity Organisation Society 1894," in *Professional Education for Social Work in Britain: An Historical Account*, edited by Marjorie Smith (1953; repr., London: George Allen and Unwin, 1965), 69–78.

97. *WUS Third Annual Report 1890*, 6.

98. "Early Leaflets on Student Training," AR2, WUS, WL.

99. *WUS Fourth Annual Report, 1891*, 8.

100. Harrow, "University Settlements," 285.

101. *WUS Nineteenth Annual Report 1906*, 15–16.

102. Constance N. Bartlett, "Women's University Settlement," *Brown Book: Lady Margaret Hall Chronicle*, June 1906, 24–26; J. Mordaunt Crook ed., *Bedford College University of London: Memories of 150 Years* (London: Royal Holloway and Bedford New College, 2001), 314.

103. Cecile Matheson, "Training for Social Work," *Journal of Education*, September 1908 in "Scrapbook of Cecile Matheson," 10/36, WL.

104. W. J. Ashley, *On Social Study* (Reprinted from the Year-Book of Social Progress, 1912); *Progress* 3 (July 1906): 231; *The Year-Book of Social Progress for 1912* (London: Thomas Nelson, 1912), 22–27.

105. "Birmingham Women's Settlement," Birmingham Daily Post, October 29, 1910 in Scrapbook of Cecile Matheson.

106. Kent, *Cambridge in South London*, 18.

107. *Report of the Trinity College Mission in St George's, Camberwell, SE* (Cambridge, 1888), 12.

108. Woods, *English Social Movements*, 86.

109. Andrews, "Reminiscences II," 271–278.

110. Alan Mayne, *The Imagined Slum: Newspaper Representation in Three Cities* (Leicester: Leicester University Press, 1993), 128.

111. Mary Bhore, "Some Impressions of England," *Indian Ladies Magazine* 1, no. 7 (January 1902): 204–212.

112. Ellen Ross, "Slum Journeys: Ladies and London Poverty 1860–1940," in *The Archaeology of Urban Landscapes,* edited by Alan Mayne and Tim Murray, 11–21 (Cambridge: CUP, 2001).
113. SCM, *Social Service in the Christian Unions* (London: SCM, 1914), 9; *Student Movement Oxford,* December 1906, 45.
114. Neil Meldrum, "The Salvation Army Social Scheme," *Student Movement* 10, no. 5 (February 1908): 110–112.
115. *Hermes,* April 1911.
116. *Hermes,* November 1919, 7.
117. *Sunflower Special Number Miss McDougall,* 8.
118. Rev. C. D. Plater, *Social Work on Leaving School* (London: Catholic Truth Society, 1911), 17.
119. *Women's University Settlement, First Annual Report 1888,* 13; *WUS Seventh Annual Report,* June 1894, 23; Kent, *Cambridge in South London,* 103.
120. "Manchester University Settlement," *Owen's College Union Magazine,* 67 (February 1901): 86.
121. Irene Bliss, "Reminiscences of Westfield College 1907–1911," Westfield College Archive, Queen Mary University of London Special Collections (QMUL), 7.
122. Hugh Legge, *Trinity College Mission in Stratford, 1888–1899* (London, 1899), 3–4.
123. Legge, *Trinity College Mission,* 10; Kent, *Cambridge in South London,* 25, 103.
124. *Manchester University Magazine* 3, no. 19 (January 1907): 101.
125. Winifred M. Gill, "At Barton Hill and at Ancoats," in *Hilda Cashmore,* 37; Jennings, *University Settlement Bristol,* 117.
126. H. G. G. Mackenzie, *Medical Control in a Boys' Club* (London: J. M. Dent and Sons, 1925); Kent, *Cambridge in South London,* 115.
127. Kent, *Cambridge in South London,* 183–185; *The Toynbee Record* 10, no. 8 (May 1898): 110; *Toynbee Hall General Information,* 14.
128. Cyril Bailey, *A Short History of the Balliol Boys' Club 1907–1950* (Oxford: OUP, 1950).
129. Kent, *Cambridge in South London,* 192.
130. Harrow, "University Settlements," 257–258.
131. "Manchester University Settlement," *Owen's College Union Magazine* no. 67 (February 1901): 86; "Ancoats University Settlement," *Owen's College Union Magazine,* 70 (May 1901): 137.
132. E. J. W. Jackson, "Memorandum on the Present State of Social Study and Practice in the Colleges," SCM A27/1, University of Birmingham Special Collections (UB).
133. Lucy M. Moor, *Girls of Yesterday and Today: The Romance of the YWCA* (London: S. W. Partridge and Co., Ltd, 1910), 92; Frederick A. Atkins, *Moral Muscle and How to Use It: A Brotherly Chat with Young Men* (London: James Nisbet and Co, 1890), 37.
134. *Women Workers Conference Report 1911,* 177.

135. H. Reinherz, "Committee Work," *Time and Talents* 13, no. 49 (January 1913): 11–13.
136. Gladys Page-Wood, "At the Training College," in *Hilda Cashmore*, 20.
137. *Young Man*, June 1912, 182.
138. F. Herbert Stead, *Handbook on Young People's Guilds* (London: Congregational Union of England and Wales, 1889), 13.
139. Geoffrey Crossick and Heinz-Gerhard Haupt, *The Petite Bourgeoisie in Europe 1780–1914: Enterprise, Family and Independence* (London: Routledge, 1995), 209–215.
140. H. G. Wells et al., *What the Worker Wants: The Daily Mail Enquiry* (London: Hodder and Stoughton, 1912).
141. John Galsworthy, "Public Schools as 'Caste' Factories." in *What the Worker Wants*, 68–71; W. T. A. Barber, "Not Patronage, but Friendship," in *What the Worker Wants*, 101.
142. George Hare Leonard, *Nobler Cares* (London: Simpkin, Marshall, Hamilton, Kent and Co., 1908), 38–39; Kent, *Cambridge in South London*, 193.
143. *The Great Appeal of the Cavendish Association to Men of the Public Schools and Universities* (London: John Murray, 1913), 79.
144. "The Universities and Social Service," *Times*, October 28, 1911, 7.
145. Kent, *Cambridge in South London*, 193.

3 CHRISTIAN INTERNATIONALISM, SOCIAL STUDY AND THE UNIVERSITIES BEFORE 1914

1. C. F. Andrews, "Possibilities of Social Service," *St Stephen's College Magazine*, November 1908, reprinted in *The Stephanian Andrews Centenary Number*, June 1971, 94–95.
2. Antoinette Burton, *Burdens of History: British Feminists, Indian Women and Imperial Culture 1865–1915* (Chapel Hill: University of North Carolina Press, 1994); Thomas Metcalf, *Ideologies of the Raj* (Cambridge: CUP, 1994).
3. Tissington Tatlow, *The Story of the Student Christian Movement* (London: SCM Press, 1933), 23.
4. Ibid, 42.
5. Andrew Porter, "Cambridge, Keswick and Late Nineteenth Century Attitudes to Africa," *Journal of Imperial and Commonwealth History* 5, no. 1 (1976): 5–34, at 19.
6. Eugene Stock, "The Student Volunteer Movement," in *Ecumenical Missionary Conference New York 1900* (New York: American Tract Society, 1900), I, 111–112.
7. The term Student Christian Movement is used throughout.
8. "Student Missionary Conference Liverpool 1908 Handbook for Delegates," SCM A23, UB, 7.
9. Ruth Rouse, "Pioneer Days among Women Students," *Student World* 27, no. 1 (1934): 54.

10. Johanna M. Selles, *A History of the World Student Christian Federation,1895–1920* (Pickwick, 2011), 91.

11. Walter Seton, "The Rise and Progress of the Student Christian Movement," *University Review* 5, no. 1 (September 1905): 465–487, at 473.

12. Walter Seton, "The Summer Conference of the Student Christian Movement," *University Review* 3, 16 (August 1906).

13. Hugh Martin, *The Student Christian Movement: A Survey of Its History and Growth* (London: Student Christian Movement, 1924), 4–5; Tatlow, *Student Christian Movement*, 15; Reason, *University and Social Settlements*, 190.

14. Stephen Band, "The Discussion at Matlock on Christian Unions and Social Problems," *Student Movement* 6, no. 1 (October 1903): 25; George Hare Leonard, "Christian Unions and College Settlements," *Student Movement* 6, no. 2 (November 1903): 40–41.

15. Rouse, "Pioneer Days," 58.

16. SCM, "Notes for Social Service Secretaries in Christian Unions," 1909, SCM A27.

17. Tatlow, *Student Christian Movement*, 379.

18. Seton, "Progress of the Student Christian Movement," 486.

19. Renate Howe, "The Australian Student Christian Movement and Women's Activism in the Asia-Pacific Region, 1890s-1920s," *Australian Feminist Studies* 16, no. 36 (2001): 316.

20. Selles, *World Student Christian Federation*, 2.

21. Ibid., 79.

22. Ruth Rouse, *The World's Student Christian Federation: A History of the First Thirty Years* (London: SCM Press, 1948), 86.

23. Lady Margaret Hall, *Lady Margaret Hall: A Short History* (London: OUP, 1923), 110–113, 141.

24. "Jubilee History of Settlement," Missionary Settlement of University Women Archive, MSS Eur F186/170, British Library (BL), 1–2.

25. *Make Jesus King: The Report of the International Students' Missionary Conference* (London: SVMU, 1896), 238; "Minutes of a Meeting Held 21 April 1896," Missionary Settlement for University Women Minute Book 1895–1898, MSS Eur F186/3, BL.

26. CMS, *Extracts from the Annual Letters of the Missionaries for 1900* (London: CMS, 1901), 410.

27. C. F. Andrews, *North India* (London: A. R. Mowbray, 1909), 103–104.

28. T. R. W. Lunt, "Report on First Years Work 1911/1912," Educational Committee File, CMS/G/E1, UB.

29. W. E. F. Ward, *Fraser of Trinity and Achimota* (Accra: Ghana Universities Press, 1965), 64; P. Edmonds, "The First Seventy Five Years," in *Edwardes College Peshawar 1900–1975 Diamond Jubilee Celebration* (Peshawar: Edwardes College, 1975), 24.

30. Rudra cited in F. F. Monk, *A History of St. Stephen's College, Delhi* (Calcutta: YMCA, 1935), 144.

31. Letter from C. F. Andrews, Delhi to Canon Cunninghan, Farnham dated February 11, 1908, SCM A21.
32. "Jubilee History of Settlement."
33. D. J. Fleming, "Social Service among Oriental Students," *Religious Education* 9, no. 3 (1914): 250–258, at 250.
34. Fleming, "Social Service among Oriental Students," 250.
35. Rouse, *World's Student Christian Federation*, 69.
36. Renate Howe, *A Century of Influence: The Australian Student Christian Movement, 1896–1996* (Sydney: University of New South Wales Press, 2009), 114.
37. Christine Berry, *The New Zealand Student Christian Movement: A Centenary History, 1986–1996* (Christchurch: SCM of Aotearoa, 1998), 9–12.
38. Fleming, "Social Service among Oriental Students," 252.
39. J. S. Burgess, "Secretary, YMCA. Peking, China Report for the Year Ending September 1915," Annual Reports of the Foreign Secretaries of the International Committee, Kautz Family YMCA Archives, University of Minnesota Libraries, accessed January 27, 2014, http://umedia.lib.umn.edu. See also Yung-chen Chiang, *Social Engineering and the Social Sciences in China, 1919–1949* (New York: CUP, 2000).
40. Georgina Brewis, "Education for Service: Social Service and Higher Education in India and Britain, 1905–1919," *History of Education Review* 42, no. 2 (2013): 119–136.
41. C. F. Andrews, "The Effect of the Japanese Victories upon India," *East and the West*, October 1905, 361–372; S. K. Rudra, "Is India Thirsting for Religious Truth," *East and the West*, January 1906, 1–8.
42. G. K. Gokhale, "Presidential Address," in *Indian National Congress Twenty-First Session Held at Benares* (Madras: G. A. Natesan, 1906), 7.
43. W. E. S. Holland, "Mission Hostels in India," in *East and the West*, July 1908, 272–282; *Madras Christian College Magazine* 24, no. 12 (June 1907): 648.
44. C. F. Andrews, *The Renaissance in India: Its Missionary Aspect* (London: Young People's Missionary Movement, 1912).
45. Andrews, *North India*, 225; Hayden A. Bellenoit, *Missionary Education and Empire in Late Colonial India, 1860–1920* (London: Pickering and Chatto, 2007), 7.
46. CMS, *Annual Letters 1907*, 312.
47. "Wilson College Students and the Influenza Epidemic," *Social Service Quarterly* 3, no. 3 (January 1919): 114–115.
48. Monk, *St. Stephen's College*, 227.
49. Brewis, "Education for Service."
50. Valentine Chirol, *Indian Unrest* (London: Macmillan, 1910), 201.
51. "College Notes," *Madras Christian College Magazine*, New series 15, no. 3 (September 1915): 136; *Madras Christian College Magazine*, New series 13, no. 4 (October 1913).

52. *Forman Christian College Notes*, New Series 3, no. 1 (January 1911): 9.
53. *Forman Christian College Monthly* 11, no. 3 (December 1919): 8.
54. J. N. Farquhar, *Modern Religious Movements in India* (New York: Macmillan, 1915).
55. Sherwood Eddy, *The New Era in Asia* (Edinburgh: Oliphant, Anderson and Ferrier: 1914).
56. Sherwood Eddy, "India's Fourfold Awakening," in *Students and the World-Wide Expansion of Christianity*, edited by Fennell P. Turner, 286 (New York: Student Volunteer Movement, 1914).
57. A. G. Fraser, "Education in India and Ceylon in View of the National Movement," *East and the West*, January 1908, 28–42.
58. *Hermes*, October 1913, 16.
59. Padmini Sengupta, *Sarojini Naidu: A Biography* (London: Asia Publishing House, 1966), 83.
60. "Social Service in India," *Progress* 13 (January 1909): 36–37; Fleming, "Social Service among Oriental Students," 250; Andrews, *Renaissance in India*, 57–58.
61. Chiang, *Social Engineering*, 35.
62. SCM, *Social Service in the Christian Unions*, 10.
63. Ibid.
64. SCM, *The Leadership of a Study Circle* (London: SCM, 1912).
65. SCM, "Social Study Statistics," SCM A27.
66. British Institute of Social Service, *Annual Report of the British Institute of Social Service, 1908*.
67. *Student Movement* 10, no. 4 (January 1908): 94; *University of London Students Handbook 1910*, 21.
68. Jose Harris, *Private Lives, Public Spirit: A Social History of Britain 1870–1914* (Oxford: OUP, 1993), 196.
69. Percy Alden, "Some Hints on Social Study," in *Conference on War Relief and Personal Service* (London: Longman's Green and Co., 1915), 76; John Martin Cleary, *Catholic Social Action in Britain, 1909–1959: A History of the Catholic Social Guild* (Oxford: Catholic Social Guild, 1961), 48.
70. Turner, *Students and the World-Wide Expansion of Christianity*, 27.
71. Michael J. Moore, "Social Service and Social Legislation in Edwardian England: The Beginning of a New Role for Philanthropy," *Albion: A Quarterly Journal Concerned with British Studies* 3, no. 1 (Spring 1971): 33–43.
72. Cecile Matheson, "Opportunities for Training for Personal Service," in *Women Workers: The Papers Read at the Conference held in Oxford 1912* (London: NUWW, 1912), 52.
73. "The Larger Work of the Guild of Help," *Progress* 3, no. 2 (April 1908): 103.
74. H. L. Woollcombe, "Development of Personal Service," in *Conference on War Relief and Personal Service* (London: Longman's Green and Co., 1915), 142.

75. Moore, "Social Service and Social Legislation," 38; *Adult School Social Service Handbook*, 54.

76. Stefan Collini, "Hobhouse, Bosanquet and the State: Philosophical Idealism and Political Argument in England 1880–1918," *Past and Present* 72 (1976): 87.

77. Frederick Rockell, "The Knights of the Long Table: An Account of the Social Work of Mansfield House University Settlement, Canning Town, London," *Millgate Monthly* 7 (February 1912): 301.

78. Richard A. Voeltz, "'A Good Jew and a Good Englishman': The Jewish Lads' Brigade, 1894–1922," *Journal of Contemporary History* 23, no. 1 (January 1988): 119–127.

79. Sharman Kadish, *A Good Jew and a Good Englishman: The Jewish Lads' and Girls' Brigade 1895–1995* (London: Valentine Mitchell, 1995), 25, 36–45.

80. *Catholic Social Year Book for 1910*, 21.

81. *Catholic Social Year Book for 1912*, 43; *Catholic Social Year Book for 1914*, 42; Rev. C. D. Plater, *Social Work on Leaving School* (London: Catholic Truth Society, 1911).

82. Peter Hinchcliff, "Religious Issues, 1870–1914," in *History of the University of Oxford* VII *Nineteenth Century Oxford*, edited by M. G. Brock and M. C. Curthoys (Oxford: OUP, 2000), Pt 2, 109.

83. Leonard, "Christian Unions and College Settlements," 40.

84. *Student Movement Oxford*, October 1906, 37; William Paton, *The Student Volunteer in College* (London: Student Christian Movement, 1913), 4.

85. SCM, *Social Service in the Christian Unions*, 10; *Social Study and Service in the Christian Unions* (London: SCM, 1917), 7; George Foulkes ed., *Eighty Years On* (Edinburgh: SRC, 1964), 38.

86. Jackson, "Social Study and Practice in the Colleges," 3.

87. Ibid., 4.

88. "A Conference of Students on Foreign Missions and Social Problems," SCM A42.

89. Hugh Martin, "Editor's Introduction," in *Citizenship: An Introductory Handbook*, edited by M. Cecile Matheson, 6 (London: Student Christian Movement, 1917).

90. Foulkes, *Eighty Years On*, 11.

91. Martin, "Introduction," 6.

92. Ibid., 4.

4   THE STUDENT CHAPTER IN POSTWAR
RECONSTRUCTION, 1920–1926

1. Ruth Rouse, *Rebuilding Europe: The Student Chapter in Post-War Reconstruction* (London: SCM Press, 1925), 20.

2. Ibid., 20, 61.

3. "Relief of Distress in Europe and Asia," Beveridge Papers Bev 7/90/6, London School of Economics Special Collections (LSE).

4. Emily Baughan, "The Imperial War Relief Fund and the All British Appeal: Commonwealth, Conflict and Conservatism within the British Humanitarian Movement, 1920–25," *Journal of Imperial and Commonwealth History* 40, no. 5 (2012): 845–861.

5. Eleanora Iredale, "Address Given at the International Committee of the Student Christian Movement, 1926: Being a Brief Record of the Work of the Universities' Relief Committee 1920–26," SCM/W11, UB; "Letter from Beveridge to Owen Smith," June 9, 1920, Bev 7/90/18.

6. Universities' Committee Minutes, September 24, 1920, SCM/W11.

7. Universities' Committee Minutes, November 26, 1920, SCM/W11.

8. G. S. M. Ellis, *The Poor Student and the University* (London: Labour Publishing Co., 1925), 16.

9. David Fowler, *Youth Culture in Modern Britain c. 1920–1970* (Basingstoke: Palgrave Macmillan, 2008), 10.

10. Keith Vernon, *Universities and the State in England, 1850–1939* (Abingdon: Routledge, 2004), 186.

11. Tissington Tatlow cited in "WUS 50 Years," *WUS in Action* 20, no 1 (February 1970): 6. I am grateful to Alan Phillips for giving me a copy of this publication.

12. Ibid., 6.

13. Ibid., 8.

14. Rouse, *Rebuilding Europe*, 34.

15. "WUS and Student Health Services," *ISS Year Book*, 1951, 32.

16. *The European Student Relief of the World's Student Christian Federation, A Brief Record of Work in Austria September 1920-April 1923* (Vienna: WSCF, 1923).

17. James Parkes, *Voyage of Discoveries* (London: Victor Gollancz, 1969), 86.

18. Rouse, *Rebuilding Europe*, 158; NUS, *The Leipzig Conference Report Issued by the National Union of Students* (London: NUS, 1922), 7.

19. Rouse, *Rebuilding Europe*, 221.

20. *ISS Year Book*, 1950, 9.

21. "The Refugee Student," SCM/N/5/2, 1.

22. Rouse, *Rebuilding Europe*, 20, 61; The Universities' Committee raised £32,645 in 1920–1921, £34,683 in 1921–1922 mainly for Russian students, £29,223 in 1922–1923 for Germany, and £22,208 in 1923–1924 again for Germany.

23. Iredale, "Address," 5.

24. Robert Mackie, "The Growth of WUS a Personal Impression" in "WUS 50 Years," 7.

25. "A Letter from the Archbishop of Canterbury," Bev 7/90/234, 1.

26. Ruth Rouse, "European Student Relief," *The East and the West* 21, no. 82 (April 1923): 155–168, at 168.

27. Iredale, "Address," 5; "Imperial War Relief Fund: Universities Committee Leeds," *The Gryphon* New Series 5, no. 1 (October 1923): 23.
28. "Letter from George Cadbury to Tissington Tatlow," March 20, 1920, SCM/W11.
29. "Glasgow University's Infirmaries Day," *Glasgow University Magazine* 32, no. 5 (January 19, 1921): 200.
30. "Infirmaries Day," *Glasgow University Magazine* 32, no. 6 (February 23, 1921): 235–236.
31. "Carnival: From Medical Society to Guild," *Mermaid* New Series 7, no. 5 (May 1937): 106.
32. Universities' Committee Minutes, April 19, 1921, Bev 7/90/113, 2, 9.
33. Universities' Committee Minutes, October 3, 1921, Bev 7/90/152; "The European Students' Relief Fund," *Dragon* 47, no. 2 (March 1925): 124.
34. Universities' Committee Minutes, April 19, 1921, Bev 7/90/113, 5.
35. Universities' Committee Minutes, May 1, 1922, Bev 7/90/113, 2.
36. "Suggestions as to how to raise funds," Bev 7/90/4, 2.
37. Universities' Committee Minutes, January 12, 1922, Bev 7/90/199, 4.
38. Universities' Committee Minutes, May 1, 1922, Bev 7/90/216, 2.
39. Universities' Committee Minutes, April 19, 1921, Bev 7/90/113, 4.
40. Rouse, *Rebuilding Europe*, 77.
41. Jeremy Lewis, *Shades of Greene: One Generation of an English Family* (London: Jonathan Cape, 2010), 52–53.
42. Iredale, "Address," 12.
43. "Review," *Serpent* 10, no. 1 (November 1925): 20.
44. Harold Abrahams, "Report of Mr Harold Abrahams," Appendix A to Universities' Committee Minutes, May 1, 1922, Bev 7/90/216, 9–10.
45. R. I. Jardine, "The Student and the Future: International Student Service and the Pacific," *Pacific Affairs* 4, no. 2 (February 1931): 113–119, at 113.
46. Ibid., 114.
47. Universities' Committee Minutes, May 1, 1922, Bev 7/90/216, 3.
48. C. P. Blacker, *Central European Universities After the War* (London: Privately printed, 1922), 57–58.
49. Rouse, *Rebuilding Europe*, 62.
50. Mackie, "The Growth of WUS," 7.
51. C. W. Guillebaud, "The Mount Holyoke Conference of International Student Service," *The University* 24 (Michaelmas 1931): 13–16; "Letter from J. Kathleen Teasdel and Gywn Williams," *Cap and Gown* 23, no. 1 (November 1925): 45–46; "The University Looks at the World," *Tamesis* 25, no. 8 (Autumn term 1926): 127–129.
52. Parkes, *Voyage of Discoveries*, 80.
53. "The Geneva Conference," *Serpent* 10, no. 1 (November 1925): 4.
54. Universities' Committee Minutes, December 14, 1923, Bev 7/90/245, 4.
55. A. Michael Critchley, "International Student Service Conference, August, 1926," *Nonesuch* 46 (November 1926): 36–37.

56. For a discussion see Peter Shapely, "Urban Charity, Class Relations and Social Cohesion: Charitable Responses to the Cotton Famine," *Urban History* 28, no. 1 (2001): 46–64 and Georgina Brewis, "'Fill Full the Mouth of Famine': Voluntary Action in Indian Famine Relief 1896–1901," *Modern Asian Studies* 44, no. 4 (Spring 2010): 887–918.
57. "The End of an Experiment," *Headway* 7, no 8 (August 1925): 155.
58. Helen McCarthy, *The British People and the League of Nations: Democracy, Citizenship and Internationalism, c. 1918–1945* (Manchester: MUP, 2011).
59. *Headway* 2, no. 7 (April–May 1920): 128; "Calendar," *Glasgow University Magazine* 32, no. 2 (December 1, 1920): 106.
60. *Headway* 2, no. 10 (July–August 1920): 182; *Headway* 3, no. 15 (December 1920): 78.
61. *Headway* 3, no. 15 (December 1920): 78.
62. "League of Nations Society," *Cap and Gown* 23, no. 2 (Lent term 1926): 42; "League of Nations Society," *Cap and Gown* 24, no. 2 (1926): 49.
63. "The Oxford Assembly," *Headway*, New Series 3, no. 12 (December 1921): 63.
64. Parkes, *Voyage of Discoveries*, 60.
65. *Headway* 3, no. 14 (November–Dececember 1920): 70.
66. Mike Day, "'Respected not Respectable: A New History of the NUS," Unpublished manuscript, 9.
67. This group evolved into the Scottish Union of Students in 1935, remaining independent until it merged with NUS in 1971. From 1971 the group was known as NUS Scotland.
68. *Gryphon* (July 1939): 5.
69. Ivison S. Macadam, *Youth in the Universities: A Paper on National and International Students' Organisations* (London: NUS, 1922), 18.
70. NUS, "Facing the Facts" c. 1923, WP 7260, British Library.
71. NUS, *Special Tours in Germany and Hungary* (London: NUS, 1922).
72. NUS, "The National Union of Students," 1928, WP 7260, British Library Pamphlet Collection.
73. NUS, *Annual Report of the Council 1925–1926* (London: NUS, 1926), 8.
74. "The National Union of Students," *Cap and Gown* 23, no. 1 (November 1925): 13.
75. *Northerner* 29, no. 2 (March 1929): 43.
76. NUS, *Universities Congress Oxford, March-April 1925* (NUS: London, 1925), 11.
77. "Minutes of a Meeting of the Universities' Committee," October 2, 1922, Bev7/90/227, 2.
78. "Informal Weekend Conference," Bev7/90/259, 3.
79. Parkes, *Voyage of Discoveries*, 59.
80. "Christian Unity in Youth: The Student Movement Opening of Liverpool Conference," *Manchester Guardian* (January 3, 1929): 12.

81. "A Short Report on the Work of the Student Christian Movement, 1927–8," SCM/N5, 12.
82. *Christ and the Student World: A Review of the World's Student Christian Federation* (London: SCM, 1922), 31.
83. F. G. Thomas, "A Review of Union Activities," *Gryphon*, New Series 5, no. 6 (July 1924): 198.
84. Parkes, *Voyage of Discoveries*, 58.
85. "The Geneva Conference," *Serpent* 10, no. 1 (November 1925): 4.
86. *NUS Report of the Council for the session 1927–1928*, 11.
87. "A Chronological History of ISS," in *International Student Service: The Year in Retrospect 1947–1948* (London: British Cooperating Committee of ISS, 1949), 31–42.
88. Blacker, *Central European Universities*, 61.
89. Harold Silver, *Higher Education and Opinion Making in Twentieth-century England* (London: Frank Cass, 2003), 23.
90. "Exeter and Oxford," *Ram*, Summer 1936, 13–14.
91. WUS, *WUS Yearbook 1956* (London: WUS, 1957), 29; "International Student Service: General Secretary's Visit to Scotland," *The Scotsman*, December 3, 1936, 7; In 1943, these committees merged into one ISS Committee for Britain and Northern Ireland.

5 NO LONGER THE PRIVILEGE OF THE WELL-TO-DO? STUDENT CULTURE, STRIKES AND SELF-HELP, 1926–1932

1. NUS, *A Survey of Seven Years Development* (London: NUS, 1930), 18.
2. Donald Grant, *The European Student Relief of the World's Student Christian Federation, A Brief Record of Work in Austria September 1920-April 1923* (Vienna: WSCF, 1923).
3. "International Student Service Occasional Papers 2," November 1927, L217, London School of Economics Pamphlet Collection (LSE).
4. Harold Silver, *Higher Education and Opinion Making in Twentieth-century England* (London: Frank Cass, 2003), 30.
5. T. W. Bamford, *The University of Hull: The First Fifty Years* (Oxford: OUP, 1978), 48–49, 64.
6. Mabel Tylecote, *The Education of Women at the Manchester University 1883–1933* (Manchester: MUP, 1941), 118.
7. Joan Webbe, "A Chapter on Women," in *Young Minds for Old: Fourteen Young University Writers on Modern Problems*, edited by Lincoln Ralphs (London: Frederick Muller, 1936).
8. L. Doreen Whiteley, *The Poor Student and the University* (London: George Allen and Unwin, 1933), 30.
9. Phoebe Sheavyn, *Higher Education for Women in Great Britain* (London: International Federation of University Women, 1922), 19–21.
10. Brian Simon, *A Student's View of the Universities* (London: Longmans, 1943), 124.

11. Ibid., 39.
12. Carol Dyhouse, "Going to University in England between the Wars: Access and Funding," *History of Education* 31, no. 1, (2002): 1–14; Pat Thane, "Girton Graduates: Earning and Learning, 1920s-1980s," *Women's History Review* 13, no. 3 (2004): 347–361.
13. "Questionnaire Sent to Students by the Union Society of Queen Mary College, London March 1938," SIM/4/7/7, Brian Simon Papers, Institute of Education Archives (IOE), 4.
14. "Occupations of parents of students who entered [King's College London] Medical School in October 1938," SIM/4/7/2/1.
15. Leta Jones, *Coward's Custard* (London: Minerva Press, 1998), 51.
16. J. R. Peddie, *The Carnegie Trust for the Universities of Scotland: The First Fifty Years* (Edinburgh: Pillans and Wilson, 1951), 57.
17. Michael Moss, J. Forbes Munro and Richard H. Trainor, *University, City and State: The University of Glasgow since 1970* (Edinburgh: Edinburgh University Press, 2000), 155.
18. University College of Wales Aberystwyth, "Parental Occupations of Students Entering in October 1938," SIM/4/7/2/1.
19. J. Gwynn Williams, *The University of Wales 1893–1939* (Cardiff: University of Wales Press, 1997).
20. T. Kenneth Rees, "Graduate Employment in Wales," *Evidence submitted by the NUS to Youth Hearing, January 1939*, SIM/4/7/7, 8.
21. W. Moelwyn Merchant, "Undergraduate and the Crisis," in Ralphs, *Young Minds for Old*, 36.
22. "Oxford University Enquiry Commission, Preliminary Report, June 1939," SIM4/7/8 1 of 2.
23. Kenneth Sinclair Loutit, "Cambridge (1930–1934)," Chapter of his autobiography *Very Little Luggage*, written in 1995 and published posthumously in 2009 online at http://www.spartacus.schoolnet. co.uk. I am grateful to John Simkin for sending me a copy.
24. Keith Vernon, *Universities and the State in England, 1850–1939* (Abingdon: Routledge, 2004), 192.
25. Whiteley, *Poor Student*, 17,
26. Vernon, *Universities and the State*, 194.
27. John Murray, "The Structure of University Education," in *The Yearbook of Education 1932*, edited by Lord Eustace Percy (London: Evans Brothers, 1931), 406.
28. Whiteley, *Poor Student*, 12.
29. David Daiches, "Edinburgh and Oxford," *Focus 25: Reflections on Education and University Life* (University of Sussex, no date), KDC/ J1–12, WL.
30. Whiteley, *Poor Student*, 12–13.
31. D. T. Edwards, "The Non-Resident Student – Problems and Possibilities," *New University* New Series 19 (March 1937): 7; "Conditions at the University: Evidence submitted by the NUS to Youth Hearing, January 1939," SIM/4/7/7, 3.

32. "Conditions at the University," 3.
33. "University of Liverpool Scout Club," *Boy* 11 (Christmas 1924): 21.
34. "The Apathetic Student," *New University* New Series 11 (January 1936): 14.
35. Tantalus, "Our Present Needs in Armstrong," *Northerner* 27, no. 1 (November 1927): 6–7.
36. Ibid., 6.
37. James Robb, *The Carnegie Trust for the Universities of Scotland, 1901–1926* (Edinburgh: Oliver and Boyd, 1927), 15.
38. National Union of Students, *Report of the Council for the session 1927–1928* (London: NUS, 1928), 21–22; Ralph Nunn May, "NUS – Past and Present," *New University* 1, no. 6 (June 1939): 13–14.
39. NUS, *Annual Report of the Council 1925–1926* (London: NUS, 1926), 15.
40. *University College Magazine* 7, no. 1 (December 1929), 2.
41. David Daiches, *Two Worlds* (1956; Edinburgh: Canongate Classics, 1997), 146.
42. Janet Howarth, "Women," in *History of the University of Oxford: Volume VII The Twentieth Century*, edited by Brian Harrison (Oxford: Clarendon, 1994), 362–363.
43. Daiches, "Edinburgh and Oxford," 5.
44. Eric Hobsbawm, *Interesting Times: A Twentieth Century Life* (London: Penguin, 2002), 105.
45. David Paton, "A Modern University in England," *Student World* 31, no. 1 (1938), 49–55.
46. Eric Ashby and Mary Anderson, *The Rise of the Student Estate in Britain* (London: Macmillan and Co., 1970), 69.
47. Rachelle Hope Saltzman, *A Lark for the Sake of Their Country: The 1926 General Strike Volunteers in Folklore and Memory* (Manchester: MUP, 2012).
48. Julian Symons, *The General Strike: A Historical Portrait* (London: Cresset Press, 1957), 68.
49. Ian MacDougall, "Some Aspects of the General Strike in Scotland," in *Essays in Scottish Labour History: A Tribute to W. H. Marwick*, edited by Ian MacDougall (Edinburgh: John Donald, 1978), 170–206, at 180.
50. P. S. Havens, "The General Strike of 1926: A Reminiscence," *University College Record 1979*, 267–273.
51. MacDougall, "Some Aspects."
52. "Oxford and the Strike," *Times*, May 19, 1926, 12.
53. Symons, *General Strike*, 68; MacDougall, "Some Aspects," 180–182.
54. Saltzman, *Lark*, 174.
55. Ashby and Anderson, *Student Estate*, 69.
56. "Students and the Strike", *Northerner* 26, no. 4 (June 1926): 110–113.
57. Saltzman, *Lark*, 72.
58. Symons, *General Strike*, 103.

59. "Students and the Strike," 110.
60. Ibid., 111.
61. Sylvia Makower cited in Saltzman, *Lark*, 76.
62. Kit Meredith, "Comments on the Student Movement During the 1930s," October 11, 1986, SIM/4/7/3, IOE, 7.
63. "Students and the Strike," 112.
64. "Spluttering Age," *University College Magazine* 4, no. 3 (July 1926): 8.
65. "Special Strike Issue," [Birmingham] *University Gazette* 2, no. 9 (May 1926): 2.
66. "Students and the Strike," 112.
67. Jack Gaster interviewed by Roy Gore and Louise Brodie, *Labour Oral History Project*, June 1994, British Library Sound & Moving Image Catalogue reference C609/06.
68. Magaret Cole, *Growing Up into Revolution* (London: Longmans, 1949), 123.
69. John Jones, *Balliol College: A History* (Oxford: OUP, 1988), 263.
70. "Editorial Notes," *British Independent* 1, Tuesday, May 11, 1926, 3; The Appeal was eventually broadcast by the BBC four days after it had been issued.
71. "Editorial Notes," *British Independent* 1, Tuesday, May 11, 1926, 3.
72. "Union Notes," *Floreamus* 12, 87 (June 1926): 267, 272.
73. A. H. Halsey and Stephen Marks, "British Student Politics," *Daedalus* 97, no. 1 (Winter 1968): 116—136, at 121.
74. "Students and the Strike," 112.
75. "SCM," *Floreamus* 13, no. 92 (March 1928): 484.
76. "NUS Notes," *The Dragon* 48, no. 2 (March 1926): 96–97.
77. Kitty Lewis, "Report on Self-Help in Wales Up to July 1929," File 25, Papers of Kitty Idwal-Jones, National Library of Wales (NLW); NUS, *Report of Council 1927–1928*, 18.
78. NUS, *Twenty-One Years* (London: NUS, 1943), 4.
79. "The International Student Service," *Mermaid* 3, no. 3 (December 1932): 66–67; *Serpent* 12, no. 2 (December 1927): 43; NUS, *Report of Council 1926–1927*, 9; "Visit of Dr Kotschnig," *The University* 12 (Winter 1927), 30.
80. "Student Self-help Institute, Second International Student Self-Help Study Week, Dresden July 2–10, 1929."
81. SCM, *SCM Annual Report 1928–1929* (London: SCM Press, 1929), 48–49.
82. *Student Service in Five Continents* (Geneva: ISS, 1929), 10.
83. Lewis, "Report on Self-Help in Wales up to July 1929"; "The Self-Help Movement in Wales," *Dragon* 52, no. 1 (Michaelmas 1929): 33.
84. *Student Service in Five Continents* (Geneva: ISS, 1929), 18.
85. Ibid., 10.
86. Catherine E. Lewis, "Self-Help," *Cap and Gown* 27, no. 2 (June 1930): 25–26.

87. Bernard Harris, "Government and Charity in the Distressed Mining Areas of England and Wales, 1928–1930," *Medicine and Charity Before the Welfare State*, edited by Jonathan Barry and Colin Jones (London: Routledge, 1991), 207–224, at 218.
88. "NUS Special Supplement," *Serpent* 12, no. 3 (February 1928): 97; NUS, *Report of Council 1927–1928*, 5.
89. "Memo on the Work of the NUS of the Universities and University Colleges of England and Wales Submitted to the LSE, January 1930," NUS2/1930/1, NUS Scotland Offices.
90. NUS, *Annual Report for 1936–37*, 13.
91. NUS – A Criticism, *New University* New Series 14 (May 1936): 5.
92. Day, "Respected not Respectable," 41.
93. *Northerner* 29, no. 2 (March 1929): 50.
94. *Northerner* 31, no. 1 (Nov 1930): 27.
95. *Northerner* 30, no. 3 (March 1930): 27.
96. Ralph Nunn May, "Vacation Work for Undergraduates," *Times*, June 10, 1929, 12.
97. Catherine E. Lewis, "Self-Help," *Cap and Gown* 27, no. 2 (June 1930): 25–26. *NUS News Bulletin*, February–March 1932, 6.
98. "The Summer Vacation," *New University* 26 (Summer 1932): 15.
99. Dyhouse, "Going to University," 6.
100. NUS, *Twenty-One Years*, 4.
101. *New University* New Series 24 (February 1938): 5; Hansard HC Deb December 23, 1937 Vol 330 c2193W.
102. Student Self-Help Institute, *Second International Student Self-Help Study Week, Dresden July 2–10, 1929*, 38.
103. Ibid.
104. NUS, *Seven Years Development*, 18; "Open Platform," *Dragon* 62, no. 1 (Michaelmas 1939): 27.
105. Lewis, "Self-Help," 25.
106. "SRC Accounts," *Northerner* 33, no. 1 (December 1932): face 33.
107. Simon, *Student's View*, 68.
108. *Serpent* 10, no. 1 (November 1925): 27.
109. NUS, *Annual Report of Council 1925–1926*, 14.
110. "The University Looks at the World," *Tamesis* 25, no. 8 (Autumn 1926): 128.
111. NUS, *NUS Year Book 1938–9*, 16.
112. "The 1927 Rag," *Northerner* 27, no. 4 (June 1927): 143.
113. Carol Dyhouse, *Students: A Gendered History* (Abingdon: Routledge, 2006), 187.
114. Ralph Nunn May, "Student Social Service to the Community," Report Presented at Committee of Representatives of International Student Organisations, Paris, April 18–20, 1932, ED 25/80, The National Archives (TNA), 15.
115. *Mermaid*, New Series 1, no. 1 (October 1930): 27–28.
116. *Mermaid*, New Series 1, no. 3 (January 1931): 80.

117. H. G. G. Herklots, *The New Universities* (London: Ernest Benn, 1928), 105–108.
118. T. E. Lawrenson, *Hall of Residence: St Anslem Hall in the University of Manchester, 1907–1957* (Manchester: St Anslem Hall Association, 2007).
119. *NUS News Bulletin*, October 30, 1931, 4.
120. George Foulkes ed., *Eighty Years On* (Edinburgh: SRC, 1964), 22.
121. Herklots, *New Universities,* 105–108.
122. See also Simon, *Student's View*, 86.
123. "Rationalise Our Rags," *The University* 17 (Summer 1929): 25.
124. "University Notes," *NUS News Bulletin* 9 (January 1932): 5.
125. Simon, *Student's View*, 86.
126. Paton, 'Modern University', 49.
127. Jones, *Coward's Custard*, 60–61.
128. "NUS Executive Meeting," *NUS News Bulletin* 9 (January 1932): 1.
129. NUS, *Report of the Council 1937–1938*, 13; "Rags," *New University*, December 1937, 8.
130. Nunn May, "Student Social Service," 18.
131. Frank A. Rhodes, *The National Union of Students 1922–1967* (1968; Published Coventry: SUSOC, 1990), 32.

6   DIGGING WITH THE UNEMPLOYED: THE RISE OF A STUDENT
SOCIAL CONSCIOUSNESS? 1932–1939

1. H. H., "Towards a New University," *ULU Magazine*, October 1933, 9.
2. "Universities and Social Service: An International Discussion," *New University* 26 (Summer 1932): 5–6.
3. Brian Simon, "The Student Movement in England and Wales During the 1930s," *History of Education* 16, no. 3 (1987): 190; Kit Meredith, "Comments on the Student Movement During the 1930s," October 11, 1986, SIM/4/7/3, IOE, 3.
4. Reginald D. Smith, "The Socialist Solution," in *Young Minds for Old: Fourteen Young University Writers on Modern Problems*, edited by Lincoln Ralphs, 4 (London: Frederick Muller, 1936).
5. A. H. Halsey and Stephen Marks, "British Student Politics,"*Daedalus* 97, no. 1 (Winter 1968): 116–136, at Eric Ashby and Mary Anderson, *The Rise of the Student Estate in Britain* (London: Macmillan and Co., 1970). 77–79.
6. Evidence of Frank Strauss Meyer to MI5, 1952, KV2/3501, TNA.
7. Andrew Sinclair, *The Red and the Blue: Intelligence, Treason and the Universities* (London: Weidenfield and Nicolson, 1986), 34.
8. John Cornford, "Communism in the Universities," in *Young Minds for Old*, 19–31; Francis Beckett, *Enemy within: The Rise and Fall of the British Communist Party* (Woodbridge: Merlin Press, 1998), 84.
9. Brian Simon, "Jack Cohen 1905–1982," SIM/3/1 and "James Klugmann," *Marxism Today*, November 1977, SIM/3/1; See also Jack Cohen's MI5 file, KV2/1060, TNA.

10. "Letter from MI5 to British Embassy," Washington, November 28, 1951, KV2/3501, TNA.
11. "Federation of Student Societies," *Student Vanguard* 1, no. 5 (May 1933): 20.
12. *Federation of Student Societies Conference Report*, January 6–7, 1934.
13. *21 Years of the University Labour Federation: The Coming of Age Conference, Leeds 1941* (Cambridge: ULF, 1941), 22.
14. Smith, "Socialist Solution," 13.
15. John Stevenson and Chris Cook, *Britain in the Depression: Society and Politics 1929–1939* (Harlow: Longman, 1994), 153–154.
16. Nicholas Deakin, "Middle-Class Recruits to Communism in the 1930s," Lecture delivered March 7, 2013 at Gresham College, http://www.gresham.ac.uk/lectures-and-events/middle-class-recruits-to-communism-in-the-1930s.
17. Philip Toynbee, "Journal," in *The Distant Drum: Reflections on the Spanish Civil War*, edited by Toynbee, 147 (London: Sidgwick and Jackson, 1976).
18. "The Socialist Society," *Ram*, Autumn 1935, 31.
19. "The Use of Leisure and Social Life," *Torch* 2, no. 9 (March 1936): 8.
20. Lucy Crewe Chambers, "Conversations in Conservatism," in *Young Minds for Old*, 113–124, at 118.
21. "Questionnaire for Study by Universities and Colleges in Preparation for Northern English Council, April 1937," SIM/4/7/6/1, IOE.
22. Brian Simon, *A Student's View of the Universities* (London: Longmans, 1943), 86.
23. Meredith, "Comments on the Student Movement," 5.
24. W. Moelwyn Merchant, "Undergraduate and the Crisis," in *Young Minds for Old*, 35–48.
25. J. S. C., "Reflections of an Out-of-Work," *New University* 4 (Michaelmas 1933): 9–10.
26. Bernard Harris, "Responding to Adversity: Government-Charity Relations and the Relief of Unemployment in Inter-War Britain," *Contemporary Record* 9, no. 3 (Winter 1995): 529–561, at 532.
27. Elizabeth Macadam, *The New Philanthropy: A Study of the Relations between the Statutory and Voluntary Social Services* (London: George Allen and Unwin, 1934).
28. Margaret Brasnett, *Voluntary Social Action: A History of the National Council of Social Service* (London: NCSS, 1969), 68.
29. Harris, "Responding to Adversity," 535–537.
30. "Youth and Social Service: The Prince of Wales's Message," *Times*, January 28, 1932, 12; "Opportunities for Service," NCSS leaflet. 1932, British Library.
31. A. D. Lindsay, "Unemployment the "Meanwhile" Problem," *Contemporary Review* 163 (January–June 1933): 687–695, at 694.
32. Brasnett, *Voluntary Social Action*, 70.
33. Stevenson and Cook, *Britain in the Depression*, 83–86.

34. *Kith and Kin* 1, no. 1 (March 1933).
35. "Universities and Social Service: An International Discussion," 6.
36. Jenny Harrow, "The Development of University Settlements in England, 1884–1939," PhD Thesis, London 1987, 1.
37. "The University Settlement," *Nonesuch* 32 (Autumn 1921): 25.
38. Gwendolen Freeman, *Alma Mater: Memoirs of Girton College, 1926–1929* (Cambridge: Girton College, 1990), 28–29.
39. "Settlement Association," *The Nonesuch* 44 (Autumn 1925), 225.
40. Robert Hamilton and Jean Macleay, *Glasgow University Settlement: A Centennial History* (Glasgow: University of Glasgow, 1998), 43.
41. "Ancoats Settlement," *Serpent* 10, no. 5 (May 1926): 139.
42. *WUS Annual Report 1921*, 10; *WUS Annual Report 1930*, 22.
43. J. V. Markam, "The Oxford House in Bethnal Green," *Social Service Review* 20, no. 6 (June 1939): 193–200, at 199.
44. "Warden's Report" in *Liverpool University Settlement Annual Report, 1929*, D7/3, 8.
45. *Cambridge House 26th Annual Report* (1922–1923), 5; *WUS Annual Report 1921*, 10.
46. SCM, "Social Study in the Christian Unions" c. 1921, SCM A21; SCM, "Openings for Social Service," SCM A21.
47. BARS, *Annual Report 1934–5* (Plymouth: BARS, 1935); *Student Forum* 3, no. 7 (8 March 1939): 8.
48. "The Social Service Conference," *Gryphon*, New Series 14, no. 3 (December 1932): 101–102.
49. Edward Bradby, "International Student Service," *Review: ULU Magazine* 1, no. 6 (June 1935): 164–165; *Sphinx* 43 (July 1937): 10.
50. Gertrude Mary Truscott, "The Birmingham Settlement," *Social Service Review* 20, no. 3 (March 1939): 105–108.
51. *Guide to the University Labour Federation* (Cambridge: ULF, 1943); "Student Action," *Student Vanguard* 2, no. 5, 12.
52. Meredith, "Comments on the Student Movement," 7.
53. Sinclair Loutit, "Cambridge (1930–1934)."
54. Barbara Pym, *A Very Private Eye: The Diaries, Letters and Notebooks of Barbara Pym,* edited by Hazel Holt and Hilary Pym (London: Macmillan, 1984), 35.
55. Sinclair Loutit, "Cambridge (1930–1934)."
56. Field, "Service Learning in Britain," 195.
57. Ethelwyn Best and Bernard Pike, *International Voluntary Service for Peace, 1920–1946* (London: Allen and Unwin, 1948), 6–34.
58. C. W. Guillebaud, "The Mount Holyoke Conference of International Student Service," *The University* 24 (Michaelmas 1931): 13–16.
59. ISS, *International Student Service: The Year in Retrospect 1947–1948* (London: British Cooperating Committee of ISS, 1949), 34.
60. Guy Fletcher, "A Student-Work Camp in Switzerland," *New University* 23 (December 1937): 7.

61. Kenneth Holland, *Youth in European Labor Camps: A Report to the American Youth Commission* (Washington, DC: American Council on Education, 1939).

62. *Youth Demands a Peaceful World: Report of the Second World Youth Congress* (New York, 1938), 29.

63. Nicholas Gillett, *Abolishing War: One Man's Attempt* (London: William Sessions, 2005), 69.

64. "Report of International Service Camp at Brynmawr," IVS J/23, IVS Archives, Hull History Centre (HH); "Pick and Shovel Peace Work," *Manchester Guardian* July 2, 1931, Offprint in IVS P/9.

65. "International Service Camp at Brynmawr," 3.

66. "The Brynmawr Experiment 1928–1933," IVS J25.

67. Best and Pike, *International Voluntary Service for Peace*, 38.

68. Donald Bentley, "SCI at Outbreak of War," c. 1967, IVS J/5.

69. "Depressed Areas Conference," *Mermaid*, New Series 6, no. 5 (April 1936): 117.

70. Howard Marshall, "Digging for a New England," *Listener*, February 3, 1937, 204–206.

71. John S. Hoyland, *Digging for a New England: The Co-operative Farm for Unemployed Men* (London: Jonathan Cape, 1936), 13, 22.

72. "Leeds Students and Others v War and Unemployment," *Gryphon*, New Series 14, no. 4 (February 1933): 148.

73. "Birmingham Settlement, Kingstanding Workcamp, July 1933, Statement of Accounts," SCM A197; See also Hoyland, *Digging for a New England*, 38–45.

74. "Memo on Students' Work-camp and Evangelistic Campaign, Swanwick, 1935," SCM A197.

75. Rolf Gardiner, "The Triple Function of Work Camps and Work Service in Europe," repr. in *Water Springing from the Ground: An Anthology of the Writings of Rolf Gardiner*, edited by Andrew Best (Springhead, 1972), 119.

76. John S. Hoyland, *Digging with the Unemployed* (London: Student Christian Movement Press, 1934).

77. Gillett, *Abolishing War*, 70.

78. Holland, *European Labor Camps*, 32.

79. IVS, "A Message to Our Friends at Oakengates," IVS J/23, "International Voluntary Service, 1934," IVS J/23, 2.

80. "International Service Camp at Brynmawr," 6.

81. Malcolm Chase, "Heartbreak Hill: Environment, Unemployment and 'Back to the Land' in Inter-war Cleveland," *Oral History* 28, no. 1 (Spring 2000): 33–42.

82. "International Voluntary Service in 1931," IVS J25.

83. "Holiday with a Purpose," *Gryphon* Third series 3, no. 1 (October 1937): 71–72.

84. Best and Pike, *International Voluntary Service for Peace*, 36, 130–131; Oliver Tomkins, "Memo on the Work Camp and Campaign," 1936, SCM/A197.

85. Holland, *European Labor Camps*, 149.
86. Michael Sims Williams, *Camps for Men* (Cambridge: Universities Council for Unemployed Camps, 1933), 3.
87. "UCUC Annual Report for 1934 and Appeal for 1935," Min IX 69 24, Cambridge University Archives (CUL).
88. "Cambridge Camps Annual Report for 1938 and Appeal for 1939," 9.
89. Harold L. Hunter, "Universities' Unemployed Camps: A General Review," in "Social Service and the University Student," supplement to *New University*, February 1939, 22.
90. Sims Williams, *Camps for Men*, 14–15.
91. "UCUC Cambridge Camps Annual Report for 1938 and Appeal for 1939," 7.
92. "Report from St John's UCUC Camp at Harome," Min IX 69 6 43.
93. *New University* New Series 1, no. 6 (June 1939): 16.
94. Harold H. Munro, "Nationalism in the North," in *Young Minds for Old*, 83–94.
95. *The Bickerton Camp Scheme* (Liverpool: LUP, 1935).
96. Leta Jones, "Summer Camps for Unemployed," c. 1988, Leta Jones Papers, D452 6/5 Liverpool University Archives, 1.
97. Leta Jones, "Report," D452 6/5.
98. University Social Service Group [Cardiff], "Holiday Camp for Unemployed Men, 1934," SCM A197.
99. "Holidays for Workless: Camps Organized by Welsh Students," *Times*, November 25, 1935, 19.
100. "University Social Service Group," *Dragon* 58, no. 2 (Lent 1936): 48.
101. A. W. Wilkinson, "Unemployed Camps in South Wales," "Social Service and the University Student," supplement to *New University*, February 1939, 24.
102. Alun Davies, "Utopia Studentium," *Dragon* 58, no. 2 (Lent 1936): 40; Merchant, "Undergraduate and the Crisis," 46.
103. Wilkinson, "Unemployed Camps in South Wales," 24.
104. Merchant, "Undergraduate and the Crisis," 46.
105. "Report, June 24–July 24 1936," Min IX 69 48, 1.
106. Ibid., 2.
107. "UCUC Cambridge Camps Annual Report for 1937 and Appeal for 1938," 8.
108. "UCUC Recommendations Made by Camp Chiefs of the Cambridge Camps, 1936," Min IX 69 5b.
109. Leta Jones, *Coward's Custard* (London: Minerva Press, 1998), 80.
110. Jones, "Summer Camps for Unemployed"; Jones, *Coward's Custard*, 79.
111. "Cambridge Camps Annual Report for 1936 and Appeal for 1937," Min IX 69 27, 6.
112. *Bredon Bunkum* 3, no. 1 (July 1937), Min IX 69 6 54.
113. "UCUC Cambridge Camps Annual Report for 1937 and Appeal for 1938," 6.

114. Harry Rée interviewed by Liz Peretz in 1988, "Leaders of National Life Collection," British Library Sound Archive.
115. UCUC, "Cambridge Camps Annual Report 1936," 4–5.
116. [J. R. Maxwell Lefroy] "Report of the Camp Chief, Trinity College Camp, 26 Oct 1936," Min IX 69 44.
117. *Bickerton Camp Scheme*, 8.
118. "Letter from Eileen Waring to Leta Jones," August 12, 1934.
119. Harrow, "University Settlements," 580.
120. "Social Service and the University Student," *New University*, February 1939, 13–24; "NUS Congress, Oxford," *New University* 1, no. 5 (May 1939): 8.
121. NUS, *Congress Report 1939* (London: NUS, 1939), 35–37.
122. *The SCM News Sheet*, 1 (November 1934): 5.
123. Harris, "Responding to Adversity," 550.
124. Mary Morris, *Voluntary Organisations and Social Progress* (London: Victor Gollancz, 1955), 182; *Voluntary Service and the State: A Study of the Needs of the Hospital Service* (London: NCSS and King Edward's Hospital Fund for London, 1952), 14.
125. Brian Harrison, "College Life, 1918–1939," in *History of the University of Oxford: Volume VII*, 96.

7   STUDENTS IN ACTION: STUDENTS AND ANTIFASCIST
RELIEF EFFORTS, 1933–1939

1. *Youth Demands a Peaceful World: Report of the Second World Youth Congress* (New York, 1938), 30.
2. Adrian Gregory, *Silence of Memory: Armistice Day 1919–1946* (Oxford: Berg, 1994), 119–120.
3. "Willingham Peace Ballot", *Cambridge Independent Press*, March 24, 1933, Cutting, SCM A169, 1/3, UB.
4. "Report of the ISS Committee for England and Wales, 1935–36," SCM W11, 7; "The Fight Against War and Fascism in the University of London," *ULU Magazine*, December 1933, 55–56; "What Is the British Youth Peace Assembly," Y.D.2006 a.6964, British Library.
5. *The League of Nations Union Yearbook 1933* (London: LNU, 1933); Donald S. Birn, *The League of Nations Union, 1918–1945* (Oxford: Clarendon Press, 1981), 140; "Report on the Work of the Society July-December 1931," November 16, 1931, LNU/6/2, LSE.
6. "Undergraduate Speakers," Supplement to *Headway* 13, no. 1 (January 1931): ii; *League of Nations Union Yearbook 1934*, 41.
7. *League of Nations Union Yearbook 1933*, 37.
8. See "Student Activities," *Student Vanguard* 2 (December 1932): 24–25.
9. Peter Stansky and William Abrahams, *Journey to the Frontier: Two Roads to the Spanish Civil War* (London: Constable, 1966), 107.
10. Ibid.

11. Martin Ceadal, "The 'King and Country' Debate, 1933: Student Politics, Pacifism and the Dictators," *Historical Journal* 22, no. 2 (June 1979): 397–422 at 422.
12. Mike Day, "'Respected not Respectable: A New History of the NUS," Unpublished manuscript, 60–61.
13. N. Poole, "The Universities and International Affairs," *New University* 3 (Summer 1933): 15.
14. *The Gryphon*, New Series 14, no. 3 (December 1932): 103.
15. "The Fight Against War and Fascism in the University of London," *ULU Magazine*, December 1933, 55–56.
16. Martin Pugh, "Pacifism and Politics in Britain, 1931–1935," *Historical Journal* 23, no. 3 (September 1980): 641–656, at 645.
17. Ceadal, "'King and Country" Debate," 418–419.
18. Evidence of Frank Strauss Meyer to MI5, 1952, KV2/3501, TNA.
19. *Student Vanguard* 1, no. 6 (June–July 1933): 12–13.
20. Minutes of the 22nd Meeting of the Executive Committee of the British University League of Nations Society July 21, 1933, League of Nations Union Archive, LSE.
21. *Gong* 23, no. 2 (Easter 1934): 40; *Gong* 23, no. 3 (Summer 1934): 41; *Gong* 25, no. 2 (Easter term 1936): 33.
22. *The Student Movement* 36, no. 1 (October 1933): 2.
23. R. V. Spathaky, "Anti-War," *New University*, New Series 6 (March 1935): 11.
24. *Student Front*, November 1934.
25. Leta Jones, *Coward's Custard* (London: Minerva Press, 1998), 61.
26. *Cap and Gown* 32, no. 1 (January 1935): 1–2.
27. Sinclair Loutit, "Cambridge."
28. "Straight Words on the OTC," *Ram*, Autumn 1936, 15–16.
29. Hansard, HC Deb 23 March 1936 vol. 310 c880.
30. "The Editor Writes Further on the Subject of War and Peace," *Northerner* 34, no. 1 (December 1933): 7.
31. Elizabeth Shields Collins, "Student Socialists in Conference," *New University*, New Series 12 (February 1936): 13.
32. *Student Front*, November 1935, 4; "Air Raid Drill," *Ram,* Summer 1935, 25; On gas tests see Gabriel Moshenska, "Government Gas Vans and School Gas Chambers: Preparedness and Paranoia in Britain, 1936–1941," *Medicine, Conflict and Survival* 26, no. 3 (2010): 223–234.
33. *Student Front*, January 1935, 3.
34. Lieve Gevers and Louis Vos, "Student Movements," in *A History of the University in Europe: Universities in the Nineteenth and Early Twentieth Centuries (1800–1945)*, Vol. 3, edited by Walter Rüegg, 358 (Cambridge: Cambridge University Press, 2004).
35. *Youth Plans a New World: Being the Official Record of the First World Youth Congress Geneva 1936*, 2nd edition (Geneva, 1937), 36;

"Minutes of a Meeting of the Executive Committee of the BULNS," September 17, 1936.

36. "What is the British Youth Peace Assembly."
37. *Student Forum* 3, no. 4 (January 1939): 1.
38. "Jack Cohen," Special Branch Observation July 2, 1938, KV2/1060, TNA.
39. "Letter from Margaret R. Bates to General Secretary, NUWT," September 6, 1937, National Union of Women Teachers Archive, Institute of Education, University of London.
40. Brian Simon, "The Student Movement in England and Wales During the 1930s," *History of Education* 16, no. 3 (1987): 201.
41. ISS, "German Refugee Students: A Report of Two Years Work 1933–1935," SCM W29 2/2.
42. *The Third Meeting of the Governing Body of the High Commission for Refugees* (London: Office of the High Commissioner, 1934), 10.
43. Norman Bentwich, *The Rescue and Achievement of Refugee Scholars: The Story of Displaced Scholars and Scientists, 1933–1952* (The Hague: Martinus Nijhoff, 1953); Jeremy Seabrook, *The Refuge and the Fortress: Britain and the Flight from Tyranny* (Basingstoke:, Palgrave, 2009); Shula Marks, Paul Weindling and Laura Wintour eds., *In Defence of Learning; The Plight, Persecution and Placement of Academic Refugees, 1933–1980s* (London: OUP for the British Academy, 2011).
44. Susan Cohen, "Crossing Borders: Academic Refugee Women, Education and the British Federation of University Women During the Nazi Era," *History of Education* 39, no. 2 (2010): 175–182; By June 1940 the BFUW had spent £1,500 on assisting 365 cases, "The Refugees," *University Women's Review* 30 (June 1940), 7–8.
45. Shula Marks, "Introduction," in *In Defence of Learning*, 3.
46. This section has been reconstructed from incomplete ISS papers contained within the SCM archive at Birmingham. Prewar papers for the British branch of ISS are presumed lost.
47. Gevers and Vos, "Student Movements," 348–349.
48. *WUS 50 Years*, 15.
49. Ibid., 351.
50. Bentwich, *Refugee Scholars*, 23.
51. "ISS and German Student Relief," *New University* 4 (Michaelmas 1933): 9–10.
52. Ibid., 17.
53. Published as *The Conflict between the Church and the Synagogue.*
54. James Parkes, *Voyage of Discoveries* (London: Victor Gollancz, 1969), 108.
55. Ernest Barker, "The Wandering Scholars: Help for Students in Exile," *Times*, October 26, 1935, 7.
56. "Refugees from Germany," *Times*, November 17, 1933, 10; "Refugee Students from Germany," *Manchester Guardian*, November 5, 1936, 20.

57. "Lord Mayor's Czech Refugees Fund: Final Report," *Times,* July 14, 1939, 7; "ISS Activities, 1937–8," *Student Movement* 41, no. 1 (October 1938): 25.
58. *New University,* New Series 1, no. 3 (February 1939): 26.
59. *New University,* New Series 1, no. 3 (February 1939): 25.
60. ISS, "International Student Service: A Brief Survey 1934," SCM W29 2/2; "University Women Refugees," *University Women's Review* 26 (October 1938): 12.
61. SCM, *SCM Annual Report, 1938–39,* 26.
62. Cohen, "Crossing Borders," 178.
63. ISS, "German Refugee Students: A Report of Two Years Work 1933–1935," SCM W29 2/2.
64. *Cap and Gown* 36, no. 2 (March 1939): 3.
65. "Minutes of a Meeting of the ISS Cooperating Committee for England and Wales, 29 May 1933," SCM A169 3/3, 3.
66. Geoffrey D. M. Block, "Jewish Students at the Universities of Great Britain and Ireland – Excluding London 1936–1939," *Sociological Review* 34, no.3–4 (July–October 1942): 183–197.
67. *New University,* New Series 1, no. 3 (February 1939): 12; *Sphinx* 42, no. 3 (March 1936).
68. Eric Ives, Diane Drummond and Leonard Scwartz, *The First Civic University: Birmingham 1880–1980: An Introductory History* (Birmingham: Birmingham University Press, 2000), 282.
69. "The Refugees," *Dragon* 61, no. 3 (Summer 1939): 33.
70. "International University Week," *Gong* 26, no. 2 (Easter 1937): 7.
71. A. E. Bowen, "Germany's Justification," *Ram,* Autumn 1936, 35–37.
72. "Fascism in the English Universities," *Student Vanguard* 1, no. 6 (June–July 1933): 5–7; Frank Hardie, "Youth and Politics," in *Growing Opinions: A Symposium of British Youth Outlook,* edited by Alan Campbell Johnson, 177–197, at 185–189 (London: Methuen, 1935).
73. Edwin Barker, "British University Students and the Class War," *Student World* 27, no. 3 (1934).
74. Elizabeth Longford, "Riot at Mosley Meeting," *Sunday Times,* August 10, 1986.
75. "Socialist Group," *Torch* 2, no. 6 (March 1935): 34.
76. "A Protest from Oxford," *Times,* November 17, 1938, 9.
77. Note from Betty Matthews to Brian Simon, October 23, 1986, SIM/4/7/3.
78. ISS, "German Refugee Students: A Report of Two Years Work 1933–1935," SCM W29 2/2.
79. "Letters to the Editor," *Dragon* 62, no. 3 (Easter term 1940): 43.
80. E Walter Kellermann, *A Physicist's Labour in War and Peace: Memoirs 1933–1999* (Hertford: M-Y Books, 2007), 46.
81. "Minutes of a Meeting of the ISS Cooperating Committee for England and Wales," May 29, 1933, SCM A169 3/3.
82. "New German Culture," *Times,* August 15, 1933, 9.

83. *WUS 50 Years*, 15.
84. Alban Hull, "The Sixteenth Annual Conference of the ISS," *Gryphon* Third Series 3, no. 1 (October 1937): 46.
85. *ISS Bulletin* cited in *WUS 50 Years*, 15.
86. Tom Buchanan, *Britain and the Spanish Civil War* (Cambridge: CUP, 1997), 150.
87. Jim Fyrth, *The Signal Was Spain: The Spanish Aid Movement in Britain, 1936–39* (London: Lawrence and Wishart, 1986), 22.
88. Frank A. Rhodes, *The National Union of Students 1922–1967* (1968; Published Coventry: SUSOC, 1990), 142; "Spanish Relief," *New University*, 1, no. 2 (December 1938): 7.
89. Kit Meredith, "Comments on the Student Movement During the 1930s," October 11, 1986, SIM/4/7/3, IOE, 7,, 7.
90. M. Hookham, "Two Decades," *Luciad* 13 (March 1956): 36.
91. "Joint Committee for Spanish Relief," *Gong* 28, no. 1 (Christmas term 1938): 32; "Joint Committee for Spanish Relief," *Gong* 28, no. 2 (Easter term 1939): 38.
92. Buchanan, *Britain and the Spanish Civil War*, 93.
93. NUS, *Report of the Annual Congress*, 1939, 28–29.
94. "Minutes of Meeting of Standing Committee of ISS, London, 14–15 November 1936," SCM W29, 6.
95. "What is the British Youth Peace Assembly."
96. British Youth Peace Assembly, "Food Tickets for Spain," IVS J/19.
97. "Student News," *New University* 1, no. 3 (February 1939): 25.
98. "Minutes of Birmingham SCM Committee Meeting," November 30, 1936, SCM M102; "Joint Committee for Spanish Relief," *Gong* 28, no. 1 (Christmas term 1938): 32; University College Magazine 14, no. 3 (June 1937): 329.
99. "Extract from Scotland Yard Report, 23 March 1938," in "Indian Students and Societies at Oxford and Cambridge: Scotland Yard Reports on Individuals and Conferences," February 1936–April 1946, IOR/L/PJ/12/4, TNA.
100. "Food for Spain: Cambridge University Campaign," November 24, 1938, 7.
101. *New University*, New Series 1, no. 5 (May 1939): 20.
102. Ronald R. S. Ward, "The Second World Youth Congress," *New University*, New Series 1, no. 1 (November 1938): 17–19; See also letters page, 23.
103. "Spain Term," *Serpent* 23, no. 3 (February 1939): 61.
104. "SUS Expects," *Cap and Gown* 36, no. 1 (December 1938): 3.
105. "Student News," *New University* 1, no. 3 (February 1939): 25; "Student News," *New University* 1, no. 4 (March 1939): 25.
106. Fyrth, *Signal Was Spain*, 223.
107. "Material available for Anniversary Campaign," Spain 1938, IVS J/19.

108. "University College," *Hull Daily Mail*, February 6, 1939, 7.
109. *Student Forum* 3, no. 5 (February 8, 1939): 3.
110. Simon, "Student Movement," 197.
111. *Spain Assailed: Student Delegates to Spain Report* (London: Student Delegation to Spain, no date, [1937]).
112. Philip Toynbee, "Journal," in *The Distant Drum: Reflections on the Spanish Civil War*, edited by Toynbee, 155 (London: Sidgwick and Jackson, 1976).
113. Ibid., 150–151.
114. "Student Mission Returns from Spanish Front," *Student Forum* 1, no. 2 (February 1937): 1.
115. "Report dated 23.11.37" in "Indian Students and Societies."
116. Toynbee, "Journal," 177.
117. *Spain Assailed*, 30.
118. "University Intelligence," *New University*, New Series 19 (March 1937): 4.
119. Simon, "Student Movement," 193.
120. The other students were George Stent, (Oxford, BULNS), Richard Simonds (Peace Pledge Union), and Derek Tasker (Liberal). See NUS, *Annual Report for the session 1937–8*, 19.
121. "Starving Spanish Children: University Students Report from Barcelona," *Student Forum*, January 3, 1939, 6.
122. *New University*, New Series 1, no. 3 (February 1939): 12.
123. John Davison, "The League Cause in the Universities," *Headway* 19, no. 2 (February 1937): 28.
124. See, for example, "John Cornford," *Sphinx* 43 (March 1937): 8.
125. Eric Hobsbawm, *Interesting Times: A Twentieth Century Life* (London: Penguin, 2002), 111.
126. Fyrth, *Signal Was Spain*, 207.
127. Simon, "Student Movement," 189.
128. Tom Buchanan, *The Impact of the Spanish Civil War on Britain* (Brighton: Sussex Academic Press, 2007), 44.
129. Sinclair Loutit, *Very Little Luggage*.
130. Hobsbawm, *Interesting Times*, 119.
131. Simon, "Student Movement," 202.
132. John Simmonds, *Students in Action: The Story of a Life Against Fascism* (Cambridge: University Labour Federation: [1944]), 16.
133. Edward Heath, "What We Found in Spain," *Student Forum* 3, no. 1 (October 19, 1938): 2.
134. "Chinese University Relief Appeal," *New University*, New Series 22 (November 1937): 11–13.
135. "Japan's Attack on Chinese Cultural Life," *Manchester Guardian*, October 15, 1937.
136. Arthur Clegg, *Aid China 1937–1949: A Memoir of a Forgotten Campaign* (Beijing: New World Press, 1989), 29–30.

137. Ibid., 29.
138. "Chinese University Relief Appeal," 13; Bertha Woodall, "ISS News," *Student Movement*, 40, no. 3 (December 1937); "Chinese Universities Relief Fund," *University Women's Review* 25 (June 1938): 5.
139. "Chinese University Relief Draft Minute" c. 1938, SCM W29, 2/2.
140. ISS, "Help for Chinese Students in Great Britain," April 25, 1938, SCM W29, 2/2; "Chinese Universities Relief Fund," *The Scotsman*, January 27, 1938, 13.
141. "Aid for Chinese Students," *Manchester Guardian*, November 22, 1937, 7; "Appeal for Chinese Universities," *Manchester Guardian*, June 3, 1938, 20.
142. "Aiding Chinese Students: British Support for Appeal Fund," *Times*, November 23, 1937, 17.
143. "Appeal for Chinese Universities," *Manchester Guardian*, June 3, 1938, 20.
144. *Mermaid*, New Series 8, no. 3 (May 1938): 53.
145. Ibid.
146. *Gryphon*, Third Series 4, no. 6 (May 1939): 629.
147. Ronald R. S. Ward, "The Second World Youth Congress," *New University*, New Series 1, no. 1 (November 1938): 17–19.
148. "Student News from Home and Abroad," *New University*, New Series 1, no. 2 (December 1938): 18–19; Bernard Floud, "Chinese Students in War-Time," *New University*, New Series 1, no. 2 (December 1938): 22–23.
149. Clegg, *Aid China*, 54.
150. Brian Simon, *A Student's View of the Universities* (London: Longmans, 1943), 101; *University College Magazine* 15, no. 2 (1938): 177.
151. *Student Forum* 2, no. 3 (February 1938): 8.
152. Simmonds, *Students in Action*, 16.
153. *Times*, October 13, 1937, 16.
154. *Student Forum* 3, no. 5 (February 8, 1939): 1; *New University*, New Series 1, no. 3 (February 1939): 9.
155. Ernest Simon, "Education for Democratic Leadership: The World Students' Conference," *Manchester Guardian*, August 1939.
156. Howe, *Century of Influence*, 211.
157. NUS, *Annual Report for the session 1936–37*, 15; SCM, *SCM Annual Report, 1938–1939*, 23, 26.
158. Brian Simon, "Dramatic Happenings in Endsleigh Street: The NUS Crisis of 1940," Draft MS marked Final New Master, 1998, SIM/4/7/1, 6.
159. "Editorial," *University College Magazine* 16, no. 1 (Autumn 1938), 5.
160. Simmonds, *Students in Action*, 4.
161. SCM, *SCM Annual Report, 1938–39*, 26.
162. SCM, *SCM Annual Report 1940–41*, 6.
163. Meredith, "Comments on the Student Movement During the 1930s," 5; Brian Simon, "Youth Hearing," *Dragon* 61, no. 1 (Michaelmas term 1938): 40–41.

164. NUS, *Annual Report of the Executive Committee to the Council 1938–39*, 6; Henry W. Nevinson, "Youth Steps Out", *Headway* 1, no. 6 (March 1939): 24–25.

8 THE STUDENTS' CONTRIBUTION TO VICTORY: VOLUNTARY WORK IN THE SECOND WORLD WAR AND AFTER

1. "34 Help Rescue Squads," *Student News* 10 (February 7, 1941): 2.
2. *Students and the Blitz* (London: ULU, 1941), 13–15.
3. *Student News* 13 (November 10, 1941): 3.
4. Brian Simon, *A Student's View of the Universities* (London: Longmans, 1943), 124.
5. *Serpent* 24, no. 1 (December 1939): 21.
6. Paul Addison, "Oxford and the Second World War," in *The History of the University of Oxford Volume VIII: The Twentieth Century*, edited by Brian Harrison (Oxford: Oxford University Press, 1994), 169.
7. "London University," *Times*, September 26, 1939, 4.
8. Eric W. Vincent and Percival Hinton, *The University of Birmingham: Its History and Significance* (Birmingham: Cornish Brothers, 1947), 216.
9. "Home University News," *Universities Review* 12, no. 1 (November 1939): 30.
10. Mike Day, "'Respected not Respectable: A New History of the NUS," Unpublished manuscript.
11. *The New Northman* 8, 2 (Summer 1940): 1.
12. "Evacuation Hits Universities," *Student News* 1 (October 19, 1939): 1.
13. "London Meets Wales: Unions Carry On," *Student News* 1 (October 19, 1939): 2.
14. "Home University News," *Universities Review* 12, no. 1 (November 1939): 30.
15. "Evacuation Hits Universities," 1; "Phineas in Exile," *New Phineas*, Autumn 1939, 25.
16. "Urgent Problems of Medical Education," 1939, U DSM/4/1, Socialist Health Association Archive, Hull History Centre.
17. Brian Simon, "Dramatic Happenings in Endsleigh Street: The NUS Crisis of 1940," Draft MS marked Final New Master, 1998, SIM/4/7/1, 16.
18. "Home University News," *Universities Review* 12, no. 2 (May 1940); Student News, February 5, 1940, 2.
19. "Open Platform," *Dragon* 62, no. 1 (Michaelmas 1939): 24–25.
20. G. A. Sutherland, *Dalton Hall: A Quaker Venture* (London: Bannisdale Press, 1963), 97; T. E. Lawrenson, *Hall of Residence: St Anslem Hall in the University of Manchester, 1907–1957* (Manchester: St Anslem Hall Association, 2007), 81; *Ashburne Hall: The First Fifty Years 1899–1949* (Manchester, Privately printed); M. J. Crossley Evans and A. Sulston, *A History of Wills Hall University of Bristol* (Bristol: University of Bristol

Press, 1994), 33; "The JCR in Peace and War," [Lady Margaret Hall] *Brown Book*, December 1941, 7–10.

21. "Editorial," *New Phineas*, Spring 1940, 3.

22. "Oxford Letter," *Brown Book*, December 1941, 6.

23. Nina Bawden in *My Oxford*, edited by Ann Thwaite (London: Robson Books, 1977), 167.

24. "Oxford Letter," *Brown Book*, December 1940, 5.

25. J. J. Kipling, "War Diary No. 5," November 26, 1939, Mass Observation Archive (MO), www.massobs.org.uk.

26. "JCR in Peace and War," 8–10.

27. "Home University News," *Universities Review*, 12 no. 1 (November 1939): 26.

28. Universities Athletics Union, *Fifty Years of University Sport* (Privately published, 1969), 14.

29. "Restrictions Shock Delegates: Early Closing Resented," *Student News* 1 (November 9, 1939): 1; "Open Platform," *Dragon* 62, no. 1 (Michaelmas 1939): 26; "Home University News," *Universities Review* 12, no. 1 (November 1939): 24–35.

30. "The ULF and the Students," 20th Annual Conference of the University Labour Federation, Liverpool 1940, SIM4//7/5, IOE.

31. "Youth Carries On," *Times*, September 16, 1939, 9.

32. "Pie-Eating Stunt Raises Money," *Student News* 7 (May 2, 1940): 1.

33. "Long Live the Spirit of Carnival," *Guild News*, October 24, 1940, 1; *Guild News*, November 21, 1940, 1.

34. *Women's University Settlement Southwark Annual Report 1940* (London: WUS, 1940), 16.

35. "Home University News," *Universities Review*, 12 no. 2 (May 1940): 91.

36. Universities Athletics Union, *Fifty Years of University Sport*, 14.

37. Goldsmiths College Report to General Committee 1939–1940.

38. "Bristol Share Out with King's," *Student News*, February 5, 1940, 2.

39. Mass Observation, "Survey of Oxford University," File Report 777, July 1941, MO.

40. "Students and Evacuees," *New Phineas*, Summer 1941, 39.

41. "Volunteers Run Sports and Shows," *Student News* 3 (November 30, 1939): 2; "Oxford Letter," *The Brown Book LMH Chronicle*, December 1939, 12.

42. "Evacuees," *Dragon* 62, no. 3 (Easter 1940): 25–26.

43. Mass Observation, "Survey of Oxford University," 8.

44. "The Women's Union Society," *New Phineas*, Spring 1941, 43.

45. Simon, "Dramatic Happenings," 158.

46. "The Causes of the War: Statement by the University Labour Federation," *The Causes of the Present War: Study Memoranda Issued by the Co-ordinating Committee of British Student Organisations* (1940), 12.

47. Francis Beckett, *Enemy within: The Rise and Fall of the British Communist Party* (Woodbridge: Merlin Press, 1998), 98.

48. *21 Years of the University Labour Federation*, 28.

49. "Mr Arthur Greenwood's Resolution," *Times,* January 2, 1940, 6.
50. "War for What?" *Student News* 1 (October 1939): 3.
51. "Universities in War," *Guild News,* January 16, 1940, 5.
52. J. J. Kipling, "Wartime Diary no 13," June 21, 1940.
53. "Celts meet English," *Student News* 2 (November 1939): 2; *Student News* 6 (March 1940): 2.
54. "The First Term of War," *Student Movement* 42, no. 3 (December 1939): 68–70.
55. Ibid., 69.
56. Simon, "Student Movement," 198.
57. NUS, *Report of Executive Committee, 1939–1940,* 2.
58. "The British Student Congress at Leeds," *Student Movement* 42 (May 1940): 175–176.
59. "The Conscription Ballot," *Serpent* 23, no. 5 (June 1939): 124.
60. Kipling, "Wartime Diary no 7," January 1, 1940.
61. "War for What?," *Student News* 1 (October 1939): 3.
62. "Open Platform," *Dragon* 62, no. 2 (Lent term 1940): 26.
63. *Northerner* 40, no. 1 (December 1939): 20.
64. "Union Society Report," *New Phineas,* Autumn 1940, 43–44.
65. J. J. Kipling, "Directive Replies, 1940," MO.
66. "New Committee to Plan Terms Work," *Student News* 2 (October 1939): 1; NUS, *Report of Executive Committee, 1939–1940,* 5.
67. Minutes of the 44th Meeting of the Executive Committee of the BULNS, January 5, 1940, LNU Archive, LSE.
68. "The British Student Congress at Leeds," 175.
69. "Congress at Leeds," *Serpent* 24, no. 4 (May 1940): 78.
70. Mass Observation, "National Union of Students Congress," File Report 115, May 1940, MO, 13.
71. "Charter of Students Rights and Responsibilities," *Student News* 7 (May 1940): 2.
72. Ibid., 15.
73. Letter from Margot Kettle to Brian Simon, May 4, 1991, SIM/4/7/1.
74. NUS, *Students in Congress: Report of the British Students Congress held in Leeds 1940* (NUS: London, 1940), 20; *Guild News,* April 25, 1940, 2.
75. Simon, "Student Movement," 200.
76. "Charter of Rights Framed," *Student News* 7 (May 1940): 1; NUS, *Report of Executive Committee, 1939–1940,* 3; "Notes," *Universities Review* 12, no. 2 (May 1940), 51–52; *Times,* May 24, 1940, 4; *Times* June 19, 1940, 9; Simon, "Dramatic Happenings," 30.
77. "Crisis Over," *Guild News,* November 21, 1940, 3; Simon, "Dramatic Happenings," 6.
78. "A Living Answer to the Sceptics," *Student News* 12 (May 1941): 4.
79. SCM, "Students' Attitude to the War," *Student Christian Movement Annual Report 1939–1940,* 9.
80. *Student News* 13 (November 1941): 3.

81. Simon, "Dramatic Happenings," 162.
82. NUS, *Report of Executive Committee, 1939–1940*, 6.
83. "Manchester Students Are Worried," *Student News* 10 (February 1941): 2.
84. "34 Help Rescue Squads," *Student News* 10 (February 1941): 2.
85. NUS, *Twenty-One Years*, 16–17.
86. *Students and the Blitz*, 16.
87. Ibid., 3; Mary Corsellis, "Bombing in the East End," *Student News* (November 16, 1940): 2.
88. *Northerner* 41, no. 2 (March 1941): 8; "Edinburgh's Blitz Plans," *Student News* 12 (May 1941): 2.
89. F. B. Chubb, "Mass Observation Diary, September 1941," MO.
90. *Students and the Blitz*, 7.
91. Ibid., 6.
92. *SCM Annual Report 1940/41*, 12.
93. *Students and the Blitz*, 13–15.
94. *21 years of the University Labour Federation*, 27.
95. "1,500 Unite to Oppose Fascism," *Student News* 16 (May 1942): 1.
96. "Scottish Students in Conference," *Student News* (February 8, 1943): 1.
97. "We Must Put our Shoulders to the Wheel," *Student News* (November 10, 1941): 3.
98. NUS, *Students Answer Fascism: NUS Congress, Birmingham, 1942* (Cambridge: NUS, 1942); Marguerite R. Gale, "English Students at War," *Students at War: Review of the National Union of Czechoslovak Students* 2, no. 1 (February 1942): 18; *Student News* 13 (November 1941): 1.
99. "Army Unit Adopted," *Student News* 15 (March 1942): 1.
100. "NUS on the Air," *Student News* 13 (November 1941): 1.
101. *Student News* 13 (November 1941): 3.
102. Simon, *Student's View*, 124–125; *Student News* 13 (November 1941): 1.
103. *Student News* 14 (January 26, 1942): 4; "Oxford Letter," *Brown Book*, December 1942, 5.
104. *The Student's Contribution to Victory: NUS Congress, London, 1943* (London: NUS, 1943), 19; NUS, *Twenty One Years*, 23.
105. Bawden in *My Oxford*, 160.
106. James L. Henderson, "World Student Relief: The Work of International Student Service," *Nature* 153 (February 1944): 152–154.
107. ISS, *The Growth of a Service: A Report of the British Committee of International Student Service, 1945–1946* (London: ISS, 1946), 10.
108. "International Students' Day" 1943, UWT/D/238/3, IOE.
109. Norman Bentwich, *The Rescue and Achievement of Refugee Scholars: The Story of Displaced Scholars and Scientists, 1933–1952* (The Hague: Martinus Nijhoff, 1953).
110. "Interned Refugees Plight," *Student News* 9 (November 18, 1940): 4.
111. WUS, *World Student Relief 1940–1950* (Geneva: World University Service, 1952), 14; *Growth of a Service*, 8.

112. "Report of the London ISS Committee held on 27 January 1945," UN2/1/1, SHL.
113. WUS, *World Student Relief 1940–1950*, 18.
114. "Student Relief," *Student News* 26 (June 1945): 2
115. ISS, *Growth of a Service*, 12; ISS, *University Relief 1943–1945: A Report* (London: Cooperating Committee of ISS for Great Britain and Northern Ireland, 1945).
116. ISS, *Growth of a Service*, 4; "TCD Concert for Student Relief," *Irish Times*, February 16, 1946, 5; *Manchester Guardian*, May 29, 1950, 7; "How Do You Raise Money?," *Student News* 24 (March 1945), 2.
117. "ULU Secretary's Report," 1946–1947, UN2/1/1, 2.
118. ISS, *Growth of a Service*, 3.
119. ISS, *The Year in Retrospect 1947* (London: ISS, 1948), 18–20; This section relies on the *Growth of a Service* report.
120. ISS, *Growth of a Service*, 3.
121. Ibid., 2.
122. ISS, *ISS University Relief 1943–1945*, 30.
123. ISS, *Growth of a Service*, 4.
124. "Ashton Hayes," *British Journal of International Student Service* 1, no. 1 (January 1946): 19–20.
125. Adi Vries, "Meditation," *British Journal of International Student Service* 1, no. 2 (April 1946): 4.
126. "Ashton Hayes," 20.
127. Ibid., 20.
128. *Council of British Societies for Relief Abroad Report for the Year 1947* (London: 1948), 11.
129. Day, *NUS 90 Years*, 35.
130. ISS, *Growth of a Service*, 7.
131. ISS, *Growth of a Service*, 4; Andre de Blonay, "Geneva Letter," *ISS Review* 1, no. 3 (July 1946): 1.
132. "A Chronological History of ISS," "A Chronological History of ISS", *International Student Service: The Year in Retrospect 1947–1948* (London: British Cooperating Committee of ISS, 1949), 41.
133. 'What is ISS?', c. 1947, WP 15593, BL.
134. ISS, *To Build Anew: An Outline of ISS Projects for the Year 1947–48*; "An NUS Report on Germany," *Northerner* 47, no. 2 (April 1947): 5–8.
135. "ULU Secretary's Report," 1946–1947, 2.
136. "Letters from German students," 1947, DC/GER/6/3/1, German Educational Reconstruction Archive, IOE.
137. Sheila Himmel, "Report from Germany," *New Phineas*, Summer 1948, 23–24; Peter Long, "Cologne 1947," *Nonesuch News* 7 (November 1947): 2; Geoffrey Godwin, "Students' Conference: Germany's Need of Enlightenment," *Reprint from TES* 18 Jan 1947.
138. James L. Henderson, "See Germany and Die," *ISS Review* 1, no. 5 (November 1946); "Weekly report IVSP Service at Hamburg," September 1946, IVS J/43, HH.

139. *IVSP General Newsletter,* January 4, 1946; *Annual Report of ISVP 1945/6,* 6; *IVSP General Newsletter,* 41, August 14, 1946, IVS J/9.
140. "Reports on Summer Camps, Germany, 1946," IVS J/43.
141. Ethelwyn Best and Bernard Pike, *International Voluntary Service for Peace, 1920–1946* (London: Allen and Unwin, 1948), 98; John Harvey, "The Idea of Voluntary Service," International Voluntary Service for Peace *News Bulletin* 40 (April 1948).
142. WUS, *World Student Relief 1940–1950,* 6.
143. Simon, *Student's View,* 126.
144. NUS, *Twenty-One Years,* 14; Eric Ashby and Mary Anderson, *The Rise of the Student Estate in Britain* (London: Macmillan, 1970), 86.
145. *The Future of University and Higher Education: A Report Prepared by the National Union of Students, 1944* (London: NUS, 1944), 5.

9 EXPERIMENTS IN LIVING: STUDENT SOCIAL SERVICE AND SOCIAL ACTION, 1950–1965

1. "Minutes of a Meeting held on 4 February 1948," Cambridge Committee Minutes, 1938–1950, CU Min IX 69 6.
2. A. H. Halsey, "Admission," in *History of the University in Europe: Universities since 1945,* Vol. 4, edited by Walter Rüegg, 207–237 (Cambridge: CUP, 2011), 207.
3. Ibid., 229.
4. *Report of the Committee on Higher Education* [hereafter Robbins Report] (London: HMSO, 1963), 15.
5. Figures from Halsey, "Admission," 230–231. Includes full- and part-time British and overseas university students and Open University students.
6. Ibid.
7. *Robbins Report Appendix Two (B),* 251–253.
8. Eric Ashby and Mary Anderson, *The Rise of the Student Estate in Britain* (London: Macmillan and Co., 1970), 91.
9. Dates given are the dates the universities received their Charters.
10. *Robbins Report,* 8.
11. See *Robbins Report Appendix Two (B),* 3–4.
12. *Robbins Report Appendix Two (B),* 218–220.
13. "Where Do Grants Come from," *Student News,* October 2, 1958.
14. On funding see *Robbins Report Appendix Two (A),* Part VI.
15. Shelia Rowbotham, "Introduction" to Helene Curtis and Mimi Sanderson, *The Unsung Sixties: Memoirs of Social Innovation* (London: Whiting & Birch, 2004), ix.
16. Halsey, "Admission," 231.
17. Peter Marris, *The Experience of Higher Education* (London: Routledge, 1964).
18. Harold Silver and Pamela Silver. *Students: Changing Roles, Changing Lives* (Buckingham: Open University Press, 1997), 5.

19. Ferdynand Zweig, *The Student in the Age of Anxiety* (London: Heinemann, 1963), 94.
20. Marris, *Higher Education*, 138–139; Zweig, *Students*, 33.
21. Marris, *Higher Education*, 138–139.
22. "Wanted – 300 students," *Gongster*, March 2, 1956, 1.
23. *Robbins Report Appendix Two (B)*, 222.
24. Tom Hickman, *The Call-Up: A History of National Service* (London: Headline, 2004), 2.
25. See also Zweig, *Students*, 90.
26. "Around the Halls," *Gongster,* February 10, 1956, 3.
27. *University of London Union Handbook 1963/4*, UN5/1/22, 87; Clive Priestly, "Ghost Halls," *Gongster,* February 10, 1956, 7.
28. Dulcie Groves, "Dear Mum and Dad: Letters Home from a Women's Hall of Residence at the University of Nottingham 1952–1955," *History of Education* 22, no. 3 (1993): 289–301.
29. Marris, *Higher Education;* Zweig, *Students*, 23.
30. Zweig, *Students*, 104
31. SCM Annual Reports 1950s.
32. *SCM Annual Report 1958–9*, 5.
33. "Editorial," *Gryphon*, March 1960, 4; Ferdynand Zweig, *The Student in the Age of Anxiety* (London: Heinemann, 1963).
34. Michael Sanderson, *The History of the University of East Anglia, Norwich* (London: Hambledon, 2002), 127.
35. Granville Hawkins, "From the Cage: An Undergraduate View," in *The Idea of a New University: An Experiment in Sussex*, edited by David Daiches, 193–200. 2nd ed. (London: Andre Deutsch, 1970), 199.
36. E. C. Barrett, "Live for Self," *Darts,* February 18, 1960, 7.
37. Ibid.
38. "Editorial," *Social Service* 24, no. 2 (September–November 1952): 50–51.
39. *In the Service of the University: Report of the ISS Summer Conference* (Geneva: ISS, 1948), SCM W34/2/2, 71.
40. *ISS Year Book 1951*, 37.
41. Nicholas Deakin, "The Perils of Partnership: The Voluntary Sector and the State," in *An Introduction to the Voluntary Sector*, edited by Justin Davis Smith, Colin Rochester and Rodney Hedley, 40–65 (London: Routledge, 1995).
42. Viscount Samuel, House of Lords Debate, Hansard, HL Deb June 22, 1949 vol. 163 cc75–136.
43. Lord Pakenham, ibid.
44. Gladys Barrett, *Blackfriars Settlement: A Short History, 1887–1987* (London: Blackfriars Settlement, 1985), 22.
45. "Cambridge House Minutes of a Meeting of the Executive Committee of the 5 June 1952," Cambridge House Archive, privately held. I am grateful to Clare Gilhooly for providing access.
46. Marie Lewis, "Developments in Settlements," *Social Service Quarterly* 36, no. 2 (Autumn 1962): 52–55; Christine Keynon Jones, *King's*

College London: In the Service of Society (London: King's College London, 2004), 114; "University Settlement Can Widen Your Horizon," *Nonesuch News,* February 26, 1952, 3.

47. William Beveridge and A. F. Wells, *The Evidence for Voluntary Action* (London: George Allen and Unwin, 1949), 122.

48. Barrett, *Blackfriars Settlement,* 23; *Cambridge House Annual Report 1958/9*; Hamilton and Macleay, *Glasgow University Settlement,* 56–57.

49. *Cambridge House Annual Report 1958/9.*

50. *Liverpool University Settlement Annual Report 1971–72,* D7/3; *Cambridge House Annual Report,* 1970.

51. *Cambridge House Annual Report, 1970.*

52. Bradley, *Poverty and Philanthropy,* 195.

53. Mary Morris, *Voluntary Work in the Welfare State* (London: Routledge, 1969), 226.

54. Georgina Brewis, "Youth in Action? British Young People and Voluntary Service 1958 – 1970," in *Beveridge and Voluntary Action in Britain and the Wider British World,* edited by Melanie Oppenheimer and Nicholas Deakin, 94–108 (Manchester: MUP, 2011).

55. Mike Thomas cited in Eileen Younghusband, *Social Work in Britain: 1950–1975,* Vol. 1 (London: George Allen and Unwin, 1978), 273.

56. Tim Dartington, *Task Force* (London: Mitchell Beazley, 1971), 9; Jos Sheard, "Volunteering and Society, 1960–1990," in *Volunteering and Society: Principles and Practices,* edited by Rodney Hedley and Justin Davis Smith, 11–32 (London: NCVO, 1992); Jos Sheard, "From Lady Bountiful to Active Citizen," in *An Introduction to the Voluntary Sector,* 114–127.

57. Sheard, "Volunteering and Society," 11–13.

58. Georgina Brewis, "Towards a New Understanding of Volunteering Before 1960," *Institute for Volunteering Research Working Paper* (London: IVR, 2013), http://www.ivr.org.uk/ivr-projects/ivr-current-projects/ivr-working-papers.

59. See Kate Bradley, "Juvenile Delinquency and the Public Sphere: Exploring Local and National Discourse in England, c. 1940–1969," *Social History* 37, no. 1 (February 2012): 19–35.

60. *The Youth Service in England and Wales* (London: HMSO, 1958), 106.

61. "Rag Money Benefits Belfast," *Student News* (October 20, 1958): 1.

62. *Which University? 1964* (London: Cornmarket, 1964), 63.

63. Zweig, *Student,* 24.

64. John G. Esplen, "Adults in Boys' Clubs," *The Boy* 30, no. 1 (Spring 1957): 8–9; Patrick Coldstream, *Learning Things: A Memoir* (Yeadon: Privately published, 2007), 245.

65. Letters Page, *Guardian,* February 16, 1960, 8.

66. "Camp with Borstal Boys," *Student News* (March 5, 1959): 7.

67. "Oxford-Borstal Camps," AE2013/96, Exeter College Archives, Oxford. I am grateful to Sara Fernandez for helping with the research here.

68. Michael Hollings, "Oxford Borstal Camps," *The Tablet*, 13 August 1960, 5.
69. "Oxford-Borstal Camps Annual Report 1964–5," AE2013/96, 1.
70. Chris Brearley, "The Trinity-Usk Borstal Camp – An Undergraduate Remembers," *Trinity College Oxford Report 2009–10*, 90.
71. Coldstream, *Learning Things*, 245.
72. Jill Manthorpe, "'It Was the Best of Times and the Worst of Times': On Being the Organiser of Student Volunteers," *Voluntary Action* 4, no. 1 (Winter 2001): 83–96.
73. G. Dowell, "Christian Action," *Darts*, May 5, 1960, 5.
74. NUS, "NUS Announced Community Action Programme," Press release November 12, 1969, MSS 280/86/3, NUS Archive, Modern Records Centre, University of Warwick.
75. Michael Dower, "Dirt Behind the Fingernails," *Challenge* 4, no. 1 (January 1963): 12–19.
76. See Brewis, "Youth in Action?"
77. See also Hoefferle, *British Student Activism*.
78. "Students from Hungary," *Times*, January 2, 1957, 9; *SCM Annual Report 1956–1957*, 7.
79. "Editorial," *Gryphon*, March 1960, 4.
80. "We Protest," *Sennet*, November 13, 1956, 1.
81. "Students in Hungary Protest," *Times*, November 12, 1956, 4; "We Protest," *Sennet*, November 13, 1956, 1; "Silent March to Cenotaph," *Nonesuch News*, November 23, 1956, 1; Magda Czigány, *"Just Like Other Students": Reception of the 1956 Hungarian Refugee Students in Britain* (Newcastle: Cambridge Scholars, 2009), 26.
82. "Silent March to Cenotaph," *Nonesuch News*, November 23, 1956, 1.
83. "Hungarian Exiles Answer Students' Questions," *Manchester Guardian*, October 31, 1956, 3.
84. "20,000 Fighting Fools," *Darts*, November 15, 1956, 1.
85. "Hungary – Bravo King's," *Sennet*, November 20, 1956, 1; "Housework," *Sennet*, February 12, 1957, 2.
86. Czigány, *Like Other Students*, 34.
87. *SCM Annual Report 1956/7*, 15.
88. "Socialist Purge," *Gilmorehill Guardian*, February 8, 1957, 1.
89. "Open Letter," *Darts*, February 7, 1957, 1.
90. Hoefferle, *British Student Activism*, 24.
91. With thanks to Nicholas Deakin for his personal recollections here.
92. "We Protest," *Sennet*, November 13, 1956, 1
93. *ISS Year Book 1951* (London: ISS, 1951), 24.
94. "A Note on the Present Position of Refugee Hungarian Students in the United Kingdom," March 1957, UoL/CB/3/6/1, Records of the Committee for Hungarian Students, Special Collections, Senate House Library.
95. *Nonesuch News* December 7, 1956, 1; "Hungary – Bravo Kings," *Sennet*, November 20, 1956, 1; "WUS Meeting 8 November 1956,"

Liverpool University WUS Minute Book, Liverpool A27/17, A231/14; "Note on Overall UK Arrangements for Helping Refugee Hungarian Students," UoL/CB/3/6/3.

96. Peter Gatrell, *Free World? The Campaign to Save the World's Refugees, 1956–1963* (Cambridge: Cambridge University Press, 2011), 51.

97. "Note on Overall UK Arrangements"; Alan Dare and Paul Hollander, "Hungarian Students in Great Britain," 1959. UoL/CB/3/6/11; See Czigány, *Like Other Students,* 152–154 on student numbers.

98. "Draft Report by J. F. Lockwood," UoL/CB/3/11/1/3; Committee of Vice-Chancellors and Principals Sub-Committee on Hungarian Students, December 7, 1956, UoL/CB/3/1/1.

99. "Draft Report by J. F. Lockwood."

100. "They're Here: Hungarians in London," *Sennet,* January 15, 1957, 1.

101. "Durham and Hungary," *Palatinate,* December 11, 1956, 1.

102. "Vice-Chancellor says Levy "Moral Obligation,"" *Broadsheet* 9, no. 12 (Summer 1957)· 1.

103. R. M. Young, "The Hungarian Students," *University of Edinburgh Gazette* 18 (October 1957), Offprint in UoL/CB/3/6/12, 21.

104. Young, "Hungarian Students," 24; Czigany, *Like Other Students,* 208.

105. Dare and Hollander, "Hungarian Students."

106. Ibid., 2, 66.

107. Ibid., 67.

108. Paul Hollander, "One Year in England," *Sennet,* November 19, 1957, 4.

109. See on this Gatrell, *Free World?,* 49.

110. "The Relief of Hungarian Refugee Students," UoL/CB/3/11/1/1.

111. Dare and Hollander, "Hungarian Students."

112. "Letter from Lord Mayor's Fund to Vice Chancellor of University of London," December 1, 1956, UoL/CB/3/1/1.

113. "WUS in Britain," *WUS Yearbook 1956,* 13.

114. Burkett, *Post-Imperial Britain,* 88.

115. "Television and Sound Will Give Rag Full Coverage," *Nonesuch News,* February 21, 1948, 1; "Profits Soar; Carnival Mixture as Before," *Student News* (December 3, 1959).

116. "Survey of Charities," *Gilmore Guardian,* October 31, 1958, 1.

117. *Broadsheet* 10, no. 10 (March 13, 1958): 2.

118. Gatrell, *Free World?,* 92–93.

119. Timothy Raison, "Student Campaigners Collect WRY Jackpot," *Student News* (May 19, 1960): 3.

120. "War on Want," *Student News,* April 30, 1959, 4.

121. *Nonesuch News,* January 29, 1960, 3; *Nonesuch News,* February 2, 1960.

122. *Guardian,* March 17, 1960, 23.

123. Raison, "Student Campaigners," 3.

124. "WUS Carnival Report," November 12, 1959, UN2/1/3, 2; "Minutes of President's Council Meeting," June 27, 1960, 7.

125. "Britain's share of Refugee Fund," *Times,* May 24, 1962, 10; Gatrell, *Free World,* 248, 250.

126. "WUS 50 Years," 36–7,

127. "Is This Nothing But a Gesture?" *Student News* (January 19, 1961): 11.

128. "Entire Student Body to Make Effort," *Student News* (February 1963): 4.

129. In particular see Burkett, *Post-Imperial Britain*; Hoefferle, *British Student Activism*.

130. *SCM Annual Report 1959–1960*, 10; Zweig, *Students*, 70–73, 139–144.

131. The universities surveyed were Aberdeen, St Andrews, Cardiff, Kings (Newcastle), Keele, Leicester and Nottingham. "CUCaND Survey," CND8/2, 3, CND Archive, London School of Economics (LSE).

132. Ibid.

133. "The Student Movement Since 1960," *Sennet*, February 2, 1970, 6; Foulkes, *Eighty Years On*, 37.

134. "The Student Movement Since 1960," 6.

135. Burkett, *Post-Imperial Britain*, 79.

136. "Colleges and Universities CND Report of Annual Conference, 1962," CND/8/14.

137. "CUCaND Notice to all Groups," January 19, 1962, CND/8/15/33.

138. *Sennet*, February 12, 1957, 3.

139. *Student News* (February 12, 1959): 1; *SCM Annual Report 1958–1959*, 14.

140. "Boycott: The First Steps," *Student News* (December 3, 1959): 1; *Nonesuch News*, January 29, 1960, 5; "South African Boycott," *Darts*, February 18, 1960, 1.

141. "No to Discrimination," *Student News* (April 30, 1959): 12.

142. "Dissenters on the March," *Palatinate*, December 4, 1959, 1.

143. "The Boycott," *Broadsheet*, March 3, 1960, 5.

144. "Editorial," *Palatinate,* November 20, 1959.

145. Roger Fieldhouse, *Anti-Apartheid: A History of the Movement in Britain. A Study in Pressure Group Politics* (London: Merlin, 2005), 329–334.

146. "Appeal for Amnesty," *Nonesuch News,* January 25, 1963, 3.

147. *Amnesty First Annual Report 1961–1962*, 16.

148. Tom Buchanan, "'The Truth Will Set You Free': The Making of Amnesty International," *Journal of Contemporary History* 37, no. 4 (October 2002): 575–597, at 592.

149. Ian Hopwood, "Report and Review of Third World First," November 1972, People & Planet papers, Oxford (P&P). I am grateful to Jamie Clarke and colleagues at People & Planet for allowing me access to this privately held collection.

150. Curtis and Sanderson, *Unsung Sixties,* vii.

10   From Service to Action? Rethinking Student Voluntarism, 1965–1980

1. Alan Barr, *Student Community Action* (London: National Council for Social Service, 1972), 5.

2. "3W1 – Third World First" c. 1970, People & Planet Papers, Oxford (P&P).
3. Barr, *Student Community Action*, 5.
4. "Introducing NUS" c. 1957, WP 7560, British Library, 23; International Voluntary Service for Peace, *Annual Report 1956*; Sir John Lockwood, "The Call for Volunteer Service Overseas," *Social Service Quarterly* 37, no 2 (Autumn 1963): 50.
5. David Wainwright, *The Volunteers: The Story of Overseas Voluntary Service* (London: Macdonald, 1965), 74; *The Hidden Force: A Report of the International Conference on Middle Level Manpower* (New York: Harper and Row, 1963).
6. Jemma Purdey, *From Vienna to Yogyakarta: The Life of Herb Frith* (Sydney: University of New South Wales Press, 2011), 74–84.
7. Robert Morris, *Overseas Volunteer Programs* (Lexington, MA: Lexington Books, 1973), 13.
8. Alec Dickson, *A Chance to Serve*, edited by Mora Dickson (London: Dennis Dobson, 1976), 80–81.
9. Ibid., 88.
10. Dick Bird, *Never the Same Again: A History of VSO* (London: VSO, 1998), 23.
11. *The Establishment of a Commonwealth Youth Trust* (1959), CAB 144/4, TNA, 16–17; Andrew Rutter, "Workcamping in New Areas," *International Voluntary Service*, Summer 1959; "A Year in the Commonwealth for Young Volunteers," *Times*, Tuesday December 1, 1959, 4.
12. Morris, *Overseas Volunteer Programs*, 5.
13. "Kennedy Plan," *New York Times*, December 19, 1960, Accessed December 23, 2013 http://peacecorps.umich.edu/documents/NYT _Dec_18_1960.pdf.
14. See Morris, *Overseas Volunteer Programs*, 253.
15. Tom Stacey, "The Peace Volunteers," *Sunday Times*, February 25, 1962.
16. Ferdynand Zweig, *The Student in the Age of Anxiety* (London: Heinemann, 1963), 203.
17. Wainwright, *Volunteers*, 87.
18. J. M. Lee, "No Peace Corps for the Commonwealth?" *Round Table* 336 (October 1995): 455–467.
19. The initial sending agencies were VSO, IVS, United Nations Association for International Service, the NUS, and the Scottish Union of Students.
20. Philip Zealey, "Need and Response in Overseas Service," *Social Service Quarterly* 36, no. 3 (Winter 1963): 109–111; *Hansard*, Fifth Series, Vol. 712, Session 1964–1965, May 14, 1965 cc. 906–907; Lockwood Committee Minutes, July 18, 1962, Box 40, Returned Volunteer Association Archive, LSE.
21. Lockwood Minutes, April 26, 1963, RVA.

22. "VSO Provides Skill," *Sennet*, November 23, 1965, 8–9; "Why Not Work Overseas," Student News, January 1963, 11; "Operation 1963 – Service," *Student News*, February 1963, 3.

23. Frank A. Rhodes, The *National Union of Students 1922 – 1967* (Coventary: Warwick Students' Union, 1990), 144–145; *Student News,* June 1963, 9.

24. Lockwood Committee Minutes LSE; Rhodes, *National Union of Students*, 145.

25. Rhodes, *National Union of Students*, 144–145.

26. "Volunteering Overseas," in *Ways and Means: A Directory of Alternative Information* (London: SCANUS, 1978), 52.

27. Bill Randall, "The Crusade," *Inside Housing*, June 25, 2004, 20–21.

28. SCM, "Christ's Call to Service Now," 1963, SCM N9.

29. Helene Curtis and Mimi Sanderson eds., *The Unsung Sixties: Memoirs of Social Innovation* (London: Whiting & Birch, 2004), 25.

30. "Letter from Rev F J Glendenning to Rev David Head," July 5, 1967, SCM A381.

31. Caroline Jackson in Georgina Brewis ed., "Students Volunteering and Community Action, 1960–2000: A Witness Seminar," held on June 24, 2010, London. https://www.academia.edu/1765846/Students _Volunteering_and_Community_Action_1960–2000_A_Witness _Seminar, 29.

32. "Students Will Visit Mental Hospital," *Student News,* March 16, 1965, 3.

33. "Tim Berry Obituary," *York Grapevine*, Autumn 2007, 8.

34. Barr, in "Witness Seminar," 30; See also Michael Sanderson, *The History of the University of East Anglia, Norwich* (London: Hambledon, 2002), 127..

35. Barr, *Student Community Action*, 11–13.

36. Michael Beloff, *The Plateglass Universities* (London: Secker and Warburg, 1968), 34.

37. "Rag Blasts Off," *Wvyern* 3 (March 5, 1965): 1.

38. Editorial, *Wvyern* 3 (March 5, 1965): 2.

39. Marion McClintock, *Shaping the Future: A History of the University of Lancaster 1961–2011* (Lancaster: University of Lancaster, 2011), 90, 101.

40. "Undergraduate Service Committee Terms of Reference," 1966/7, A231/6, Community Service Committee, UL.

41. Derek Palmer, "Rag Must Go," *New Student* 3 (March 1968): 17; Barr, *Student Community Action*, 129; Pauline Clark, "Social Works May Oust Rag Days," *Guardian,* March 29, 1968, 5.

42. "Letters," *New Student* 4 (May 1968): 20.

43. Palmer, "Rag Must Go," 17.

44. Ray Phillips, *Student Community Action: Report of the Pilot Programme of the NUS Student Community Action Project 1971–1974* (London: NUS, 1974); NUS, "Annual Conference Margate 1969, Amendments to Agenda," NUS MSS 280/86/3.

45. "What is a Social Worker?," *Sennet*, November 3, 1969, 6–7.
46. Digby Jacks, *Student Politics and Higher Education* (London: Lawrence and Wishart, 1975), 141.
47. Barr, *Student Community Action*, 62,
48. A. H. Halsey and Stephen Marks, "British Student Politics,"*Daedalus* 97, no. 1 (Winter 1968): 116–136, at 127.; Eric Ashby and Mary Anderson, *The Rise of the Student Estate in Britain* (London: Macmillan and Co., 1970)..
49. Caroline M. Hoefferle, *British Student Activism in the Long Sixties* (Abingdon: Routledge, 2013), 62–65.
50. Ibid., 81.
51. Mike Day, *National Union of Students, 1922–2012*(London: Regal Press, 2012), 49; Louis Vos, "Student Movements and Political Activism" in *History of the University in Europe*, Vol. 4, 276–318, at 293.
52. Nick Thomas, "Challenging Myths of the 1960s: The Case of Student Protest in Britain," *Twentieth Century British History* 13, no. 3 (2002): 277–297.
53. Hoefferle, *British Student Activism*, 82.
54. David Gilles, "NUS Conference, Margate, November 21–24, 1969," NUS MSS 280/86/3; "Letter from Ruth Bundey," NUS MSS 280/86/1.
55. "Students in Social Service," *Times*, July 4, 1968, 9.
56. Barr, *Student Community Action*, 18.
57. Peter Wilby, "Student Leaders Have New Target," *Observer*, November 9, 1969, 21.
58. B. MacArthur, "The Success of the Sit-in in Britain," *Times*, June 17, 1970, 9.
59. Lord Beaumont of Whitley, HL Deb April 23, 1969 Hansard Vol. 301 cc460.
60. Beloff, *Plateglass*, 67.
61. NUS, "NUS Announced Community Action Programme."
62. "Community Action," *Sennet*, March 2, 1971, 6–7.
63. The motion is reproduced in Barr, *Student Community Action*, 131–133.
64. Ibid., 66.
65. Letter sent to Trusts by NUS President, June 1970. Reproduced in *SCANUS*, June 1973, 7. The program was funded by the Calouste-Gulbenkian Foundation and the King George Jubilee Trust.
66. Maggie Black, *A Cause for Our Times: Oxfam the first 50 Years* (Oxfam, 1992), 157.
67. "Third World First," *Colossus*, Spring 1972, 3.
68. Ian Hopwood, "Report and Review of Third World First," November 1972, People &Planet papers, Oxford (P&P).
69. John Murphy, "Community Action and Liberal "Third-Worldism,"", *SCANUS*, November 1973, 2–3.
70. "News from Groups," c. 1970–1971, P&P.

71. Peter Taylor-Goobly, "Save Biafra!" *Sennet*, January 26, 1970, 4; "News from groups," c.1970–1971, P&P.

72. Og Thomas, "Evaluation of 3W1, 1976–1979," P&P.

73. T. S. Bowles, *Survey of Attitudes towards Overseas Development* (London: HMSO, 1978), 13.

74. Ibid., 47.

75. *Cambridge House Annual Report 1970.*

76. *Student Community Action Resources Programme, Annual Report 1978–9.* SCA reports and newsletters are now held at the London School of Economics, Volunteering England/7/1–2.

77. "Student Community Action: Submission to the Voluntary Services Unit at the Home Office," 1978, Volunteering England/7/1.

78. "Glasgow OSCA," *COMMUNUS* 30 (November 1974): 14.

79. *Student Community Action Newsletter* 2, no. 1 (1971).

80. *Student Community Action Newsletter* (December 1971), 3.

81. "Working Together in Action Groups," *SCANUS* May 1973, 10–12.

82. Richard Crossman, "The Role of the Volunteer in the Modern Social Service," in *Traditions of Social Policy: Essays in Honour of Violet Butler*, edited by A. H. Halsey, 259–285, at 259 (Oxford: Basil Blackwell, 1976).

83. Nick Plant in "Witness Seminar," 26.

84. *Community Interaction Southampton University* (Southampton: Community Interaction, 1982), 24; SCADU, *Annual Report 1982–3* (London: SCADU, 1983), 2; "Community Action" (Manchester), Volunteering England/7/2.

85. Ray Phillips, *Report of the Pilot Programme of the NUS (UK) Student Community Action Project 1971–1974* (London: NUS, 1974), 4.

86. "Play," Supplement to *SCANUS*, June 1974.

87. David Stephenson, "Jacari," *Communus* 33 (June/July 1975): 12–13.

88. Sinclair Goodlad, Asad Abidi, Peter Anslow, and John Harris, "The Pimlico Connection: Undergraduates as Tutors in Schools," *Studies in Higher Education* 4, no. 2 (1979): 191–201.

89. Student Activities 1969.

90. Cambridge SCA, *Student Community Action* (Cambridge, 1980), Volunteering England/7/2.

91. Sarah Spencer ed., *Student Community Action* (Nottingham: Nottingham University Students Union Community Action Group, no date), Volunteering England/7/2.

92. Phillips, *Report of the Pilot Programme*, 5.

93. "The Stoke Park Thing – Justifiable," *Student Community Action Newsletter*, April 1972, no page no.

94. "Nottingham University Rampton Group," undated note, SCA.

95. "Rampton: New Campaign (PROPAR) Takes Off," *Student Community Action* 6 (1979): front page.

96. Jane Young, "Housing Action," *SCANUS*, February 1974, 2.

97. Nick Plant in "Witness Seminar," 19.

98. Brian Pullen with Michele Abendstern, *History of the University of Manchester, 1973–1990* (Manchester: MUP, 2004), 229.

99. World University Service, *Education for Refugees* (London: WUS, 1977).

100. "SCA and Cuts," *Student Community Action,* 10 (1980): 7.

101. Barr, *Student Community Action,* 6.

102. Alec Dickson, "Foreword" in *Education and Social Action: Community Service and the Curriculum in Higher Education,* edited by Sinclair Goodlad, 7–11 (London: George Allen and Unwin, 1975), 10.

103. Alun Richards, "Would You Let the University Get in the Way of Your Education?" *SCANUS,* September 1972, 9–10.

104. SCADU, *Annual Report 1982–3* (London: SCADU, 1983), 6; Phil Woolas, "Community Access Conference Report," in *Community Access Pack,* edited by Mike Aiken, Oliva Dix, Tommy Shepherd, Ian Wilmott, and Phil Woolas (London: NUS and SCADU, 1982).

105. Jacks, *Student Politics,* 142.

106. Ibid.

107. Robert Holman, "Students and Community Action," *Universities Quarterly: Higher Education and Society* 26, no. 2 (Spring 1973): 187–194.

108. *Current Issues in Community Work: A Study by the Community Work Group* (London: Routledge and Kegan Paul, 1973), 46.

109. Lisa Huber, "Playtime in Belfast," *SCANUS Newsletter* 1, no. 1 (September 1972): 14–16.

110. Ibid.

111. SCARP, *Taking Action in the Community* (London: SCARP, 1980), 32.

112. Richard Davies, "Glasgow SCA Reports," *SCANUS,* February 1974, 13–14.

113. "Students Take Positive Step," *Student News,* January 1963, 6.

114. "Letter to *SCARP: Student Community Action"* 5 (1979): back page.

115. Ronald Fraser, *1968: A Student Generation in Revolt* (London: Chatto and Windus, 1988).

116. Day, *National Union of Students,* 58.

117. Ibid.

118. "It Doesn't Pay to Be Gay," *Broadsheet,* Autumn 1971, 6.

119. Dave Carter, "The Closure of SCARP and Current Plans for the Future," Volunteering England/7/1.

120. SCARP collapsed in 1980 but 1981 a new, independent Student Community Action Development Unit (SCADU) was set up with funding from the VSU. It became a registered charity in 1983. Its successor body, Student Volunteering England merged with national charity Volunteering England in 2007, which itself merged with the National Council for Voluntary Organisations in 2012.

121. Maria Brenton, *The Voluntary Sector in British Social Services* (London: Longman, 1985), 46–48.

122. *Student Community Action Newsletter* 2, no. 1 (1971): 2.
123. "New from Oxfam: Bitter-Sweet Chocolate Bars," *Times,* October 6, 1972, 14.
124. "Student Movement Since 1960," 6.

11 Conclusion: Students and Social Change, 1880–1980

1. Jenny Harrow, "The Development of University Settlements in England, 1884–1939," PhD Thesis (London: London School of Economics, 1987), 636.
2. *UK Voluntary Sector Workforce Almanac 2013* (London: Skills Third Sector, 2013), http://www.3rdsectorworkforce.org.uk/

SELECT BIBLIOGRAPHY

Anderson, R. D. *Universities and Elites in Britain Since 1800*. Cambridge: Cambridge University Press, 1995.

Ashby, Eric and Anderson, Mary. *The Rise of the Student Estate in Britain*. London: Macmillan, 1970.

Barr, Alan. *Student Community Action*. London: National Council for Social Service, 1972.

Beauman, Katharine Bentley. *Women and the Settlement Movement*. London: Radcliffe Press, 1996.

Bradley, Katharine. *Poverty, Philanthropy and the State: Charities and the Working Classes in London, 1918–1979*. Manchester: Manchester University Press, 2009.

Brewis, Georgina. "From Working Parties to Social Work: Middle-Class Girls' Education and Social Service 1890–1914," *History of Education* 38, no. 6 (November 2009): 761–777.

———. "Youth in Action? British Young People and Voluntary Service 1958–1970." In *Beveridge and Voluntary Action in Britain and the Wider British World*, edited by Melanie Oppenheimer and Nicholas Deakin, 94–108. Manchester: Manchester University Press, 2011.

Buchanan, Tom. *Britain and the Spanish Civil War*. Cambridge: Cambridge University Press, 1997.

Burkett, Jodi. *Constructing Post-Imperial Britain: Britishness, Race and the Radical Left in the 1960s*. Basingstoke: Palgrave Macmillan, 2013.

Collini, Stefan. *Public Moralists: Political Thought and Intellectual Life in Britain*. Oxford: Oxford University Press, 1991.

Curtis, Helene and Sanderson, Mimi eds. *The Unsung Sixties: Memoirs of Social Innovation*. London: Whiting & Birch, 2004.

Day, Mike. *National Union of Students, 1922–2012*. London: Regal Press, 2012.

Dyhouse, Carol. *Girls Growing Up in Late Victorian and Edwardian England*. London: Routledge and Kegan Paul, 1981.

———. *Students: A Gendered History*. Abingdon: Routledge, 2006.

Field, John. "Service Learning in Britain between the Wars: University Students and Unemployed Camps," *History of Education* 41, no. 1 (March 2012): 195–212.

Fowler, David. *Youth Culture in Modern Britain c. 1920–1970*. Basingstoke: Palgrave Macmillan, 2008.

Fryth, Jim. *The Signal Was Spain: The Spanish Aid Movement in Britain, 1936–39*. London: Lawrence and Wishart, 1986.

Gatrell, Peter. *Free World? The Campaign to Save the World's Refugees, 1956–1963*. Cambridge: Cambridge University Press, 2011.

Gevers, Lieve and Vos, Louis. "Student Movements." In *A History of the University in Europe: Universities in the Nineteenth and Early Twentieth Centuries (1800–1945)*, Vol. 3, edited by Walter Rüegg, 269–363. Cambridge: Cambridge University Press, 2004.

Gibert, Julie S. "Women Students and Student Life at England's Civic Universities before the First World War," *History of Education* 23, no. 4 (1994): 405–422.

Harris, Jose. *Private Lives, Public Spirit: A Social History of Britain 1870–1914*. Oxford: Oxford University Press, 1993.

Harrison, Brian. *Seeking a Role: The United Kingdom, 1951–1970*. Oxford: Oxford University Press, 2009.

Harrow, Jenny. "The Development of University Settlements in England, 1884–1939." PhD Thesis, London: London School of Economics, 1987.

Hoefferle, Caroline M. *British Student Activism in the Long Sixties*. Abingdon: Routledge, 2013.

Howe, Renate. "The Australian Student Christian Movement and Women's Activism in the Asia-Pacific Region, 1890s–1920s," *Australian Feminist Studies* 16, no. 36 (2001): 311–323.

Lake, Meredith. "Faith in Crisis; Christian University Students in Peace and War," *Australian Journal of Politics and History* 56, no. 3 (2010): 441–454.

Lee, J. M. "No Peace Corps for the Commonwealth?" *Round Table* 336 (October 1995): 455–467.

Macdonald, Catriona M. "'To Form Citizens': Scottish Students, Governance and Politics, 1884–1948," *History of Education* 38, no. 3 (2009): 383–402.

McCulloch, Gary. *Philosophers and Kings: Education for Leadership in Modern England*. Cambridge: Cambridge University Press, 1991.

Rhodes, Frank A. *The National Union of Students 1922 – 1967*. 1968; Coventry: Warwick Students' Union, 1990.

Rouse, Ruth. *Rebuilding Europe: The Student Chapter in Post-War Reconstruction*. London: SCM Press, 1925.

———. *The World's Student Christian Federation: A History of the First Thirty Years*. London: SCM Press, 1948.

Ruegg, Walter ed. *A History of the University in Europe*. Cambridge: Cambridge University Press, 2001.

Saltzman, Rachelle Hope. *A Lark for the Sake of Their Country: The 1926 General Strike Volunteers in Folklore and Memory*. Manchester: Manchester University Press, 2012.

Scotland, Nigel. *Squires in the Slums: Settlements and Missions in Late-Victorian London*. London: I. B. Tauris, 2007.

Selles, Johanna M. *A History of the World Student Christian Federation,1895–1920: Motives, Methods and Influenctial Women.* Eugene, Or: Pickwick, 2011.

Silver, Harold. *Higher Education and Opinion Making in Twentieth-Century England.* London: Frank Cass, 2003.

Silver, Harold and Silver, Pamela. *Students: Changing Roles, Changing Lives.* Buckingham: Open University Press, 1997.

Simon, Brian. *A Student's View of the Universities.* London: Longmans, 1943.

———. "The Student Movement in England and Wales during the 1930s," *History of Education* 16, no. 3 (1987): 189–203.

Soffer, Reba N. *Discipline and Power: The University, History and the Making of an English Elite 1870–1930.* Stanford: Stanford University Press, 1994.

Tatlow, Tissington. *The Story of the Student Christian Movement.* London: SCM Press, 1933.

Thomas, Nick. "Challenging Myths of the 1960s: The Case of Student Protest in Britain," *Twentieth Century British History* 13, no. 3 (2002): 277–297.

Vernon, Keith. *Universities and the State in England, 1850–1939.* Abingdon: Routledge, 2004.

Vicinus, Martha. *Independent Women: Work and Community for Single Women, 1850–1920.* London: Virago, 1985.

Wainwright, David. *The Volunteers: The Story of Overseas Voluntary Service.* London: Macdonald, 1965.

INDEX

Aberystwyth, University of, 15, 17, 48, 58, 60, 80, 82, 105, 120, 121, 137, 139, 140, 141, 185
Abyssinian war, 111, 115, 133
after-care committees, 28, 46, 96
America. *See* United States
Amnesty International, 171, 173–4
Ancoats Settlement, 25, 31, 96
Andrews, Charles Freer, 29, 35, 40, 45
Anglo-Catholicism, 19–20
Anschluss, 118, 119
Anti-Apartheid Movement (AAM), 171, 172–4, 182
anti-Semitism, 118–22, 166
apartheid, 4, 155, 165, 171, 172–4, 182, 198
Armistice Day
  fundraising, 57, 113
  protest, 112–13
Armstrong College, Newcastle (later King's College, Newcastle), 60, 61, 71, 72, 76–7, 81, 83, 113, 115, 120, 141, 145
Athletics, university. *See* sports, university
Australia, 38, 39, 40, 41, 43, 50, 132, 148, 177
Austria, 7, 55, 58, 59, 67, 118, 121, 167

Bangor, University college of, 60, 80, 115, 137
Barnett, Samuel, 22–3, 24, 45, 198
Bedford College, 19, 37, 119
Beveridge, Sir William, 8, 52, 117, 161

Birmingham, University of, 15, 18, 19, 21, 27, 28, 57, 68, 73, 77, 82, 84, 85, 91, 96, 99, 100, 113, 120, 129, 131, 136, 138, 140, 142, 165, 166, 175, 178, 180, 181–3, 185, 191
Blitz, 135, 144–6
boycott
  of Japanese goods, 130–1, 133
  as protest technique, 8, 11, 111, 133, 172
  of South African goods and services, 172–3, 185
Bristol, University of, 15, 25, 32, 47, 59, 90, 112, 114, 115, 131, 136, 139, 165, 166, 170, 181, 189
Bristol University Settlement, 25, 30, 95
British Association of Residential Settlements, 96, 161
British Federation of University Women (BFUW), 117, 119, 130
British Independent (newspaper), 78
British Institute of Social Service, 45, 46
British Union of Fascists, 121
British Universities League of Nations Society (BULNS), 60, 63, 64, 119, 141
British Youth Peace Assembly (BYPA), 116, 123, 124, 127, 128, 130, 133
Brynmawr, 99, 102

Cambridge House, 25, 31, 161, 162, 186
Cambridge Spies, 90–1, 113

Printed in the United States of America